Bertrand Tavernier: Interviews

Conversations with Filmmakers Series
Gerald Peary, General Editor

Bertrand Tavernier
INTERVIEWS

Edited by Lynn A. Higgins and T. Jefferson Kline

University Press of Mississippi / Jackson

www.upress.state.ms.us

The University Press of Mississippi is a member of the Association of American University Presses.

Copyright © 2016 by University Press of Mississippi
All rights reserved
Manufactured in the United States of America

First printing 2016

∞

Library of Congress Cataloging-in-Publication Data

Names: Tavernier, Bertrand author. | Higgins, Lynn A. editor. | Kline, T.
   Jefferson (Thomas Jefferson), 1942– editor.
Title: Bertrand Tavernier : interviews / edited by Lynn A. Higgins and T.
   Jefferson Kline.
Description: Jackson : University Press of Mississippi, 2016. | Series:
   Conversations with filmmakers series | Includes bibliographical references
   and index. | Includes filmography.
Identifiers: LCCN 2016018260 (print) | LCCN 2016032209 (ebook) | ISBN
   9781496807687 (hardcover) | ISBN 9781496807694 (epub single) | ISBN
   9781496807700 (epub institutional) | ISBN 9781496807717 (pdf single) |
   ISBN 9781496807724 (pdf institutional)
Subjects: LCSH: Tavernier, Bertrand—Interviews. | Motion picture producers
   and directors—France—Interviews.
Classification: LCC PN1998.3.T377 A5 2016 (print) | LCC PN1998.3.T377 (ebook)
   | DDC 791.4302/33092—dc23
LC record available at https://lccn.loc.gov/2016018260

British Library Cataloging-in-Publication Data available

Contents

Introduction

Bertrand Tavernier is widely considered to be the leading light in the generation of French filmmakers who launched their careers in the 1970s, in the wake of the New Wave. In just over forty years, he has directed almost two dozen feature-length films in genres ranging from historical drama to documentary, from science fiction to neo-Western, and from intimate family portrait to, most recently as of this writing, a political satire adapted from a comic strip. The topics he chooses are equally eclectic. The memorable protagonists his fiction films have brought to life include a modest Lyonnais clockmaker, a nineteenth-century serial killer, a colonial sheriff in a West African village, a jazz saxophonist, an impressionist painter, a couple seeking to adopt a child in Cambodia, a New Orleans police lieutenant facing the chaos and corruption that followed Hurricane Katrina, members of a Parisian narcotics squad, a medieval knight, several soldiers from the First World War, and the imaginary daughter of d'Artagnan. Yet despite all this diversity in genre, historical period, and theme, Tavernier's films form a unified and coherent oeuvre. Asked to identify his driving motivation, Tavernier responded: "Above all else, it's the desire to understand."[1]

Bertrand René Maurice Tavernier was born in Lyon on April 25, 1941, the product of two established Lyonnais families. His mother, Geneviève Dumont-Cotte, descended from a dynasty of the silk-makers for which Lyon has been renowned since the Renaissance. His father, René Tavernier, came from a long line of professionals and public officials. A poet and publisher, he was an important figure in the local "Intellectual Resistance" during the German Occupation, when Louis Aragon, Elsa Triolet, and Albert Camus were among the guests at the Tavernier home on the eastern edge of the city. Lyon was also, of course, the birthplace of cinema; August and Louis Lumière made many of the first moving pictures there, including their famous *La Sortie des usines Lumière à Lyon* (1895) [*Workers Leaving the Lumière Factory in Lyon*]. As an adult, Tavernier would lobby for the preservation of the Lumière homestead and its transformation into the Institut Lumière (est. 1982), over whose museum, library, screening theaters, and annual film festival the filmmaker continues to preside. Although the family moved to Paris when Bertrand was still a child, the city's history, its traditions, and the distinctive light over the Rhone and Saône Rivers that converge there occupy a special place in his sensibility.

A shy child and not a particularly dedicated student, the young Tavernier was an omnivorous cinephile from an early age. He would escape after school to the Paris movie houses, where he sometimes attended several showings in a day. In 1960, he and a few friends created their own film society, the Nickel-Odéon, which they affiliated with the Fédération Française des Ciné-Clubs, and where they would regale themselves with whatever films they could beg or borrow, in the process acquiring a formidable knowledge of world cinema. Movies—especially American ones—were his sentimental and political education. "I began to discover politics thanks to American cinema," he later confided in an interview. "I learned about the New Deal from *The Grapes of Wrath*. I wanted to know more about Prohibition, the Wilson presidency, the Democrats and Republicans from watching gangster movies and about the Indian genocide from westerns by Delmer Daves."[2] He also learned about his predecessors' struggles for freedom of expression, and he studied the visual language they used to express their worldview. Tavernier's own films show a burning interest in French history and politics—the prelude to the 1789 Revolution, the Belle Epoque, the legacies of the World Wars, and especially the French colonial past and its continuing aftermath.

Young Bertrand's apprenticeship as a voracious moviegoer closely paralleled the development of postwar cinephilia in the country at large. During the Occupation, the German authorities had exercised tight control over what films could be imported and shown, but the Liberation opened theaters to previously banned French films of the 1930s as well as a flood of British, Italian, Soviet, and especially American films of all genres and qualities. The abovementioned national Ciné-Club organization, founded by Louis Delluc in 1935, had gone dormant during the Occupation as well but flourished with renewed vigor after the Liberation. The terms of the May 1946 Blum-Byrnes agreement meant that France would receive postwar reconstruction loans in exchange for opening the door to an influx of American cultural products. Discovery of John Ford, Orson Welles, and Gary Cooper was a revelation to Tavernier and other postwar youth, as were newly available albums by jazz greats such as Sidney Bechet, Louis Armstrong, Bud Powell, Lester Young, and Charlie Parker. October of 1946 saw the creation of the Centre National de la Cinématographie (CNC), its state aid to filmmakers designed to promote production and export of French movies. Cinema was a high profile and accessible form of entertainment, and the public flocked to the theaters in even greater numbers than during the Occupation. 1947—the year the Tavernier family moved to Paris—was and remains a record year for movie attendance. In 1958, the new Ministry of Culture, under André Malraux, launched a policy of encouraging first-time filmmakers by offering advances on box office receipts. This quickly led to the explosion of young talent that was the New Wave.

That a child with Bertrand's interests growing up in the postwar cinematic effervescence just described would aspire to a career as a filmmaker—even despite parental opposition—is not surprising. The young Tavernier got his start when he defied parental injunction to study law and found himself on his own dime, earning his way writing movie reviews for local publications and eventually articles for important venues such as *Positif, Cahiers du cinéma*, and *Télérama*. He was inspired by Jean-Pierre Melville's *Bob le flambeur* (1956), and his essay-interview championing Melville impressed the older filmmaker sufficiently to offer the young journalist-cinephile a position as assistant for his next film, *Léon Morin, Prêtre* (1961) [*Léon Morin, Priest*]. These activities in turn drew the attention of Georges de Beauregard, one of the most visionary and powerful producers of the era. Associated with the rise of the *Nouvelle Vague*, he had promoted, in addition to Melville, the careers of such rising directors as Jean-Luc Godard, Claude Chabrol, Jacques Rivette, Agnès Varda, and cinematographer Raoûl Coutard. In 1961, de Beauregard hired Tavernier as press attaché, and then in 1963 and 1964 invited him to contribute original short subjects to two collective "films à sketches." Although the critical response to Tavernier's contributions was positive, he continued to work as a press attaché and journalist until 1972. During this time, he conducted some of the interviews he would later publish through the auspices of the Institut Lumière under the title *American Friends: Interviews with Great Hollywood Directors* (2008). In 1970, with Jean-Pierre Coursodon, he published an encyclopedia of American cinema, *30 Years of American Cinema*. The revised edition of 1995—*50 Years of American Cinema*—contains over 1100 pages of film history filmographies, and insightful analyses of individual artists and films. Undoubtedly one factor explaining the richness of the many published conversations with Tavernier, including those collected here, is that he started his career by mastering the art of the interview.

Unlike the cohort of the *Nouvelle Vague*, the new filmmakers of the 1970s did not form a movement, nor did they ride the crest of rising public enthusiasm. On the contrary, movie attendance was in decline: ticket prices had risen faster than the rate of inflation, and television offered a convenient and cheaper alternative. Filmmakers could no longer afford to focus on experimental or abstract or "difficult" work that would attract elite audiences of cinephiles or intellectuals. Tavernier's temperament ran in a different direction anyway. Although he is a filmmaker's filmmaker in the sense that his esthetic and ethical standards are extremely rigorous, and he enjoys pushing the envelope of techniques and genres, he has no interest in experimentation for its own sake. He seeks an audience that cuts across boundaries separating generations and social milieux and distinguishing high from popular culture. Even his historical films take on big and controversial contemporary topics. As already noted, he is motivated by a desire to understand, but also to probe, to advocate, to educate, to provoke. And to entertain. Every one of his films is a pleasure for the eyes, the ears, and the intellect.[3]

For his first feature, Tavernier made two choices that proved controversial. The first was his choice of location. *The Clockmaker*, released in 1974, was set in Lyon. The film's French title—*L'Horloger de Saint-Paul*—evokes the church at the heart of the city's historical district, and the gentle musical motif that recurs throughout the film is adapted from the chimes of the church's antique clock. It was not easy to find funding for the project, but when an interested producer offered to finance the film if the fledgling filmmaker would consent to relocate his story from his native city to Paris, Tavernier flatly refused. In the face of financial obstacles, lead actor Philippe Noiret, already committed to the script, invested his personal funds and the considerable weight of his own reputation to make the project possible.

A second decision that continues to raise eyebrows even today was Tavernier's choice of the veteran screenwriting team of Jean Aurenche and Pierre Bost to script the film. Aurenche and Bost had been in the business for decades. They had signed titles some of which are now considered masterpieces: René Clément's *Jeux interdits* [*Forbidden Games*] (1952), *Gervaise* (1955), and *Paris brûle-t-il?* [*Is Paris Burning?*] (1966); Jean Delannoy's *La Symphonie pastorale* [*Pastoral Symphony*] (1946); Claude Autant-Lara's *Douce* [*Love Story*] (1943), and *La Traversée de Paris* [*Four Bags Full*] (1956). But the pair had also become associated with the so-called "Cinema of Quality," part of a postwar cultural policy designed to raise the profile of French national cinema to counterbalance the postwar American influx (implicitly a "cinema of quantity"). Many of these films were indeed static, declamatory, and uninspired adaptations of French literary classics, in a style the "young Turks" of the New Wave rebelled against. The charge was led by Truffaut, who specifically targeted Aurenche and Bost in a hot-headed and misguided 1954 manifesto, published in the *Cahiers du Cinéma*: "A Certain Tendency in French Cinema." Truffaut, who later confessed he had acted somewhat dishonorably, mobilized the intergenerational tensions brewing at the time by dismissing his elders' work and designating it as a "Cinéma de Papa." His tirade served as a rallying cry, and Aurenche and Bost were effectively blacklisted by many leading filmmakers and producers for almost two decades.

Working with his chosen scriptwriting team, Tavernier adapted *The Clockmaker* from a novel by Georges Simenon, shifting the setting from 1950s Connecticut to post-1968 France. The film tells a story about a young man who commits a crime and his father who tries to understand, and who gradually learns to question authority and stand by his son. The father's evolution in consciousness enlarges his family's drama to encompass its political and historical dimension, the sort of narrative complexity that appeals to Tavernier and at which Aurenche and Bost excelled. Tavernier explains that as a young filmmaker, he needed input from an older generation for this project of intergenerational (mis)communication, and Aurenche and Bost fit the bill perfectly. Moreover, Tavernier was impressed with the scriptwriters' sparkling talent and their political and social vision, notably in *Love Story*, an Occupation-era film directed by Autant-Lara, into which the scriptwriters had daringly inserted covert provocations to revolt.

The Clockmaker won the prestigious Louis Delluc prize awarded annually, often to exceptionally promising first-time directors. His debut film set in place many of the themes and preoccupations for which he has become well known: the centrality and richness of his character portraits, for example, and his inspired work with actors. Philippe Noiret, a cinematic legend by any standard, recognized Tavernier's talent from the start and would go on to play lead roles in in six additional Tavernier features, a corpus of work the actor considered the highlight of his long and prolific career. Other actors were either discovered by Tavernier (e.g., fellow Lyon native Christine Pascal), were enticed away from the theater (Philippe Torreton of *Capitaine Conan* and *Ça commence aujourd'hui* [*It All Starts Today*], for example), or gave the best performances of their careers in Tavernier films (Jean Galabru in *Le Juge et l'assassin* [*The Judge and the Assassin*], Thierry Lhermite in *Quai d'Orsay* [*The French Minister*]).

Tavernier's next two films, also scripted by Aurenche and Bost, couldn't have been more different from the first. *Que La Fête commence* [*Let Joy Reign Supreme*] offers a portrait of the Regent Philippe d'Orléans, who governed the realm during the minority of the future King Louis XV. Like his historical model, Noiret's regent is an intelligent and good-hearted man too weak-willed to avoid the looming catastrophes, spending his time instead in dissolute debaucheries. Thanks to an extraordinary trio of actors—Jean Rochefort and Jean-Pierre Marielle along with Noiret—the "fête" of the title can also serve to describe the film itself—a visual feast. *The Judge and the Assassin* (Noiret and Galabru respectively) pits a deranged serial killer against the judge who tracks him down. Set against the rich political and social canvas of the Belle Epoque, with its Dreyfus Affair, anarchism hysteria, hypertrophied class and gender hierarchies, and colonial anxieties, the film's social critique was in tune with the prevailing intellectual spirit of its own era. In the wake of the 1968 revolts, leading figures such as Michel Foucault, Roland Barthes, Michel de Certeau, and others were challenging patriarchal institutions like the church, the law, and the traditional family, and Tavernier's films extended those investigations in an imaginative register. Anchored by the historical juncture at which he began his career, Tavernier would continue to probe historical moments of instability and transition in his fiction films: the end of the Middle Ages (*La Passion Béatrice* [*Beatrice*]), the sixteenth-century Wars of Religion (*La Princesse de Montpensier* [*The Princess of Montpensier*]), the waning of the Belle Epoque (*Un*

Dimanche à la campagne [*A Sunday in the Country*]), the aftermath of the First World War (*La Vie et rien d'autre* [*Life and Nothing But*]; *Capitaine Conan*), the ominous prelude to the Second World War and the bloody conflicts of decolonization (*Coup de Torchon* [*Clean Slate*]). In all these historical dramas, meticulous attention to period setting and "mentalities" coexists with inescapable contemporary relevance.

Tavernier's final film of the 1970s turns in yet another direction. Angered by abusively raised rents and evictions in his corporation-owned apartment building, Tavernier had written a letter to new Prime Minister Jacques Chirac threatening to make a movie about the episode. The result was *Des Enfants gâtés* [*Spoiled Children*]. In the film, scriptwriter Bernard Rougerie (Michel Piccoli) takes an apartment in order to work without distractions, but his middle-aged complacency is shaken by his involvement in the politics of everyday life: a rent strike in his building and an amorous entanglement with one of the protesters.

In connection with *Spoiled Children*, Tavernier launched his own production company with a couple of friends. That company, called Little Bear (after his then wife Colo's nickname for him), afforded the filmmaker the artistic and financial autonomy he needed to put forward his own social agenda and to support projects he believed in. Among its many ventures, Little Bear has produced films by Tavernier's son, Nils, a talented filmmaker in his own right; it provided funds to Tavernier's assistant director in his first two films, Laurent Heynemann, to make *La Question*, a filmed dramatization of a clandestine 1958 book of the same title that exposed the use of torture by the French military in Algeria; and it financed a collective film, *Lumières sur un massacre*, organized by Handicap International to draw attention to continuing casualties from leftover landmines in war zones all over the world. Little Bear has also produced or co-produced most of Tavernier's own films.

Spoiled Children—and the outrage that fueled the film's creation—launched two threads that Tavernier would develop throughout his future career. A substantial section of his filmography, primarily during the 1980s, is devoted to portraits of professional artists. After Bernard Rougerie, Tavernier's artist figures include an elderly painter (in *A Sunday in the Country*) who agonizes over whether by avoiding risks, he has achieved less than his potential; an ailing American jazz saxophonist (*Autour de Minuit* ['*Round Midnight*]) who worries that his talent is exhausted; a novelist (in *Daddy Nostalgie*) who abandons her writing to care for her dying father. These and other artist figures struggle to keep their self-doubt at bay and to balance commitments to art, family, and society. In a recent interview, Tavernier realized that almost all his films are about people's relation to their work.[4] Clearly, he sets artists among other workers (teachers, soldiers, narcotics police, even a regent and a government minister), all of whom struggle with responsibility to self and others and who strive to believe their contribution makes a difference.

A second thread that can be identified as early as *Spoiled Children* is an engage-ment with documentary modes of storytelling, a dimension of Tavernier's oeuvre that became more pronounced and insistent toward the end of the Mitterrand presidency and into the 1990s. The filmmaker attributes this shift in emphasis to the rise of the extreme Right and his need to respond with a more explicit politi-cal engagement, a more direct intervention in public events.[5] While continuing to make purely fictional films, he began to make more actual documentaries and also to experiment with the kind of hybrid of documentary and fiction he had first deployed in response to his renters' strike. Tavernier believes—as he explains repeatedly here in these interviews—that films are not *reflections* of personal and social and political reality; they are *part* of that reality, and that therefore public debates about cinema should not be restricted—"ghettoized"[6]—to the entertain-ment section.

Of Tavernier's numerous documentaries, some were shot quickly, in the heat of events. In this category we might mention *Histoires de vies brisées: les "double peine" de Lyon* (2001), co-directed with son Nils, which exposed the de facto double jeopardy inflicted on undocumented immigrants sent to prison for minor crimes and then deported. For *De L'Autre Côté du Périph'* [*The Other Side of the Tracks*] in 1997, Tavernier and Nils spent several months interviewing residents of a hous-ing project in Montreuil, beyond the "boulevard périphérique" (Paris beltway). Made in response to an insulting challenge by the minister of the interior and in the context of a movement protesting a law requiring citizens to inform on undocumented immigrants, the film unrolls a litany of official discrimination and neglect. Others were the fruit of careful planning. One example is *Lyon, le regard intérieur* [*Lyon Inside Out*] (1988), a television documentary about the filmmaker's native city, for which Tavernier conducted a leisurely interview with his father. An-other example is the 1984 *Mississippi Blues*, also known as *Pays d'Octobre* [*October Country*], a quest through the American Deep South for the source of the blues. Undoubtedly Tavernier's most durable documentary, however, is *La Guerre sans nom* [*The Undeclared War*] (1992), which marked the thirtieth anniversary of the Evian Accords that ended France's war in Algeria. That four-hour film, made with historian Patrick Rotman, consists entirely of interviews with ordinary French soldiers who fought in Algeria, many of whom had never before spoken about their experiences. Tavernier is a listener. Motivated by his "desire to understand," his documentaries are deeply democratic, in the sense that his camera serves to help ordinary people gain access to the public ear and have their say.

Tavernier has also pursued his documentary inclinations and filming styles within fiction films. For example, *L.627* (1992) recreates the daily dangers and frus-trations faced by a brigade of anti-drug cops. *L'Appât* [*Fresh Bait*] (1995) is adapted from a true-crime book about a trio of teenagers who robbed and murdered several men in the hopes of emigrating to America and launching their own ready-to-wear clothing business. Increasingly, Tavernier has experimented with investigating real situations in real locales in films that are nevertheless (minimally) scripted, with most, but not all of the roles played by actors. *It All Starts Today* (1999) follows the daily challenges faced by a kindergarten teacher in a depressed mining town. The protagonist, a teacher, is an actor (Philippe Torreton), but the children and other teachers play themselves. *Holy Lola* (2004) details the bureaucratic obstacles faced by a couple seeking to adopt a child in Cambodia. In all of these stories (as in some of the purely fictional films such as *Life and Nothing But*), the enemy is any malignant or mindless bureaucracy, and the "heroes" (such as they are—Tavernier is wary of heroic narratives) are ordinary people trying to do the right thing. What is innovative and fresh about these films is the way they weave together real situations with invented anecdotes. Tavernier encouraged his actors to contribute to the elaboration of the story and the dialogues and to engage with the issues and the real people in the real situations depicted. To a great extent, they did just that, so that when interviewed, the actors frequently marvel that they lost track of whether they were acting or not. These films were widely discussed. They raised public awareness, provoked debate, and some even succeeded in bringing about real change.

Tavernier is a man who wears many hats. His desire to understand—and intervene—manifests itself in his activities that extend and complement his directing career, and his conception of filmmaking as a form of exploration or investigation brings together his roles as artist, critic, historian, and public activist. Like his films, he is deeply engaged with the pressing issues facing France and the world: the value of work, the consequences of war, colonialism and its continuing aftermath, the price of heroism, the power of art. An insatiable cinephile who began his career as a publicist, he is immensely knowledgeable and passionate about world cinema and advocates tirelessly on behalf of the films he loves. The Institut Lumière he helped establish hosts retrospectives and festivals. In short, he sees his career as following in the lineage of the Lumière brothers themselves, in that his goal, like theirs, is to "show the world to the world." His films try (and succeed, mostly) to avoid explanatory and expository and polemical interventions that would distance us from characters, who always remain central. But speaking as himself, Tavernier is happy to explain, to theorize, to take a stand. (As he remarks herein, you have to be prepared "to come down out of your ivory tower and consent to having a few dust-ups over your ideas."[7]) Taken together, his films and his interviews paint the portrait of an artist engaged with the issues and personalities of his time and place.

This perhaps excessively serious overview of Tavernier's career would not be complete, however, without evoking his sense of fun. Still a Lyonnais at heart, he enjoys a good meal and a good laugh, and his films contain liberal doses of both. His humor is not Rabelaisian, however; in fact, by contemporary standards, he's somewhat of a prude. An astute and sensitive observer of human behavior, he has a highly developed sense of irony: carefully targeted, mordant, and self-aware. A kind and gentle man, he nevertheless lets no bureaucratic or official absurdity go unchallenged. You do not want to be on the receiving end of his sardonic wit. In his films, in writing, and in person, he doesn't pull punches, but he is also a charming and lively conversationalist.

It is no surprise, then, that an interview with Tavernier is a treat. Beginning with discussions of his own films, the interviews you will discover in this volume cover a vast panorama of topics. At the core are his thoughts about the ways cinema can inspire the imagination and contribute to the broadest and richest possible public conversation.

LAH

Notes

1. Antoine Royer, "Interview with Bertrand Tavernier on *Death Watch*," in this volume, p. 267.

2. Jean-Claude Raspiengeas, *Bertrand Tavernier* (Paris: Flammarion, 2001), 70–71.

3. Even with its ups and downs, Tavernier's approach has been a success, as reflected in his many awards (see Filmography).

4. "Tavernier: 'Les diplomates de connaissent pas les 35 heures" [On *The French Minister*], *Le Figaro*, Nov. 5, 2013.

5. Richard Phillips, "An Interview with Bertrand Tavernier," in this volume, p. 210.

6. Jacques Demeure and Paul-Louis Thirard, "Conversation with Bertrand Tavernier," in this volume, p. 44.

7. Demeure and Thirard, p. 38.

Chronology

1941   Bertrand René Maurice Tavernier is born April 25 in Lyon to philosopher and poet René Tavernier and Geneviève Dumont-Cotte. The family lives on the rue Chambovet, and from there Bertrand will make his first visits to the cinema with his grandmother Hélène Tavernier.

1947   The Tavernier family moves to Paris.

1952   Worried by their son's mediocre academic record, his parents send Bertrand to be educated by the Oratorians in Pontoise, where he is unhappy and feels exiled from his family. On weekends he takes the bus to Paris and spends his time at the movies.

1957   Tavernier enrolls at the Lycée Henri IV in Paris and is happy to have the Paris Cinémathèque on the nearby rue d'Ulm.

1960   Tavernier and some friends found the Nickel-Odéon which they affiliate with the Fédération Française des Ciné-Clubs. Tavernier publishes a glowing review of Jean-Pierre Melville's films in *L'Etrave*, a student journal. Melville hires Tavernier as his assistant for *Léon Morin, Prêtre*.

1961   Georges de Beauregard hires Tavernier as his press attaché.

1963   Tavernier contributes a short film sketch to an ensemble film, *Les Baisers*.

1964   Tavernier's second short film is included in *La Chance et l'amour*.

1965   Tavernier marries Claudine (Colo) O'Hagan, whose parents are friends of the Taverniers. Son Nils is born on September 1.

1967   Birth of daughter, Tiffany, on May 3.

1968   Tavernier follows the "Events of '68" in Paris but does not take an active role in the demonstrations.

1972   Tavernier contacts Jean Aurenche, and together they pursue Georges Simenon for the rights to his novel which will become Tavernier's first feature-length film, *L'Horloger de Saint-Paul* [*The Clockmaker*], starring Philippe Noiret.

1974   Tavernier's first film is awarded the Prix Louis-Delluc.

1975   Tavernier and Aurenche create a historical drama based on the life of

Louis XIV's Regent Philippe d'Orléans. *Que la Fête commence* [*Let Joy Reign Supreme*] premiers on March 26 to rave reviews.

1976 Fascinated by the life of Joseph Bouvier, who killed twelve children in different regions of France between 1893 and 1898, Tavernier creates *Le Juge et l'assassin* [*The Judge and the Assassin*] which will be awarded several Césars: for best actor, best scenario, and best music. Tavernier creates his own production company, Little Bear.

1977 Colo and Bertrand's experiences as members of a renters' collective lead them to write and direct *Des Enfants gâtés* [*Spoiled Children*]. Sadly, Tavernier's stormy on-set relationship with Christine Pascal will become public.

1979 A reading of David Compton's *The Continuous Katherine Mortenhoe* will inspire Tavernier to make an Orwellian film about a woman whose death is watched by millions thanks to the ingenious insertion of a camera in the eye of a man who becomes her confidant. Tavernier engages Romy Schneider and Harvey Keitel to interpret the major roles in *La Mort en direct* [*Death Watch*], a psychological sci-fi written by Tavernier and David Rayfiel and filmed in Glasgow.

1980 Tavernier returns to Lyon for his inspiration, and, with Colo as his co-scenarist, writes *Une Semaine de vacances* [*A Week's Vacation*] and films it in six weeks along the banks of the Rhône. The film will be selected for the 33rd Cannes Festival but turns out to be one of the director's least appreciated films. Tavernier and Luc Béraud are elected co-presidents of the Society of Film Directors.

1981 Colo and Bertrand decide to separate. He adapts Jim Thompson's *Pop. 1280* for the screen. After ten months of negotiations for the rights, Tavernier joins with Jean Aurenche again and travels to Senegal to create *Coup de torchon* [*Clean Slate*]. The film opens to mixed reviews despite a brilliant performance by Philippe Noiret. The film ends up being a financial and critical success.

1982 Commissioned by television Channel 3, Tavernier films nine days of conversations with the Surrealist poet Philippe Soupault. Originally planned to be fifty-two minutes long, the film will end up three hours long.

1984 Tavernier contacts his old friend, the American director Robert Parrish, who hadn't directed a film in ten years, and they agree to make a documentary about the American South and the blues. They begin in Oxford, Mississippi, following Faulkner's traces. The result is a lengthy travelogue entitled *Mississippi Blues*. During a chance encounter of Martin Scorsese, Irwin Winkler, and Tavernier, the three

hatch a plan to make a film about the history of American jazz players in Paris in the fifties. The filmmaker discovers Pierre Bost's *Monsieur Ladmiral va bientôt mourir* and asks Colo to join him in writing
a screenplay of the novel. Together they discover the seventy-three-
year-old theater actor, Louis Ducreux, and team him up with Sabine
Azéma as the father-daughter pair in the delightful *Un Dimanche à la
campagne* [*A Sunday in the Country*]. The film will win the grand prize
at Cannes for its mise en scène.

1985   At seventy-two years of age, Dexter Gordon agrees to play the role
of the semi-fictional saxophonist, Dale Turner, in *Autour de Minuit*
['*Round Midnight*], and shooting begins in July at Epinay Studios.
Gordon's drinking on set and off creates huge problems for the
production.

1986   '*Round Midnight* is released. Tavernier returns to the US to do a publicity tour for the film, visiting Baltimore, Detroit, Los Angeles, and
a dozen other cities. Herbie Hancock will receive an Oscar for the
best musical score. This French film on American jazz will be more
celebrated in the States than in France.

1987   Tavernier shoots *La Passion Béatrice* [*Beatrice*], based on a scenario by
Colo about the life of Beatrice Cenci, who had her abusive husband
murdered in 1577 and his body thrown off her balcony to make the
murder look like an accident. The film is a failure at the box office. In
a moment of depression, the director wonders whether he ought to
call it quits. Instead, as a kind of therapy, Tavernier returns to Lyon
to film *Lyon, le regard intérieur*, a fifty-two-minute television documentary in which Bertrand interviews his father, René, about the
city.

1989   Tavernier and Jean Cosmos create a script that joins a tangled web
of life stories about the Great War with a panorama of the postwar
efforts to identify the some 350,000 "missing" from that war. Tavernier also unites Philippe Noiret and Sabine Azéma in a love story
constructed in and through the search for the unknown soldier. The
result is the monumental *La Vie et rien d'autre* [*Life and Nothing But*].
Shot around Verdun in the fall and winter of 1988, the film will attract an audience of nearly two million. Bertrand's father, René Tavernier, dies at age seventy-four on December 14.

1990   After this great grand panorama, Bertrand and Colo turn to Jane
Birkin and Dirk Bogarde to portray the father and daughter in an
intimate drama entitled *Daddy Nostalgie*. The film opens to mixed
reviews.

1991   Tavernier publishes *Thirty Years of American Cinema* summing up the author's thoughts about film. The book is an immediate success.

1992   Commissioned to make a ninety-minute documentary on the Algerian war, Tavernier produces a four-hour film. Faced with his producers' rage at the length of this film, the director shouts, "I won't cut a thing!" *The Undeclared War* will be programmed only twice, but Tavernier obtains the rights to the work and brings it out on videocassette. While working on the documentary, Tavernier prepares *L.627*, a film about a police brigade struggling with the drug traffic in Paris. At the film's release, Tavernier is attacked by the French minister of the interior for his exposé of this problem. The film's success at the box office is thereby assured.

1994   Initially only the producer of *La Fille de d'Artagnan* [*D'Artagnan's Daughter*], Tavernier is unhappy with octogenarian Ricardo Freda's direction and steps in to finish the film himself, turning it into a parody of the Dumas novel. The critical reaction is mixed at best.

1995   Fascinated by a 1984 news story about three teenagers who torture and kill two businessmen in a ten-day period, Tavernier and Colo create a script entitled *L'Appât* [*Fresh Bait*] to portray the amorality and insouciance of these three seemingly normal kids. The film wins the Golden Bear at the Berlin Film Festival.

1996   Since the early nineties, Tavernier had been interested in a historical anomaly: after the armistice ending the First World War had been signed in 1918, French troops continued to fight on the Macedonian Front as part of the Allied intervention in the Russian Civil War. In 1934, Roger Vercel had brought this anomaly to life in his Goncourt-winning novel *Capitaine Conan*, and both Tavernier and Jean Cosmos had taken a fancy to this story at the same time. The fruit of their collaboration is an epic film of the same title that premieres in October to very unenthusiastic reviews.

1997   Given the strong public feelings about undocumented immigrants in France and the violent demonstrations that had occurred on both sides of the issue, it was only natural that Tavernier should make a documentary sympathetic to the plight of these "unclassifiables." The result is a contentious documentary that Bertrand and his son Nils premiered in October: *De L'Autre Côté du Périph'* [*The Other Side of the Tracks*].

1999   Once engaged in the plight of the "disinherited" in France, Tavernier examines the problems of the schools and the inadequacy of the social services in France's depressed northern mining district. *Ça commence aujourd'hui* [*It All Starts Today*] provides a stirring fictionalized account of the enormous difficulties faced by the young director of one such school. The film is highly acclaimed outside France.

2000   With his son Nils, Tavernier makes *Histoires de vies brisées: les 'double peine' de Lyon*, a "small" film about legal immigrants threatened with deportation.

2002   From his work with scriptwriter Jean Aurenche, Tavernier is convinced that Aurenche's story of filmmaking during the German occupation needs telling. The result is *Laissez-Passer* [*Safe Conduct*], a gripping narrative about the difficulties of filming under German control.

2004   When Tavernier asks his daughter, Tiffany, if she'd like to direct a film, she demurs but suggests he adapt a novel she'd written about a French couple who seek to adopt a child in Cambodia. *Holy Lola*, filmed in Cambodia, recounts the many frustrations and ultimate success of that venture.

2009   Fascinated by James Lee Burke's *In the Electric Mist with Confederate Dead*, Tavernier returns to the American South—this time to a post-Katrina Louisiana—to adapt Burke's novel for the screen. Tommy Lee Jones not only plays the main character, Dave Robicheaux, but helps the director with casting and local color for *Dans La Brume électrique* [*In the Electric Mist*].

2010   Perhaps in part because of his love of the American Western, coupled with his love of historical dramas, Tavernier brings Madame de La Fayette's short novel *The Princess of Montpensier* to the screen. The story allows the director to move outdoors and film dramatic battle scenes between Huguenots and Catholics, as well as "hell for leather" cross-country gallops reminiscent of the best of John Ford and company.

2013   For his latest film, Tavernier turns to satire. The result: *Quai d'Orsay* [*The French Minister*]. The film receives three nominations at the French Césars. Niels Arestrup wins the award for Best Supporting Actor.

2014   Bertrand Tavernier enthusiastically endorses a book of interviews to be published by the University Press of Mississippi, where he'd come to shoot *Mississippi Blues* thirty years previously!

Filmography

"LA CHANCE EXPLOSIVE" in LA CHANCE ET L'AMOUR (1964)
(UK/USA: CHANCE AT LOVE)
Director: **Bertrand Tavernier**
Screenplay: **Bertrand Tavernier**
Dialogues: Nicolas Vogel
Producer: Georges de Beauregard
Cinematography: Alain Levent
Editing: Armand Psenny
Sound: Jean-Claude Marchetti
Music: Antoine Duhamel
Cast: Michel Auclair (Alain Lorrière), Bernard Blier (Camilly), Iran Evry (Sophie), Bob Morel (un truand), Gérard Tichy (un truand), Jack Léonard (un truand), Antonello Campodifiori (un truand), Edouard F. Médard (un truand)
105 minutes (entire film), b/w

"BAISER DE JUDAS" in LES BAISERS (1965)
Director: **Bertrand Tavernier**
Assistant Director: Volker Schlöndorff
Screenplay: Claude Nahon, Roger Tailleur
Producer: Georges de Beauregard
Cinematography: Raoul Coutard
Editing: Etiennette Muse
Music: Eddie Vartan
Cast: Leticia Roman (Tiffany), Bernard Rousselet (Robert), Judy Del Carril (Sylvie), William Sabatier (Inspector Beroy), Guy Sauval (l'inconnu?)
97 minutes (entire film), b/w

L'HORLOGER DE SAINT-PAUL (1974)
(UK: THE WATCHMAKER OF SAINT PAUL; USA: THE CLOCKMAKER OF SAINT PAUL)
Director: **Bertrand Tavernier**

Screenplay: Jean Aurenche, Pierre Bost, **Bertrand Tavernier**; based on the novel
L'Horloger d'Everton by Georges Simenon
Producer: Raymond Danon; Lira Films
Cinematography: Pierre-William Glenn
Editing: Armand Psenny
Sound: Michel Desrois, Harald Maury
Music: Philippe Sarde
Cast: Philippe Noiret (Michel Descombes), Jean Rochefort (Commissaire Guil-
boud), Jacques Denis (Antoine), Yves Afonso (Commissaire Bricard), Julien
Bertheau (Edouard), Jacques Hilling (Costes), Clotilde Joano (Janine Boitard),
Andrée Tainsy (Madeleine Fourmet)
Filmed in and around Lyon
105 minutes, color
Awards: Prix Louis Delluc (Bertrand Tavernier, 1973); OCIC Award (Bertrand Tav-
ernier, Berlin, 1974); Silver Berlin Bear (Bertrand Tavernier, Special Jury Prize,
Berlin, 1974)

QUE LA FETE COMMENCE (1975)
(USA: LET JOY REIGN SUPREME)
Director: **Bertrand Tavernier**
Screenplay: Jean Aurenche, **Bertrand Tavernier**
Producers: Alain Belmondo, Michèle de Broca, Yves Robert; Fildebroc, Les Produc-
tions de la Guéville, Universal Pictures France (UPF)
Cinematography: Pierre-William Glenn
Editing: Armand Psenny
Sound: Michel Desrois
Music: Antoine Duhamel, based on the manuscripts of Philippe d'Orléans
Cast: Philippe Noiret (Philippe d'Orléans), Jean Rochefort (L'abbé Dubois), Jean-
Pierre Marielle (Le marquis de Pontcallec), Marina Vlady (Madame de Parabère),
Christine Pascal (Emilie), Gérard Desarthe (Le duc de Bourbon), Alfred Adam (Vil-
leroi), Jean-Roger Caussimon (Le cardinal)
114 minutes, color
Awards: SFCC Critics Award (Bertrand Tavernier, Best Film, 1976); César (Bertrand
Tavernier, Best Director, 1976); César (Pierre Guffroy, Best Production Design,
1976); César (Jean Rochefort, Best Supporting Actor, 1976); César (Jean Aurenche
and Bertrand Tavernier, Best Writing, 1976)

LE JUGE ET L'ASSASSIN (1976)
(UK/USA: THE JUDGE AND THE ASSASSIN)
Director: **Bertrand Tavernier**

Producers: Raymond Danon, France 3 Cinéma, Société Française de Production, Lira Films
Cinematography: Pierre-William Glenn
Editing: Armand Psenny
Sound: Michel Desrois
Music: Philippe Sarde
Cast: Philippe Noiret (Judge Rousseau), Michel Galabru (Joseph Bouvier), Isabelle Huppert (Rose), Jean-Claude Brialy (Attorney of Villedieu), Renée Faure (Madame Rousseau), Cécile Vassort (Louise Lesueur), Yves Robert (Professor Degueldre), Jean-Roger Caussimon (Street Singer), Jean Bretonnière (Deputy), Monique Chaumette (Louise's Mother)
Filmed in Ardèche, France
110 minutes, color
Awards: César (Michel Galabru, Best Actor, 1977); César (Jean Aurenche and Bertrand Tavernier, Best Writing, 1977)

DES ENFANTS GATES (1977)
(UK/USA: SPOILED CHILDREN)
Director: **Bertrand Tavernier**
Screenplay: Charlotte Dubreuil, Christine Pascal, **Bertrand Tavernier**
Producers: Daniel Toscan du Plantier, Alain Sarde, Film 66, Little Bear, Sara Films
Cinematography: Alain Levent
Editing: Armand Psenny
Sound: Michel Desrois
Music: Philippe Sarde
Cast: Michel Piccoli (Bernard Rougerie), Christine Pascal (Anne Torrini), Michel Aumont (Pierre), Gérard Jugnot (Marcel Bonfils), Arlette Bonnard (Catherine Rougerie), Geneviève Mnich (Guite Bonfils), Gérard Zimmermann (Patrice Joffroy), Liza Braconnier (Danièle Joffroy)
Filmed in Paris, France
113 minutes, color

LA MORT EN DIRECT (1980)
(UK/USA: DEATH WATCH)
Director: **Bertrand Tavernier**
Screenplay: **Bertrand Tavernier**, David Rayfiel; based on the novel *The Continuous Katherine Mortenhoe, or The Unsleeping Eye* by David Compton
Producers: Jean-Serge Breton, Elie Kfouri, **Bertrand Tavernier**, Gabriel Roustani, Janine Rubeiz, Antenne 2, Gaumont International, Little Bear, Sara Films, Selta Films, SFP Cinéma, TV13 Filmproduktion (Münich)

Cinematography: Pierre-William Glenn
Editing: Michael Ellis, Armand Psenny
Sound: Michel Desrois
Music: Antoine Duhamel
Cast: Romy Schneider (Katherine Mortenhoe), Harvey Keitel (Roddy), Harry Dean Stanton (Vincent Ferriman), Thérèse Liotard (Tracey), Max von Sydow (Gerald Mortenhoe), Caroline Langrishe (Girl in the Bar), William Russell (Dr. Mason), Vadim Glowna (Harry Graves)
Filmed in Glasgow and Mull of Kintyre, Scotland
128 minutes, color

UNE SEMAINE DE VACANCES (1980)
(UK: A WEEK'S HOLIDAY; USA: A WEEK'S VACATION)
Director: **Bertrand Tavernier**
Screenplay: Marie-Françoise Hans, **Bertrand Tavernier**, Colo Tavernier
Producers: Christine Gozlan, **Bertrand Tavernier** Antenne 2, Little Bear, Sara Films
Cinematography: Pierre-William Glenn
Editing: Armand Psenny
Sound: Michel Desrois
Music: Eddy Mitchell, Pierre Papadiamandis
Cast: Nathalie Baye (Laurence), Gérard Lanvin (Pierre), Michel Galabru (Mancheron), Flore Fitzgerald (Anne), Philippe Léotard (Sabouret), Jean Dasté (Laurence's father), Philippe Delaigue (Jacques), Marie-Louise Ebeli (Laurence's mother)
102 minutes, color

COUP DE TORCHON (1981)
(UK: CLEAN UP; USA: CLEAN SLATE)
Director: **Bertrand Tavernier**
Screenplay: Jean Aurenche, **Bertrand Tavernier**; based on the novel *Pop. 1280* by Jim Thompson
Producers: Henri Lassa, Adolphe Viezzi, Les Films de la Tour, Films A2, Little Bear
Cinematography: Pierre-William Glenn
Editing: Armand Psenny
Sound: Michel Desrois, Dominique Levert
Music: **Bertrand Tavernier**, Philippe Sarde
Cast: Philippe Noiret (Lucien Cordier), Isabelle Huppert (Rose), Jean-Pierre Marielle (Le Peron and his brother), Stéphane Audran (Huguette Cordier), Eddy Mitchell (Nono), Guy Marchand (Marcel Chavasson), Irène Skobline (Anne), Michel Beaune (Vanderbrouck)

Filmed in Sénégal
128 minutes, color
Awards: SFCC Critics Award (Bertrand Tavernier, Best Film, 1982); Silver Ribbon, Italian National Syndicate of Film Journalists (Philippe Noiret, Best Actor—Foreign Film, 1986)

PHILIPPE SOUPAULT (1982)
Director: **Bertrand Tavernier**
Producers: FR 3 (Series: Témoins), Ministry of Culture
Cinematography: Jean-Francis Gondre
Editing: Luce Grunenwaldt
Sound: Harald Maury
Cast: Philippe Soupault (himself), Jean Aurenche (himself)
163 minutes, b/w

MISSISSIPPI BLUES (1983, Canada; 1984, France)
Directors: Robert Parrish, **Bertrand Tavernier**
Producers: Yannick Bernard, **Bertrand Tavernier**; Films A2, Little Bear, Sara Films
Cinematography: Pierre-William Glenn
Editing: Ariane Boeglin, Agnès Vaurigaud
Sound: Michel Desrois, Dominique Levert
Filmed in Mississippi
96 minutes, color

UN DIMANCHE A LA CAMPAGNE (1984)
(UK/USA: A SUNDAY IN THE COUNTRY)
Director: **Bertrand Tavernier**
Screenplay: **Bertrand Tavernier**, Colo Tavernier; based on the novel *Monsieur Ladmiral va bientôt mourir* by Pierre Bost
Producers: Alain Sarde, **Bertrand Tavernier;** Films A2, Little Bear, Sara Films
Cinematography: Bruno de Keyzer
Editing: Armand Psenny
Sound: Guillaume Sciama
Music: Philippe Sarde
Cast: Louis Ducreux (Monsieur Ladmiral), Sabine Azéma (Irène), Michel Aumont (Gonzague, Edouard), Geneviève Mnich (Marie-Thérèse), Monique Chaumette (Mercédès), Claude Winter (Madame Ladmiral), Thomas Duval (Emile), Katia Wostrikoff (Mireille)
90 minutes, color

Awards: Boston Society of Film Critics Awards (BSFC Award, Bertrand Tavernier, Best Director, 1985); Boston Society of Film Critics Awards (BSFC Award, Best Foreign Language Film, 1985); Cannes Film Festival (Best Director, Bertrand Tavernier, 1984); César (Sabine Azéma, Best Actress, 1985); César (Bruno de Keyzer, Best Cinematography, 1985); César (Bertrand Tavernier and Colo Tavernier, Best Writing—Adaptation, 1985); Kansas City Film Critics Circle Awards (KCFCC Award, Best Foreign Film, 1985); London Critics Circle Film Awards (ALFS Award, Foreign Language Film of the Year, 1985); Mainichi Film Concours (Bertrand Tavernier, Best Foreign Language Film, 1986); National Board of Review, USA (NBR Award, Best Foreign Language Film, 1984); National Board of Review, USA (Sabine Azéma, NBR Award, Best Supporting Actress, 1984); New York Film Critics Circle Awards (NYFCC Award, Best Foreign Language Film, 1984); Grand Prix du Cinéma Français (Meilleur Film)

AUTOUR DE MINUIT (1986)
(UK/USA: 'ROUND MIDNIGHT)
Director: **Bertrand Tavernier**
Screenplay: **Bertrand Tavernier,** David Rayfiel; based on the work by Francis Paudras and Bud Powell
Producer: Irwin Winkler; Little Bear, Productions et Editions Cinématographiques Françaises
Cinematography: Bruno de Keyzer
Editing: Armand Psenny
Sound: Michel Desrois, William Flageollet
Music: Herbie Hancock
Cast: Dexter Gordon (Dale Turner), François Cluzet (Francis Borier), Sandra Reeves-Phillips (Buttercup), Gabrielle Haker (Bérangère), Lonette McKee (Darcey Leigh), Christine Pascal (Sylvie), Herbie Hancock (Eddie Wayne)
Filmed in Paris, New York City, and Lyon
133 minutes, color
Awards: Academy Award (Herbie Hancock, Best Music, Original Score, 1987); Bodil Awards (Bertrand Tavernier, Best European Film, 1988); César (Herbie Hancock, Best Music Written for a Film, 1987); César (Bernard Leroux, Claude Villand, Michel Desrois, William Flageollet, Best Sound, 1987); David di Donatello Awards (Dexter Gordon, Best Foreign Actor, 1987); Italian National Syndicate of Film Journalists (Silver Ribbon, Dexter Gordon, Best Actor—Foreign Film, 1987); Italian National Syndicate of Film Journalists (Silver Ribbon, Bertrand Tavernier, Best Director—Foreign Film, 1987); Los Angeles Film Critics Associate Awards (LAFCA Award, Herbie Hancock, Dexter Gordon, Best Music, 1986); Sant Jordi Awards (Dexter Gordon, Best Foreign Actor, 1988)

LA PASSION BEATRICE (1987)
(UK/USA: BEATRICE)
Director: **Bertrand Tavernier**
Screenplay: Colo Tavernier
Producers: Adolphe Viezzi, AMLF, Cléa Productions, Les Films de la Tour, Little
Bear, Scena film, TF1 Films Productions
Cinematography: Bruno de Keyzer
Editing: Armand Psenny
Sound: Michel Desrois
Music: Ron Carter
Cast: Bernard-Pierre Donnadieu (François de Cortemart), Julie Delpy (Béatrice),
Nils Tavernier (Arnaud), Monique Chaumette (François's mother), Robert Dhéry
(Raoul), Michèle Gleizer (Hélène), Maxime Leroux (Richard), Jean-Claude Adelin
(Bertrand Lemartin), Jean-Louis Grinfeld (maître Blanche)
130 minutes, color
Awards: César (Jacqueline Moreau, Best Costume Design, 1988)

LYON, LE REGARD INTERIEUR (1988)
(UK/USA: LYON INSIDE OUT)
Director: **Bertrand Tavernier**
Screenplay: **Bertrand Tavernier**
Producer: Jean-Claude Bringuier: Little Bear
Cast: René Tavernier (himself), Pierre Mérindol (himself)
57 minutes, color

LA VIE ET RIEN D'AUTRE (1989)
(UK/USA: LIFE AND NOTHING BUT)
Director: **Bertrand Tavernier**
Screenplay: Jean Cosmos, **Bertrand Tavernier**
Producers: René Cleitman, Frédéric Bourboulon, Albert Prévost, AB Films Produc-
tions, Europe 1, Hachette Première, Films A2, Little Bear
Cinematography: Bruno de Keyzer
Editing: Armand Psenny
Sound: Michel Desrois, William Flageollet
Music: Oswald D'Andrea
Cast: Philippe Noiret (Dellaplane), Sabine Azéma (Irène), Pascale Vignal (Alice),
Maurice Barrier (Mercadot), François Perrot (Perrin), Jean-Pol Dubois (André),
Daniel Russo (Lieutenant Trévisse), Michel Duchaussoy (General Villerieux)
Filmed around Verdun
135 minutes, color

Awards: BAFTA Awards (René Cleitman, Bertrand Tavernier, Best Film not in the English Language, 1990); César (Philippe Noiret, Best Actor, 1990); César (Oswald D'Andrea, Best Music Written for a Film, 1990); David di Donatello Awards (Philippe Noiret, Best Foreign Actor, 1990); European Film Awards (Philippe Noiret, Best Actor, 1989); European Film Awards (Bertrand Tavernier, Special Prize of the Jury); Los Angeles Film Critics Association Awards (LAFCA Award, Best Foreign Film, 1990); Tokyo International Film Festival (Bertrand Tavernier, Best Artistic Contribution Award, 1989); Prix Georges de Beauregard (Meilleur film français)

DADDY NOSTALGIE (1990)
(UK/USA: DADDY NOSTALGIA)
Director: **Bertrand Tavernier**
Screenplay: **Bertrand Tavernier**, Colo Tavernier
Producers: Adolphe Viezzi, Cléa Productions, Little Bear, Solyfic, Eurisma
Cinematography: Denis Lenoir
Editing: Ariane Boeglin
Sound: Michel Desrois
Music: Antoine Duhamel
Cast: Dirk Bogarde (Daddy), Jane Birkin (Caroline), Odette Laure (Miche), Emmanuelle Bataille (Juliette), Charlotte Kady (Barbara), Michele Minns (Caroline, as a child)
Filmed in Bandol and Sanary-sur-Mer, France
105 minutes, color
Awards: Valladolid International Film Festival (Dirk Bogarde, Best Actor, 1990)

LA GUERRE SANS NOM (1992)
(UK/USA: THE UNDECLARED WAR)
Director: **Bertrand Tavernier**
Screenplay: Patrick Rotman, **Bertrand Tavernier**
Producers: Jean-Pierre Guérin; GMT Productions, Little Bear, Le Studio Canal +
Cinematography: Alain Choquart
Editing: Luce Grunenwaldt
Sound: Michel Desrois
Cast: Patrick Rotman (interviewer), **Bertrand Tavernier** (interviewer)
240 minutes, color
Awards: Bergamo Film Meeting (Bertrand Tavernier, Special Mention, 1992)

"POUR AUNG SAN KYI, MYANMAR" in CONTRE L'OUBLI (1991)
(UK/USA: AGAINST OBLIVION or LEST WE FORGET)

Director: **Bertrand Tavernier**
Producers: GMT Productions, Little Bear, Le Studio Canal +, Amnesty International, Les Films du Paradoxe
110 minutes (entire film), color

L.627 (1992)
Director: **Bertrand Tavernier**
Screenplay: Michel Alexandre, **Bertrand Tavernier**
Producers: Frédéric Bourboulon, Alain Sarde; Canal+, Les Films Alain Sarde, Little Bear
Cinematography: Alain Choquart
Editing: Ariane Boeglin
Sound: Michel Desrois, Gérard Lamps
Music: Philippe Sarde
Cast: Didier Bezace (Lucien "Lulu" Marguet), Jean-Paul Comart (Dominique "Dodo" Henriot), Charlotte Kady (Marie), Jean-Roger Milo (Manuel), Nils Tavernier (Vincent), Philippe Torreton (Antoine Cantoni), Lara Guirao (Cécile Rousselin), Cécile Garcia-Fogel (Kathy)
Filmed in Paris, France
145 minutes, color

LA FILLE DE D'ARTAGNAN (1994)
(UK/USA: D'ARTAGNAN'S DAUGHER)
Director: **Bertrand Tavernier**
Screenplay: Jean Cosmos, Michel Léviant, **Bertrand Tavernier;** based on an original idea of Riccardo Freda and Eric Poindron
Producers: Ciby 2000, Little Bear, TF1 Films Productions
Cinematography: Patrick Blossier
Editing: Ariane Boeglin
Sound: Michel Desrois, Gérard Lamps
Music: Philippe Sarde
Cast: Sophie Marceau (Eloïse), Philippe Noiret (D'Artagnan), Nils Tavernier (Quentin), Jean-Luc Bideau (Athos), Raoul Billerey (Porthos), Sami Frey (Aramis), Charlotte Kady (Lady in Red), Claude Rich (Duke of Crassac)
125 minutes, color

L'APPAT (1995)
(UK/USA: FRESH BAIT)
Director: **Bertrand Tavernier**
Screenplay: **Bertrand Tavernier**, Colo Tavernier

Producers: Frédéric Bourboulon, René Cleitman, Canal+, France 2 Cinéma, Hachette Première, M6 Films
Cinematography: Alain Choquart
Editing: Luce Grunenwaldt
Sound: Michel Desrois, Gérard Lamps
Music: Philippe Haïm
Cast: Marie Gillain (Nathalie), Olivier Sitruk (Eric), Bruno Putzulu (Bruno), Richard Berry (Alain), Philippe Duclos (Antoine), Marie Ravel (Karine), Clotilde Courau (Patricia)
115 minutes, color
Awards: Berlin International Film Festival (Bertrand Tavernier, Golden Berlin Bear, 1995); Gramado Film Festival Golden Kikito (Marie Gillain, Best Actress, 1995); Gramado Film Festival Golden Kikito (Luce Grunenwaldt, Best Editing, 1995)

CAPITAINE CONAN (1996)
(UK/USA: CAPTAIN CONAN)
Director: **Bertrand Tavernier**
Screenplay: Jean Cosmos, **Bertrand Tavernier**
Producers: Frédéric Bourboulon, Alain Sarde, Les Films Alain Sarde, Little Bear, TF1 Films Productions
Cinematography: Alain Choquart
Editing: Khadicha Bariha, Laure Blancherie, Luce Grunenwaldt
Sound: Michel Desrois, Gérard Lamps
Music: Oswald d'Andréa
Cast: Philippe Torreton (Conan), Samuel Le Bihan (Norbert), Bernard Le Coq (De Sève), Catherine Rich (Madeleine Erlane), Claude Rich (General Pitard de Lauzier), François Berléand (Commandant Bouvier), Claude Brosset (Père Dubreuil), André Falcon (Col. Voirin)
129 minutes, color
Awards: Cabourg Romantic Film Festival (Philippe Torreton, Best Actor, 1997); Cannes Film Festival (DVD Design Award, tied with *The Sixth Sense* [1999], 2003); César (Philippe Torreton, Best Actor, 1997); César (Bertrand Tavernier, Best Director, tied with Patrice Leconte for *Ridicule*, 1997); Denver International Film Festival (Bertrand Tavernier, Krzysztof Kieslowski Award, 1997); Denver International Film Festival (Bertrand Tavernier, Feature Film, People's Choice Award, 1997); French Syndicate of Cinema Critics (Bertrand Tavernier, Best Film, Critics Award, 1997); San Sebastián International Film Festival (Bertrand Tavernier, FIPRESCI Prize, tied with *Qin song* [1996], 1996); San Sebastián International Film Festival

(Bertrand Tavernier, Solidarity Award, 1996); San Sebastián International Film Festival (Guy-Claude François, Special Mention, Best Production Design, 1996)

DE L'AUTRE COTE DU PERIPH' (1997)
(USA: THE OTHER SIDE OF THE TRACKS)
Directors: **Bertrand Tavernier**, Nils Tavernier
Producer: Little Bear
150 minutes, color

ÇA COMMENCE AUJOURD'HUI (1999)
(UK/USA: IT ALL STARTS TODAY)
Director: **Bertrand Tavernier**
Screenplay: Dominique Sampiero, **Bertrand Tavernier**, Tiffany Tavernier
Producers: Frédéric Bourboulon, Alain Sarde; Les Films Alain Sarde, Little Bear
Cinematography: Alain Choquart
Editing: Sophie Brunet, Sophie Mandonnet
Sound: Michel Desrois, Gérard Lamps
Music: Louis Sclavis
Cast: Philippe Torreton (Daniel), Maria Pitarresi (Valeria), Nadia Kaci (Samia), Véronique Ataly (Madame Liénard), Nathalie Bécue (Cathy), Emmanuelle Bercot (Madame Tiévaux), Françoise Bette (Madame Delacourt), Christine Citti (Madame Baudoin)
Filmed in Anzin, Pas-de-Calais, France
117 minutes, color
Awards: Berlin International Film Festival (Bertrand Tavernier, FIPRESCI Prize, 1999); Berlin International Film Festival (Bertrand Tavernier, Honorable Mention, 1999); Berlin International Film Festival (Bertrand Tavernier, Prize of the Ecumenical Jury, 1999); Fotogramas de Plata (Bertrand Tavernier, Best Foreign Film, 2000); Lumiere Awards, France (Philippe Torreton, Lumiere Award, Best Actor, 2000); Norwegian International Film Festival (Bertrand Tavernier, Ecumenical Film Award, 1999); San Sebastián International Film Festival (Bertrand Tavernier, Audience Award, 1999); Sant Jordi Awards (Philippe Torreton, Best Foreign Actor, 2000); Sant Jordi Awards (Bertrand Tavernier, Best Foreign Film, 2000)

HISTOIRES DE VIES BRISEES: LES "DOUBLE PEINE" DE LYON (2001)
Directors: **Bertrand Tavernier** with Nils Tavernier
Producer: Little Bear
Cinematography: Alain Choquart, Eric Philbert, Nils Tavernier
Editing: Sophie Brunet, Sophie Mandonnet, Marie Deroudille

Sound: Alain Choquart, Eric Philbert, Nils Tavernier
Music: Louis Sclavis, Zebda
110 minutes, color

LAISSEZ-PASSER (2002)
(UK/USA: SAFE CONDUCT)
Director: **Bertrand Tavernier**
Screenplay: Jean Cosmos, **Bertrand Tavernier;** after the memoirs of Jean Aurenche and Jean Devaivre
Producers: Frédéric Bourboulon, Alain Sarde, Les Films Alain Sarde, France 2 Cinéma, France 3 Cinéma, KC Medien, Little Bear, Vertigo Productions
Cinematography: Alain Choquart
Editing: Sophie Brunet
Sound: Michel Desrois, Gérard Lamps, Elisabeth Paquotte
Music: Antoine Duhamel
Cast: Jacques Gamblin (Jean Devaivre), Denis Podalydès (Jean Aurenche), Marie Desgranges (Simone Devaivre), Charlotte Kady (Suzanne Raymond), Ged Marlon (Jean-Paul Le Chanois), Philippe Morier-Genoud (Maurice Tourneur), Maria Pitarresi (Reine Sorignal), Laurent Schilling (Charles Spaak)
170 minutes, color
Awards: Berlin International Film Festival (Jacques Gamblin, Silver Berlin Bear, Best Actor, 2002); Berlin Interational Film Festival (Antoine Duhamel, Silver Berlin Bear, Best Film Music, 2002); Fort Lauderdale International Film Festival (Bertrand Tavernier, Jury Award, Best Director, 2002); Fort Lauderdale International Film Festival (Bertrand Tavernier, Jury Award, Best Film, 2002); Fort Lauderdale International Film Festival (Jean Cosmos & Bertrand Tavernier, Jury Award, Best Screenplay, 2002); Fort Lauderdale International Film Festival (Denis Podalydès, Jury Award, Best Supporting Actor, 2002); Étoiles d'Or (Antoine Duhamel, Étoile d'Or, Best Composer, tied with Krishna Levy for 8 femmes [2002], 2003)

HOLY LOLA (2004)
Director: **Bertrand Tavernier**
Screenplay: Dominique Sampiero, **Bertrand Tavernier**, Tiffany Tavernier
Producers: Frédéric Bourboulon, Alain Sarde, Les Films Alain Sarde, Little Bear, TF1 Films Productions
Cinematography: Alain Choquart
Editing: Sophie Brunet
Sound: Dominique Levert
Music: Henri Texier
Cast: Jacques Gamblin (Pierre), Isabelle Carré (Géraldine), Bruno Putzulu (Marco),

Lara Guirao (Annie), Frédéric Pierrot (Xavier), Maria Pitarresi (Sandrine), Jean-Yves Roan (Michel), Séverine Caneele (Paricia)
Filmed around d'Aurillac, France, and in Cambodia
128 minutes, color
Awards: San Sebastián International Film Festival (Bertrand Tavernier, Audience Award, 2005)

IN THE ELECTRIC MIST (2008—US)
(France: DANS LA BRUME ELECTRIQUE)
Director: **Bertrand Tavernier**
Screenplay: Jerzy Kromolowski, Mary Olson-Kromolowski; based on the novel *In the Electric Mist with Confederate Dead* by James Lee Burke
Producers: Frédéric Bourboulon, Michael Fitzgerald, Ithaca Pictures, Little Bear, TF1 International
Cinematography: Bruno de Keyzer
Editing: Larry Madaras, Roberto Silvi
Sound: David Bach
Music: Marco Beltrami
Cast: Tommy Lee Jones (Dave Robicheaux), John Goodman (Julie "Baby Feet" Balboni), Peter Sarsgaard (Elrod Sykes), Kelly Macdonald (Kelly Drummond), Mary Steenburgen (Bootsie Robicheaux), Justina Machado (Rosie Gomez), Ned Beatty (Twinky LeMoyne)
Filmed in Louisiana
117 minutes, color

LA PRINCESSE DE MONTPENSIER (2010)
Director: **Bertrand Tavernier**
Screenplay: Jean Cosmos, François-Olivier Rousseau, **Bertrand Tavernier**
Producers: Marc Silam, Eric Heuman, Paradis Films, Studio Canal
Cinematography: Bruno de Keyzer
Editing: Sophie Brunet
Music: Philippe Sarde
Cast: Mélanie Theirry (Marie de Mézières), Gaspard Ulliel (Guise), Grégoire Leprince-Ringuet (Le Prince de Montpensier), Lambert Wilson (Chabannes), Raphaël Personnaz (Anjou)
139 minutes, color

QUAI D'ORSAY (2013)
(US: THE FRENCH MINISTER)
Director: **Bertrand Tavernier**

Producers: Frédéric Bourboulon, Little Bear, Pathé, France2 Cinéma
Screenplay: Christophe Blain, Abel Lanzac
Cinematography: Jérôme Alméras
Music: Philippe Sarde
Cast: Thierry Lhermite (Alexandre), Raphaël Personnaz (Arthur), Niels Arestrup (Claude), Bruno Raffaelli (Stéphane), Julie Gayet (Valérie), Anaïs Demoustier (Marina), Thomas Chabrol (Sylvain), Jane Birken (Molly), Sonia Rolland (Nathalie), Joséphine de la Baume (Isabelle)
113 minutes, color

Bertrand Tavernier: Interviews

Conversation with Bertrand Tavernier

Jacques Demeure and Paul-Louis Thirard / 1974

From *Positif*, no. 156 (February 1974). Reprinted by permission. Translated by T. Jefferson Kline.

Jacques Demeure & Paul-Louis Thirard: Did your experience as a press agent help you to make your film?

Bertrand Tavernier: Yes and no. Yes, because Pierre Rissient and I never thought of our work as press agents as simply about publicity. We always tried to make it an extension of our position on esthetic and cinephilic questions. I know that sounds pretentious, but I can say that, in the majority of cases, I used my position to defend certain filmmakers, certain films and ideas I'd championed in the journals I'd written for—though with less success. In fact that's what's a little depressing when you're writing for a journal: you have the impression you're preaching in a void and that you're not even read by the other critics who should be concerned with what you're writing. How else can you explain that after dozens of studies, interviews, critiques, you find the same idiocies, the same historical errors. The article by Marcel Martin on Ford, for example . . .

Anyway, it was in this sense that our work went beyond promoting films. We developed connections with distributors, with producers, and tried to convince them to bring out such and such a film. At times we oversaw the contracts. So we were able to get released or re-released more than a hundred films that might never have been shown. May I make a little parenthesis? The critics who complain about the system or who moan about the horrors of exploitation, should get their hands dirty. Of course it's more boring to do that than to hotly theorize about a film you've seen at the Festival of Toulon—it demands a lot of time and a lot of energy. You have to keep at it and sometimes it takes three years to get something done. You also have to come down out of your ivory tower and consent to having a few dust-ups over your ideas. It can be both exciting and depressing, but that's one of the only ways to keep a certain kind of criticism going.

Anyway, this work put me in contact with some producers and distributers who were helpful to me when I wanted to make *L'Horloger de Saint-Paul* [*The*

Clockmaker]. They'd already worked with me and had a certain amount of trust in me. Of course the negative side of this was that some of them had already labeled me as press agent and didn't take seriously my desire to make a film.

D&T: So obviously it wasn't easy?

BT: No. After having written a very short adaptation, I got Noiret to agree to work with me and found a producer. It's after that that things got difficult. Things repeatedly fell apart. I got a large advance, thanks to the people at Pathé and Sirius, who signed on after reading the first fifty pages of the synopsis. But the producer got scared and disappeared. After several failures of this kind, Raymond Danon agreed to produce the film. He told me: "You subject is not so bad." I said, "No." So he financed the scenario. When he read it, he hated it, but he told me "If the distributors are still interested, I'll go along with it. I might be mistaken." And so I did the film. He gave me complete liberty on condition that I keep to the agreed schedule, which was very tight. I had in my contract that I'd be fired if I spent more than a third of the budget in the first two weeks. But in the end, I not only kept on schedule, but finished a day early, thanks to my cameraman, Pierre-William Glenn, and the whole team. I considered staying on schedule to be a moral issue. It was in relation to other guys who would be making their first film at Lira. I've seen the scorn that can be heaped on young filmmakers when someone abuses the schedule. It can mean others' chances can get blocked. So I tried not to bungle it and to be as precise as possible.

But I'm not sure all these disappointments regarding the preparation and all those months of waiting and frustration are interesting for your readers. I think we should try to broaden the discussion; it's much more difficult to make a film on a modest budget (between two to three million) than in 1965, that's due to certain factors that would merit a serious analysis. Since 1968, the star system has taken on a growing importance and is likely to grow even more in the future, because cinema is more and more dominated by the producers and the distributors who finance the films, and who decide which ones will get made. Which is serious, because, as I've noticed on many occasions, producers cannot rid themselves of their exploitative mentality. They'll scuttle projects in which they've invested, either because it isn't going well enough for them, or because they feel they won't make enough money on it. The cost of films increasing, producers and distributors, to get their money out as fast as possible, try to increase their distribution circuits which increases the publicity costs and further diminishes the number of films being made. This disastrous policy leads to inevitable consequences: to keep the widest possible distribution, they insist on known stars, which further increases the cost of the film and necessitates an even wider distribution. It's a vicious circle.

In any case, currently, if your project isn't approved by one of the three or four major circuits (Pathé-Gaumont, UGC, or Siritzky), you'll have trouble getting it done. This policy reminds me a bit of what happened in England, where the British cinema fell completely into the hands of the Americans, which totally destroyed it.

D&T: One has the impression that a film gets written off in a year.
BT: It's true. The disappearance of the secondary theaters is a terrible thing. We'll find ourselves in the same situation as in the States, except that there they can make up their deficits thanks to TV, which pays lots of money for these films. In France we don't even have the equivalent of the German third channel which pays good money for films like Bertucelli's *Ramparts of Clay*, Solanas's *Hour of the Furnaces*, or Karmitz's *Blow for Blow* and airs them, which isn't the case for the co-productions with the ORTF.[1] This explains why so many people turn to American companies to get produced, which is, however, pretty frightening. In many of these companies, everyone is scared of getting fired and everyone is looking to cover themselves. No one dares make a decision in Paris without calling London or New York . . .

When I presented Warner Bros. with my advance, my scenario, and Noiret's agreement, they asked me to summarize the film in two pages. Eight days later I got a negative response, without ever having met, even for a minute, the head of European productions. This despite the fact that I brought them a guarantee of 1.4 million francs, that is, two-thirds of the necessary budget.

I'll say it again, we need to sound the alarm, and I feel all the freer to pull the handle on the alarm since I've been supported. But I'm thinking of a number of filmmakers, from Rouffio to de Chalonge, from Benayoun to Bernard Paul, who are having a terrible time making it. If you arrived empty-handed, they won't even talk to you. Empty-handed means without a star . . . The majority of producers don't look for projects but instead wait for you to bring them a completed scenario and the agreement from a couple of actors. And this is a great drama in France. No one will finance a script, even at the most minimal prices. Or almost no one. If the larger companies gave one tenth of their useless expenses to finance new subjects or adaptations, as they do in the US and in Italy, that would help French cinema a lot.

D&T: But you didn't consider an advance on receipts?
BT: But my advance on distribution was ten times greater than I would have gotten from the advance on receipts. That's why the example of my film is interesting. Even with this enormous advance, and the support of the producers, I had a lot of trouble.

I also have to say that this is a very important time sociologically in France: it's the dictatorship of silliness. All you have to do is look at the success of comic films and study their receipts to be terrified, especially since it's getting worse all the time. Films with Trintignant, Montand, or Piccoli attract many fewer viewers than stupid comedies. Comedies have never had as much success as they've had over the last four years. It would be interesting to compare the career of Fernandel and Bourvil with that of Louis de Funès. This obsession with silliness is taken up in the press and especially on TV. All we hear is that the principal goal of the French filmgoer is to laugh. It's enough to walk by the movie theaters the week before Christmas. Never have there been so many films belonging to the same genre.

Moreover, American companies, to counter the diminution of American films in France (down by 30 percent), are also financing comic films like Clair's *The Furious Führer*. And American films are replaced by these comedies and pornographic films. The worst part is that the press does nothing to counter this, quite the opposite! It's spending its time debating trivia.

D&T: What's the budget of your film?

BT: It's one of those films that cost between 250 and 270 million francs. On top of that there are Simenon's rights, which are pretty high (22.5 million). When you add in the salaries of Noiret, Rochefort, Auenche, and Bost, it comes out to a pretty reasonable budget, especially given the overblown costs of French stardom, which includes not only stars, but star-authors, star-directors, star-scenario writers. So we've become an industry that is in thrall to the super-pricing of actors and directors. To remedy the situation, we'll need to make some necessary changes: insist on greater participation, as some actors are doing; or, for directors, to do what seems to me absolutely logical, set a fixed percentage of receipts, let's say 5 percent of ticket prices, and a bit like SACEM does for musicians.

D&T: Like every author's society does.

BT: Exactly. And this seems to me a very important thing, since first of all, when the film is a commercial success, the director ought to get his share equitably and without possibility of fraud. That way we'd have the famous percentage of profits that you never really see. And then, certain scandals could be avoided: for example the fact that Carné or Pierre Chenal, who enjoyed considerable success as directors, are now living in the most miserable conditions imaginable. This just isn't normal, particularly in the case of Carné whose films are still continually shown.

We must do something to lower the astronomical cost of making a film. The more this cost goes up the fewer the films that get made and the greater the financial risks of those that do, given the system by which receipts are raised, the current pay scales and the enormous take of the producers. And what's really scandalous is that they take their profits with no regard whatsoever for the consumer. You know that even in the newer cinemas, the projection and sound are horrible. A film can lose up to 40 percent of its value in such conditions. What's really unbelievable is that the more we perfect the technology (new film, more sensitive lenses) the more we botch the final product.

And what's more, there's such a rush to make films that "work" that we sacrifice a bunch of others and don't wait for the word to get out about them: Tanner's *Return from Africa* was pulled after three thousand seats were sold at Saint-Séverin, in a theater that had two hundred seats. That's absolutely scandalous! Whereas a cinema that's a little more respectful of the films, or totally independent, like the one at Saint-André-des-Arts, managed to keep *The Salamander* or *Family Life* long enough to get better receipts. So we have a dramatic situation that is deteriorating even as the potential for audiences is growing. Now, if a film isn't an immediate hit within five to ten days, it's simply pulled from circulation.

So the new element in the world of film is this obsession with ticket sales, an obsession that is fed by the all the attention given to it by *France-Soir* or *Combat*. The best-selling films are publicized as if they were prizes for the best film of the week in an industry where the fate of the film director is fragile and uncertain. It's an additional pressure that's been added and which is as dictatorial as it is arbitrary, since there's no real connection between ticket sales and the price of the film. There are films that are great deals because they cost little and bring in five or six times as much. Inversely there are certain films that bring in twenty times as much, but cost thirty times more than the others.

Take the example of Sautet. Since *Max and the Junkmen* sold fewer tickets than *The Things of Life*, people said, "What a crappy film!" because Sautet went from 500,000 to 375,000 viewers, whereas, in fact, 90 percent of French filmmakers would love to sell that many tickets! And I even heard a lot of producers and movie houses that Jean Yanne's second film, *Me I Want to Have Dough*, was crap, whereas the film sold 650,000 tickets, simply because another film had just sold a million. And the critics just fall into step. It's become the reign of outbidding. It's fascinating to count the number of times Jean Yanne has been compared to Molière, Oury to Voltaire and vice versa . . . It's a wonder we hear about Keaton and Chaplin any more.

It's no longer enough to get a good review, you have to get an exceptional review to make it. To attract an audience, words like "interesting" just don't cut it; a film must be "amazing." This is not helping filmmakers or films. Everything ends up being equivalent to everything else; you can't tell the difference between one film and another any more. This excess of praise seems to call for equally violent attacks. The value of the cinema goes up and down as fast as the dollar. In *Cinéma*, in an article about Tom Gries's second film, after *Will Penny*: "Can we trust Gries any more?" After two films! You know, for the last two or three years film criticism has been waning. On the one hand, there are those who emulate *Sergent York*, those who were blown away by it and the cops in the Latin Quarter who deny twenty years of policy from one day to the next, without ever questioning what they're doing. It's not they who are wrong, it's the filmmakers who don't act exactly like the hero of Hawks's admirable film. And then there are the rest, who either like everything or tear everything down except the two or three original films of the year.

We have to shake things up, force the communist press, for example, to take a more critical position and talk about films elsewhere in the paper than the arts and entertainment section. Every time I've tried to interest the editors of the opinion page in talking about a film, whether it's in the *Nouvel Observateur*, in *L'Express*, or in *L'Humanité*, I don't get anywhere. For example, it's no good trying to get Wurmser (or someone like him) to dedicate a first page article to a film (or a play or even a TV show) to try to contest the fascist position being taken in it. When we tried to get an investigation into the situation of the Portuguese workers who were portrayed in *O Salto* we didn't see anything appear for an entire year! At the *Nouvel Observateur* it's the same: "Articles on film go on the film page." That's a kind of ghettoization that's worse than the Latin Quarter.

D&T: Let's talk about screenwriters. It's interesting to see Bost and Aurenche listed in the credits.[2]

BT: It was a deliberate choice. I'd had as a project before *The Clockmaker* a film on Bonny and Laffont; I wanted to do something on the French Gestapo. First of all, nothing like that had been done, especially regarding the economic side of it. It was a subject that was unpleasant and very difficult to do. What interested me was not just the gangsters on the rue Lauriston, but especially the people that came to see them: the bankers, the rich merchants . . .

I didn't want to try to write such a script by myself, but wanted to have the help of people who'd lived through that period, and I thought of Aurenche and Bost, since ultimately, the best film on this period, which has never been equaled is Autant-Lara's *La Traversée de Paris* [*Four Bags Full*]. When this project fell through, for reasons too complicated to explain here, I took Simenon's novel which I'd been wanting to adapt for two or three years. It was one of the five or six projects I'd most wanted to do. When I thought of Bonny and Laffont, I watched a bunch of films written by Aurenche and Bost. While I was watching Autant-Lara's *En Cas de Malheur* [*Love Is My Profession*], I was struck by the quality of the adaptation of the dialogues. I discovered that many of their films were considered outmoded by some historians of film, but it was often more because of the mise en scène than the scenario. Often the scenario struck me as extremely modern but what dated films were questions of photography or direction, for example, in *Le Diable au corps* [*Devil in the Flesh*], the panoramic shots of the fire when the lovers are embracing. But in *Douce* [*Love Story*] for example, there isn't a single line that's aged. It's an admirable film from beginning to end and that I find exemplary both in its social commentary and in the depth of its characters. And I find it amazing that in 1942, they end a scene with a guy who's leaving the lodgings of a poor friend with Marguerite Moreno's words, "Patience and resignation," and the guy says, "No! Impatience and revolt!" What I liked about Aurenche and Bost was that they didn't wait till 1968 to discover that you had to put political elements in films, give them liberal or anarchist slants.

I was also persuaded, by revisiting all these old films by so many directors and so many writers, that you could have collaborators who were very precise and very strong without losing your own personality. What struck me in a certain number of French films was that the scenario wasn't at all overdone. It wasn't overwritten like American films often are, or French films before the war, or during the war, or Italian films where you'll sometimes find in films by the greats, six, seven, eight writers listed in the credits. And I also took Aurenche and Bost because I wanted to make a French film, a very French film. What shocks me now in many films is their lack of national identity. I'm not just talking about people who imitate American film, or the people who imitate the imitators of Melville, but about all those films you see that have no contact with what is properly French. Some of the directors I like display deep French roots, like Sautet or Granier-Deferre, that I wanted to rediscover. Moreover there were recent films by Pascal Thomas, *La Veuve Couderc* [*The Widow Couderc*], Chabrol's *Le Boucher* [*The Butcher*], and a very interesting film by Guérin, *Lo Pais*.

So I benefitted from lots of difference circumstances. I chose Lyon because it was a city I loved and knew well. I wanted to take advantage of the chance to destroy some clichés about the city; to show Lyon without any shots of Fourvière or La Place Bellecour. And then the actors got completely caught up in the ambiance of Lyon. I think I benefitted from shooting everything on location. Guys like Autant-Lara certainly lost a lot of atmosphere by shooting in studios. I even wanted to shoot the interiors in Lyon, since I felt, I knew that there was an atmosphere in Lyon apartments that I would have lost, even if I'd shot in real apartments in Paris: those large, dark rooms with very high ceilings. Those courtyards, where you can hear children playing scales on the piano, the marble-topped tables in the restaurants—I wanted to recreate all of that in my film.

It was a bit of my childhood, so I put in the film a myriad of details I remembered. The entire scene with the nurse, for example, with the plate she'd won in a singing competition. I think we all let ourselves go in this film. The story of the little boy really happened to Aurenche. He told it to me one day, and I said, "We have to have that in the film! I think this story anticipates the moral of the film, encapsulates the relationship between the two men." At first glance, it doesn't add anything to the drama. But, in fact, I found it indispensable. And the whole film was constructed like that. Which goes against the reputation that Aurenche and Bost have of being very stylized writers.

And I have to say we were greatly helped by Simenon's support. He gives such an amazing social contour to his novels, rooting them so deeply in an everyday reality that it's very easy to develop the context, to eliminate literary techniques, and use his dramas as a springboard. Simenon and the provinces would be a good subject for an article . . .

D&T: But in relation to the French tradition you refer to—I don't think that you're such a cinematic traditionalist as you claim. In our tradition there's a typical scene in the courtroom. There's always a long key scene in a courtroom in French films, but you dispose of it in a single shot. That's all that remains of tradition.

BT: For me that was the only solution, right from the first draft. Aurenche and Bost agreed immediately. Trials made sense in French film before the advent of TV. The show *In Your Soul and Conscience* totally killed this type of scene. I couldn't see my way out of such a scene. So we ended up with the obligatory close-up of the judge who taps his gavel and says "I'm going to evacuate the courtroom." And then I thought about the sound track: I can't tolerate what they call in the right-hand column: "Sounds of various murmurs." It's generally added in and you hear, "Yes," "Oh," "Oooh" "OH!" or bursts of laughter after one of the lawyer's jokes. As soon as I hear the word "trial" I see the ghost of Jacques Varennes, or Jacques Monod, who killed more judges than all the anarchist gangs in the whole world . . . And then, if we'd begun to show the trial, we would have necessarily cheated or else devoted twenty-five minutes to it. And that would have destroyed the rhythm and direction of the story. I would have had to eliminate the scene on the bridge where Jacques Denis expresses the moral of the film.

So, I decided on this very simple low-angle shot in the deserted courtroom. It's one of the only low-angle shots in the film, and it was done that way to show there was no one there.

D&T: Could we talk a bit about the actors, who were so well directed, especially since there was a mix of stars—for whom I have the greatest respect—and some people who were astonishing: the young couple . . .

BT: I saw some of the actors from *Nothing to Report*, one of the rare French films played by little-known actors. To begin with, I eliminated blondes . . .

D&T: Racist! [laugher]

BT: Ok, it was an anti-romantic racism. I didn't want the son to be appealing at all at first glance. It would have been too demagogic, and his looks shouldn't serve to explain his act either. I didn't want the viewers to say, when they saw him, "Well with a face like that, it's no wonder he did that to his father! He's an idiot not to have expected it." And then, when I met Sylvain Rougerie I knew immediately he was perfect for the role. We had one or two read-throughs with Noiret and Rochefort and I felt they could work well together; the same with Jacques Denis and Noiret.

At first, between these two it was tough, because Denis is a communist and he has very set ideas about his character and about Noiret's as well. Some were spot on, some were not so good. There was a terrible dust-up and Noiret got really angry: "You're not going to use this Swiss guy!" [laughs] And then, right away in the first scene, he understood how talented Denis was. Plus it really got to me after *La Salamandre* [*The Salamander*] that everyone took Bideau and no one was interested in Denis.

As for my direction of actors, it's very pragmatic and I did about 80 percent of it before we started shooting: lunching or dining with the actors, having them tell me their stories, talking about one filmmaker or another, having discussions with Audiberti and Rochfort. It seemed to me very important especially to create a good ambiance with the actors and maintain it throughout. I felt the actors should feel completely at ease when they walked onto the set and my job was to create a mise en scène that didn't get in their way, but gave them lots of freedom. Guys like Noiret and Rochefort bring so much to the work that I just had to be sufficiently open to work their ideas into the film in such a way that it didn't undo what I was trying to do. The hardest part is to take what they give you without having their suggestions conflict with what we already had going. I have to say that I had a cameraman who used very little light, had an amazing ability to frame his shots and was ready to follow the actors when they came up with something unexpected. I remembered what Gabin told me once: during the shooting of *La Bête humaine* [*The Human Beast*], Renoir got angry at Kurant, the cameraman: "Mister Kurant, stop annoying the actors with your UFA stuff, you're there to serve them, not the other way around!" With Glenn, who worked a lot with a hand-held camera, I tried not to get in the actors' way, using more distanced shots and fewer close-ups. At the end of the first week, Glenn was using Noiret as the pivotal point for each shot. Whatever happened, you could find him exactly where he was supposed to be.

In short, I think the Lyonnais shrimp salad and sausages had a lot to do with my direction of the actors. Claude Chabrol once said that he chose his exterior shots as a function of the restaurants available. I understand that very well!

D&T: Why is the victim a factory cop?
BT: I wanted to use someone everyone dreams of killing. When you read the papers, there are always guys who seem to be protected by the powers that be or the police and their impunity makes you furious. For me, I can't stand watching

the way the cops sometime abuse the law or Marcellin is gradually turning into a fascist. For young people, factory cops are that kind of problem. I used a sentence someone said during a trial of kids who'd shot at some cops, "I didn't want it always to be the same guys who got off the hook!" At the beginning of our work on the adaptation, the son was a leftist. Aurenche and Bost made me change that: "We don't know how to write about leftists. It's not that we're against them, we just wouldn't know how to write the film." They encouraged me to make the son's act one of those obscure acts of revolt that happen a lot nowadays. This made the scenario much more rigorous and we cut a bunch of speeches that I'd written at the expense of the character, but didn't alleviate the aggressive tone he took. I think that in addition to the Brechtian films that are distanced and deconstructed, French cinema needs polemical films. Films in which the polemics unfold in the day-to-day life of France.

Notes

1. L'Office de Radio-Television Française.
2. Jean Aurenche and Pierre Bost were the screenwriters who'd been castigated by François Truffaut in his famous article "A Certain Tendency of French Cinema," which launched the politics of "auteurism" and ultimately the New Wave.

Conversation with Bertrand Tavernier

Jacques Demeure, Jean-Pierre Jeancolas, and Michel Sineux / 1977

From *Positif*, no. 197 (September 1977). Published by permission. Translated by T. Jefferson Kline.

Demeure, Jeancolas, & Sineux: After the two historical films that you've made—since the last interview published in *Positif*—tell us how the project on *Des Enfants gâtés* [*Spoiled Children*] was conceived.

Bertrand Tavernier: It came together very quickly. I wanted to do a film on day-to-day life when I was renting a place in Paris. I was even president of the Committee for the Defense of the Tenants in my building for several years. It was on the rue des Dames. And after *Le Juge et l'assassin* [*The Judge and the Assassin*], I wanted to make a film that would be the complete opposite of that one. A modern film, because after the two historical films, you feel like you're in a nightmare of TV antennas and electric poles. I couldn't go down a street without thinking: "Shit, they've modernized another building!" or see a field without saying to myself: "Another stupid electric pylon, but what can we do . . ." Now the nightmare has become different: it's the cranes and tall buildings. That's all I see now, after *Spoiled Children*. I also wanted to make a little film on a more modest subject. So that's how it began. I had two ideas: take as a character a film director—or screenwriter, since in the beginning he was a screenwriter—and throw him, according to a certain schema that you often find in Italian comedies, into a social milieu where he doesn't belong, and have him confront a series of very concrete problems, and also have him meet a much younger woman who interrogates him passionately, and forces him to re-examine his assumptions. That's how it started.

When I was working on the jury for Advances on Receipts, I read a scenario by Charlotte Dubreuil, which turned into *What do you want, Julie?* that interested me a lot. I voted for the project and then I wanted to meet the author and I asked her to work with me. She came to visit me while we were doing *The Judge and the Assassin*, and on Sundays we'd take time out to discuss various elements. We began writing, and little by little I began to feel that I needed to get someone else involved in the project: the person for whom we were writing the role of Anne, Christine Pascal. I'd worked with her on an adaptation of Theodore Sturgeon for television that never got made. I liked the way she wrote. She joined us and, thanks to her, things got shaken up a bit. She arrived with some very set opinions, sometimes a bit too rigid, but what I hoped would happen, happened: she was the spark that allowed us to go on.

From then on the writing was done almost exclusively with Christine, and Charlotte took on the role of mediator, since Christine had too theoretical an approach to things. The three of us worked well together. Christine joked that Charlotte was sort of the Bost of the operation and she was the Aurenche, which had some truth to it. Christine didn't completely write her role, nor I the role of Bernard. There are things in the character of Anne that I wrote and others in Bernard that Christine wrote. When you write a scenario you can't divvy it up the way you deal cards. Everything is tied together so inextricably that you can't really tell who did what.

Q: Yes. What characterized the first three films was that they were men's films. Women appeared in them, but they had secondary roles and were often treated symbolically.

BT: I wouldn't say symbolically. I tried in each film to make the female characters the driving force in the film. An element that constituted a moral judgment on the other characters. For example, the character of Isabelle Huppert in *The Judge*, which I mostly wrote myself, developed little by little. It's true that the stories, at the outset, were men's stories. But stories of men caught in relationships, or a lack of relationships, or in bad relationships with women. The Regent, Bouvier, the judge . . . Even if the women weren't present, they played important roles. Christine Pascal in *Let Joy Reign Supreme*, Isabelle Huppert in *The Judge* carry in themselves a judgment on all that surrounds them and this judgment is very severe. The process of moving this judgment from the background to the foreground was what I had to learn. It's what I really wanted to do in this film and is why I asked the two women to work with me on the scenario. I don't think *Spoiled Children* constitutes a break from my other films: it's more a matter of moving into the foreground elements that were less developed in the earlier films.

Q: Is what these women bring to the film as actresses more important than what the actors did in the preceding films?

BT: It's difficult to say. Christine is a character who gives so much of herself, who wants to speak, wants to explain . . . But what Noiret and Rochefort bring is extremely important to my films. Maybe less for what they explain than for their tacit understanding, a way of understanding each other without speaking. It's difficult for Philippe Noiret to open up. What he thinks of the character, of the way certain things must be changed, he can occasionally explain, but often he communicates in a very oblique way. What he and Rochefort brought to the film was also very considerable. What's funny in this film is the way that they influenced certain lines without even being there: Michel Aumont and some of the other characters end up saying things that come from Rochefort, Galabru, or Marielle. For example, Marielle said to me one day, "Women don't like jazz. When they listen to Charlier Parker they find him too piercing." It's such a terrific statement that I had to put it in the film. And then Michel Aumont had the idea of saying: "That's a phrase I heard somewhere but I can't remember who said it." He took the idea and put it in like that.

Q: So Michel Aumont, in the film's story, is a bit like Charlotte Dubreuil, between you and Christine?

BT: Michel Aumont's character comes from a lot of different things. At first, it was Claude Sautet who was going to play the role. Then Sautet, who'd read the scenario and who'd made a couple of excellent suggestions, resolved the problem of the character by refusing to play it, forcing me to find someone else. It was Piccoli and I who decided it should be Michel Aumont, but when Sautet heard that it was Aumont he was delighted and thought it was a great idea. Sautet also helped us resolve a difficulty regarding what we'd written for Bernard: in what we'd written, we had made Bernard the director and Pierre the screen writer, who'd been working together on the scenario already for some time. But we couldn't make it work that they could explain to the viewers what they'd been doing since it wasn't logical that they'd tell a story if they already knew it. So we tried using devices, like "Okay, so let's sum up what we've done . . ." which were completely wrong. It was Sautet who had the idea: "Pierre has to come along at the beginning as someone who's going to help shape up the scenario." And from then on, the writing was easy. It was Sautet who allowed us to give this character a sense of irony and to allow him some distance vis-à-vis both the work that had been done and the situation he found himself in.

Q: And the title?

BT: Ah, the title. Now it's *Spoiled Children* whereas when we started out it was *The Spoiled Children*. We thought about it a lot. We'd gotten this title from the play by Madame de Genlis that Caroline Huppert had put on with Christine. The people at Gaumont thought it was great. But after the heirs of Philippe Hériat challenged us on this, we had to change it slightly.

Q: One of the best scenes of the film is when they get into an argument: He wants to take a taxi home, but he can't and they make up. It's a scene about moods.
BT: That was a bit what the film was about. I was trying to make a film without a single dramatized scene. Certainly there are dramatic elements, like the suicide, the expulsion, but once the characters, their milieu, and the themes are set, there are no dramatic elements that are introduced from the outside. This type of scene originated in an idea we had but couldn't seem to write. Christine and I wanted there to be an argument between the two characters. But what we'd imagined turned out to be too theoretical . . . But then I found in Duneton's novel *I'm Like a Sow Who Doubts* a phrase where a student says "I want the war to start." And so with Christine we wrote that scene from there.

Claude Duneton I met when I was working with the Advance on Receipts committee. He wrote a very beautiful scenario with Guérin on the Larzac region but it never got made. He's the son of some farmers who wrote two books, *I'm Like a Sow* and *Parler croquant* in which he explains why he gave up teaching. We used a lot of different material on this film from writers like Daniel Thibon, Patrick Aujard, and others. For example after the laundromat scene, we used a very beautiful text by Thibon on how to keep from dying by holding your breath, etc.

We used lots of different texts, a little bit the way Aurenche uses phrases he's heard. It's something I learned from working with him. Aurenche is very attentive to what's happening around him whether it's amazing, silly, emotionally charged, or just simple. He told me, for example, about how Prévert died. Prévert, who didn't say a word during his last days, spoke a lot during the night. On the eve of his death, he started saying his name, "Jacques, Jacques . . ." His wife approached his bed and asked, "But Jacques, you're saying your name." And he answered, "Yes. I'm calling myself to keep me here so I don't leave." That's as beautiful as any of his poems. Aurenche was never afraid to use these kinds of things from his personal life and relationships. He wasn't worried that it would sound too much like an in-joke since people talk like that. He helped me be free in my film.

Q: To come back to the actors, we have the impression that you use two very different kinds of direction for the principal actors, like Piccoli, Christine Pascal, Arlette Bonnard, and the extras, the inhabitants of the building who are treated more like characters from old films that you love—and we love too—with Michel Aumont straddling the two worlds.
BT: Well, that's not quite the way it was. I wasn't thinking of classic French cinema, which, of course, I love—and by the way Volker Schoendorff told me that when he was reading the scenario, he thought of *Le Crime de Monsieur Lange* [*The Crime of Monsieur Lange*]. I took some things from Italian comedy and from life. Things I'd seen when I was involved with the other tenants in our building. I was

struck by certain ironic situations. Or when it wasn't things that happened to me directly, I heard stories from the tenants in our association. I didn't feel I was directing the actors differently. Or, rather, if there's a difference, I think it comes from the fact that all of the characters are seen with a certain tender irony, but that for the principal actors, there was also something else. In any case, I wasn't thinking at all about the silhouettes of French cinema, I was thinking about things I'd experienced. For example the character of the guy who receives that cream pie came from a story Christine told me about a girl and the way she talked and we put it in the film word for word. We simply added the pie to show that the girl is acting out a bit. All that came from reality. Or the television show and the guy who screws up: that happened to me a dozen times in my interviews. In Lyon, for example, a guy from France 3 asked me, "So in *Que La Fête commence* [*Let Joy Reign Supreme*] you've gotten into the realm of the French Revolution . . ." I burst out laughing uncontrollably (since the film takes place a half-century before the Revolution) and the guy says, "Get serious, we're working here!"

So I'm sensitive to things like that, to things that can happen, and I just want to put them in my film. I've met actors, like Jugnot, who have done *café-théâtre* and who are great at satirical comedy and who have a genius for gags like that. I just like to put in my films things I see around me. Like the things that I find in Prévert—an ironic way of looking at the world. But I wanted to avoid any trace of condescension. These are characters I like a lot. Even when they get a bit pretentious, I find them very touching. I want to communicate the unease they might be feeling, the difficulty of speaking or being understood.

Every one of the fifty-four characters in my film has an autonomous existence. That comes as well from the work we did on historical films and the way we shot, trying as much as possible to collaborate with our actors. All the group scenes like the one with slides, we rehearsed them several times with the people who had lines and who interrupted others. We created a complete biography for each character, with Christine and Charlotte, asking ourselves what they did, what they read. Then we gave them to the actors and let them bring to these lives what they wanted. Jugnot invented some amazing lines, for example, when he was speaking to his children. And Piccoli completely fit right in with this group. I had some heads of tenants' associations that played themselves in the film. Piccoli was totally at ease with them. So I don't think I directed anyone differently from anyone else, it's just that in the context of the film, he was outside and didn't belong to their world. He feeds off of them, watches them, is a complete phagocyte. There are people who wonder why he doesn't end up making a film about the tenants. But that's just what I wanted to avoid, because in reality things don't happen that way. The influences on us are too indirect. I would have been too simple and not right for him to say "I'm going to make a film about these tenants." On the other hand, I find it utterly believable that he say to Michel Aumont, "That's exactly how I see the characters in the film." And at this point, Aumont, who's been ironizing and making jokes, says something completely right in social and political terms: "No, that's something for privileged people."

So there are memories woven in here of conversations I'd had with Aurenche or with Sautet. Even when they're working directly on the subject, they come up with ideas that are politically correct, even if they didn't start out from a theoretical position, like "I'm going to treat this from a Marxist point of view . . ." But suddenly they'll say, "We have to bring this out more, because from a social standpoint . . ." and generally it's right. But what I wanted to avoid, was that Piccoli and Aumont's film be the mirror of my film. That seemed too academic to me . . .

Q: All the secondary characters are types and yet quite ambiguous. Jugnot's character, for example, joins the struggle against economic injustice, but when he lends money to Anne, he seems to think, at least for a moment, that this gives him certain rights with her. But Christine Pascal's character seems no less complex and more theoretical. How do you see her? Does she always know what she wants?
BT: No, absolutely not! Her character is sometimes a bit theoretical, because she has to be. It's her way of protecting herself. She's lost, confused, and anguished. She has certain very precise demands. The character of Bernard represents everything she would like to have, and, at the same time, that she wouldn't want to have. Security. She needs it, but she doesn't want it and violently rejects it. She wants to find out everything about Bernard, and also about herself. She's constantly swinging between a form of very demanding passion and a form of despair. At times, she hides behind her aggressiveness, but it's just a way of regrouping in order to move on. She's very contradictory; she has moments of tenderness and moments of complete fear, for example, when she talks about the girl who committed suicide. She identifies completely with this girl and this terrifies her . . . She's a character who represents the vulnerability and the violence that I see in many girls and that are conditioned by the social problems that face them, especially unemployment. She wants good relationships and believes that you can find good relationships by talking with people. This is a bit idealistic, but Christine is like that in life. She meets someone who takes refuge in his own life experience, in his culture, someone who can use silence and who knows how to use it to hide his feelings. He's got an entire set of habits and comforts which allow him to be "happy" and allow him to avoid taking risks. She, on the other hand, risks everything.

Q: The character of Arlette Bonnard—Piccoli's wife—is grouped with the others, in the margins.

BT: I was afraid at one point that the entire film would end up in complete despair. The tenants' struggles couldn't end up in triumph: they could only obtain small improvements, just the kind of thing you achieve these days. I don't see how any great victories would be possible . . . I liked the character of the wife because she suddenly achieved something positive with one of the children she was taking care of. She's a character who's gone through lots of changes. At first it was really important, but when we were writing these scenes we always found that when Piccoli came home, the story always turned into a triangular situation. Even if he didn't talk about his relationship with Anne, the fact that he didn't talk about it weighed down the scene. And I wanted to avoid that at all costs. I didn't want the husband-wife-mistress problem to become part of the drama. So we finally eliminated the character. Then I had the idea to have her intervene in her role as psychologist, both because it seemed to me to extend, in a metaphorical way, certain aspects of the film (these children who have trouble communicating, who don't speak . . .) and because this work that we see her do justifies Anne's phrase, when she says, "She's lucky to do that kind of work." It's true, this kind of work is useful for a girl like Anne; she can help other people. And also, because these children, who are stuck and oppressed, are a very important piece of the film. To see this woman confronted by all these people, who are already wounded and suffering, provided, in a very few scenes, a feminine character of incredible strength.

You could say it's a little idealized, but I don't think it is . . . I wanted to show as well that there is a solid connection between her and Piccoli, and that there's something bruised in her. Hence the text I used at the end: the person who wrote this text is a person of a very high degree of sensitivity . . . What she does extends the view of these apartment buildings: when we see the recreation yard, and behind it we see the child she's helping to touch the earth, it's the same . . . I'm not idealizing her: she's taking care of three or four kids, but in the shots we did, you can see dozens and dozens of other kids who live in horrible conditions. So, all her work is, after all, but a drop in the bucket. But that keeps her relationship with Bernard going in a dramatic and contradictory way.

Q: You worked with a smaller budget than you had in your two previous films.
BT: It's not an expensive film. I've never made films that required huge budgets. Maybe that's due to my experience as a press agent, which allowed me to see the economic aspect of films and to take account of it. This film was refused by AMLF They signed a contract, but when they read the first version—which, to be fair, had some weaknesses, they backed out. So we found ourselves with no distributor, no co-producer and, since everyone knew that the film was supposed to involve AMLF, when we knocked on other doors, we were received by people who knew

what had happened. Finally, Gaumont agreed to distribute the film and to co-produce it 50/50. To make a film under these conditions meant that we had only twenty-six days to shoot it. The budget was only about seventy thousand dollars. With such constraints, Piccoli and I had to take on some debts with the labs, who were to be reimbursed with our take on the film. Since we had an amazing team, both our assistants, the cameraman, and the director of production (Louis Wipf, who began his career with Carné's *Daybreak* and who'd been director of production for Grémillon, Clouzot, Autant-Lara, and Tourneur), the film was so well prepared and shot that we were under budget by nine thousand dollars, which allowed us to give a small raise to the technicians, pay off our debts and, for Piccoli and me, to make a small profit. We'd given ourselves very small salaries that would normally have been paid three months after the film premiered so they wouldn't encumber the budget. By lowering the salary of the actors and giving them a percentage of the receipts, we were able to achieve something that's having some important repercussions. Gaumont already has two films in the works that couldn't have been made before this: Francis Girod's *The Wild State* will be made thanks to *Spoiled Children*. In my opinion, given how tricky the question of participation in film production is, since three-fourths of the time the interested parties never see a dime, the idea of basing salaries on eventual receipts means that they're sure to get some reimbursement and at the same time reduces the enormous cost of making films. This would allow us to make films that aren't subjected to the threat of having to attract a minimum of four hundred thousand viewers and would permit more experimental subjects.

Q: Which leads us to think about your film in the context of current French cinema. I think we could place it among a certain number of recent trends in French film that more informal and open-ended. We see traces in *Spoiled Children* of experimental films like those of Deligny, or Charlotte Debreuil's film; treatments of the city, as in Poljinsky's film that was so militant, but was only shown once. And suddenly you arrive with a film that should have a fairly large distribution and introduce the viewing public to a certain number of preoccupations of recent French film.

BT: I was very impressed by Renaud Victor's *Ce Gamin-là* and I'd long wanted to make a film about children. There are currently a whole series of films that explore a bunch of different domains and I hate it that they don't get a wider distribution because I think they could touch a lot of people. Maybe it's because there are fewer and fewer independent cinemas, or because they have trouble programming this kind of film. But they're the same circuits of distribution that intelligently and beneficently circulated at an earlier time, a lot of art and avant-garde films. So we shouldn't imagine everything is lost. You have to understand that in France we're very privileged. When you see what's going on in Italy or Germany, when you think about Russia or the US, you realize that in France, and especially in Paris, we're really lucky: Gaumont and UGC show Werner Herzog, Dino Risi, Bergman, films that previously would have been shown in only one theater. So you can find lots of interesting films that sometimes even get screened in the provinces. But it's also true, on the other hand, that the monopoly of distribution prevents certain independent cinemas from surviving—or that survive only by showing porno films. And where TV ought to step in and broadcast these less popular films, they exhibit a very reactionary reluctance to do so. But you also have to blame a certain laziness among our viewers who should go see these films, but don't always do so. The public has to assume some responsibility here! You notice that certain films that should touch lots of people aren't seen by more than 2 percent of the potential film-going public. Take the example of Heynemann's *La Question* [*Torture*]: despite the efforts of *L'Humanité* to promote this film, there was little interest. It's also true that the monopolization of distribution makes the general situation worse and worse, especially for independent films and theaters.

Q: Nonetheless, your film explores lots of themes which, when approached differently by other filmmakers, don't get as much attention. So is it entirely the system that's to blame? Or is it also a matter of the language that's adopted to transmit certain messages?
BT: Hard to tell. I wanted to do this film because of my children and their reactions to conditions in certain parts of the city. But we wouldn't say that films that touch people are more useful than those that don't. Both kinds are useful and necessary. But some are made in a way that prevents them from having a stronger impact, perhaps because the director didn't have access to the means necessary to do so.

Q: I don't think that there are things that can't be expressed in film. Everything depends on the way the film is made. Everything that's said and doesn't succeed in convincing the viewers in other films can be found in your film and works, and, I'll go further: your film will become a model reference point for other films. This kind of thing is going on in Italy and some other countries. Why not in France?
BT: Well, it's also going on in France. It's not having instant success, but films that portray these social preoccupations continue to exert a kind of subterranean influence that is more long-term. Take Godard, for example. Certain of his films sold only twelve hundred to fifteen hundred tickets, but they continue to play a role ten years later. Films like *France. S. A.* or *The Ten Franc Cup* or *Bande à part* [*Band of Outsiders*] will continue to have a certain influence even if, initially, they didn't have the public they should have had.

Q: In France we've always deplored the split between the films that are purely for amusement, like Louis de Funès's films, and the films that "think," and we envy the Italian comedies that fuse into a single product this double preoccupation with amusement and reflection.

BT: Well there are some exceptions to your formula: how would you classify Sautet? Or Granier-Deferre's *The Widow Couderc*? Or *R.A.S.* by Boisset. Or Allio's *La Vieille Dame indigne* [*The Shameless Old Lady*]?

Q: Well you can count films like that on your fingers. There are not enough of them to establish a tendency. Let me ask the question differently. How would you situate your own films among the various genres currently illustrated by French film?

BT: I really have trouble answering that. There are certain things that excite me and I try to translate them vehemently while maintaining a certain form of humor vis-à-vis the subject. It's true that the Italians have a way of treating certain subjects that borders on disrespect and that I find very salutary. Risi, Comencini, Scola take on very serious subjects that are very specific socially and politically but without this catastrophic seriousness that drags others down. I see no reason why Duras's *The Truck*, in which there are some things that move me very much, has to have this atmosphere of a Good Friday mass. There's no reason why avant-garde cinema, which aspires to be poetic and serious, should be so sinister. The greatest poets were vibrant and ironic. I feel this deeply when I try to make my own films, but that doesn't mean I have a theory about it or all the right answers. It's just how I am. That's all.

Q: We might take a minute to talk about the problems posed by historical films, since you were absent at our round-table discussion on this subject (*Positif* no. 189).

BT: None of the historians present had anything to say about popular history: nothing was said about the peplums of Riccardo Freda, Vittorio Cottafavi. It's a pity to leave out this field of investigation, for it's a cinema that is very rich esthetically and plastically. It's a vision of history that's interesting to study from the point of view of myth, because it follows certain canons, and certain revealing tastes. A few of its films, when they succeed, reveal a sense of history that is much stronger than in certain more ambitious works. I remember a moment in *Seven Swords for the King* where you saw an adventurer in the courtyard of an inn who was drinking; there were women around him, chickens running about, etc. And during these few minutes, I had a very powerful feeling, caused by the perfect way it was framed, by the décor, the use of color, and the camera movements that we were watching history unfold at a very simple level. There were other comparable moments, like when the Cardinal was arguing about a croquet game. So it's a pity this very rich aspect of historic film wasn't discussed: films like Cottafavi's *Milady and the Musketeers*, Freda's *Seven Swords for the King* or *Hercules' Conquest of Atlantis* or the version of *The Three Musketeers* with George Sidney and Gene Kelly, or the pirate films of Michael Curtiz. The second thing that surprised me was that they gave the impression that they believed that *The Judge and the Assassin* was a history of the Ardèche region, whereas it took place in the Ain. As for the reproach that Joutard made, that I hadn't used the oral traditions of the Ardèche, it doesn't make sense, since this tradition was constituted after the events of my film. To take an example, the legend of the "Stone of Vacher," on which he is supposed to have beheaded his victims (which is false), sprang up after the execution of Vacher. It's because Aurenche is an old Ardechois and that I am from Lyon, and that the Ardèche countryside is more beautiful than that of Ain that we decided to transpose the story. I also had trouble understanding from this round table at what point a film began to be "historical."

Q: You've worked thus far with two cinematographers: Pierre-William Glenn and Alain Lèvent. Are there similarities between them?

BT: They have a wonderful quality in common: they're extraordinarily fast. Each one does his own framing. For me it's important to communicate about the photography and the framing at the same time, especially when you're working a lot with a hand-held camera. They have another quality in common: they're both cameramen who think about sound. That is, they do lighting in a certain way but if they see that there will be a problem with the boom, they'll change the lighting to make sure the sound is good. This isn't very common. There are a few cinematographers, known among the sound engineers who will say, "Those guys don't get it: as soon as we put up the boom, there are bunches of shadows." This is particularly important to me because I like to get direct sound and I've got a terrific sound man, Michel Desrois, who did the boom on *L'Horloger de Saint-Paul* [*The Clockmaker*] and managed to do both my historical films in direct sound.

The differences between Glenn and Lèvent? Glenn is more audacious, a little crazy—and sometimes can be very stubborn—but when you ask him to do things differently, and when he sees why, you can get him to do anything. Glenn is more stimulating in his way of continually rethinking the film. He takes care of everything and gets very involved with the actors and tries to get them to do particular things his way. For example, he likes very deep focus, so he'll use an 800 lens, and when I make him change it, he'll say, "No, no! It's terrific, like Pekinpah! He does everything with an 800 lens." We'll be working with a 75 or 40 lens and he say, "No, that's like Bresson, can't stand Bresson . . ." Lèvent intervenes less. He says, "It's your film." That's a little frustrating at times, since I have to assume responsibility for everything. The thing they share that's terrific is that they don't get in the actors' way. They let the actors work without markings, and end up three feet away from where they were supposed to be, and don't automatically cut. It's important that the actors don't feel this kind of technical censure. The one is a kind of formidable cowboy, who, when he's finished throwing stones at his assistants or making karate chops, manages to film an extremely complicated shot very quickly and shares his enormous enthusiasm with the team. The other is more discrete, more timid, perhaps because he's had some nasty dust-ups with violent actors, who pushed him around. With him there's a different ambiance. He creates an Olympian calm on the set, which is easier for some of the women. With the other race-car champion, we don't always have calm!

In any case, both of them can work quickly where others might take hours. There's a shot I really like in *Spoiled Children*—it's the scene where two poster hangers are working at night. Lèvent took three minutes to light it. We started at five minutes to ten. At two minutes to ten it was done. It's incredible . . . I have to say we were able to work with very good tools, Panavision lenses with very wide apertures, for example. I've made three films in Panavision, two in normal Panavision and *The Judge and the Assassin* in anamorphic Panavision. It's superb, gives you extraordinary definition and you can shoot without artificial lighting in incredible circumstances. Militant cinema should be shot with this kind of lens, but it's very expensive . . . You can shoot at night with ridiculously little lighting. For example, in the long take where Piccoli is telling the story of Marius Jacob in the car, there was just a little spot on his face, but the rest of the scene is completely sharp. It's a shot I really love. I had to start it all over to catch the sound of a little jazz ensemble that appeared for an instant. We didn't add that during the mixing, it was there at the shooting and it's pretty nice.

The idea of the film, *Spoiled Children*, is pretty simple: shoot most of the film without any zoom, using 28, 35, and 55 lenses, and on certain shots 75. Use the zoom only during the reportage for a few long shots. It was a good lesson in mise en scene to limit the use of the zoom and think more in terms of cutting. The zoom can become a crutch. Our aim in the photography was to achieve certain of the very cool and hyperreal tones of the American painters, like Edward Hopper, in exterior shots and in the close-ups of faces, like Christine in the café.

Q: How do you think about music in your films?
BT: I was sorry that in *Let Joy Reign Supreme* we didn't emphasize enough that the beautiful music was actually composed by the real Regent, Philippe d'Orleans in the eighteenth century. It added a lot to his character that he'd composed his opera with phrases like "Unhappy people, hear the prayer . . ." This opera is an adaptation of Euripides's *Bacchantes*, a very curious choice, that he'd dramatized. In doing the adaptation, Antoine Duhamel was very struck by a few mistakes in

the notation made by this amateur. These "mistakes" made the music even more interesting, and gave it an almost modern sonority.

The music in my films grows out of elements contained in the films. For *The Clockmaker*, the major theme came from the carillon of the Cathedral of Saint-Jean in Lyon. For *Let Joy Reign* it was the Regent. For *The Judge and the Assassin* the music was recorded before the film so that we could use it during the shooting. It helped the actors understand the scene at times. Here for *Spoiled Children* we started with a song that is an homage to the tradition of Fréhel. Then I suggested that Sarde listen to a theme of Marin Marais, written in 1723, and then a piece by Johnny Griffin accompanied by two bass fiddles. We took Marais's basic harmonies and added in other instruments and had Griffin play Marais. For all three films there's a predominance of bass fiddles: in *The Clockmaker*, the theme was played by six bass fiddles in unison. For *The Judge* there were fourteen of them! Here I had two bass fiddles in a score written originally for the viola da gamba . . . The musicians had a tough time with it. Rabbath asked me, "Couldn't we record this before the strings cut through to our bones?" We cut in a marvelous song by Caussimon sung by Jugnot, the "Tango of the Latinist." He sang it during the party; it was the story of a young seminarian who goes to Pigalle . . . The song with Marielle and Rochefort was great fun to do. I'd wanted to get them to sing for a long time. In fact Rochefort sings for a few seconds off-screen in *The Clockmaker* . . . As for Marielle, I'd heard him whistling the chorus of Sidney Bechet—sublime! Since both of them love Caussimon, they had great fun at it. Everything was done quickly: two hours, four takes. They articulate the libretto and understand it . . . The sound engineer liked them a lot. He's used to taking a lot of time with certain pop singers. Just to get them to sing "I love you" takes an entire afternoon. Marielle has called me several times since the shoot: "Hello, it's your favorite crooner . . ."

Blending the Personal with the Political: An Interview with Bertrand Tavernier

Leonard Quart and Lenny Rubenstein / 1978

From *Cineaste*, no. 4 (1978). Reprinted by permission.

Leonard Quart & Lenny Rubenstein: Your films seem to operate on both a political and psychological level. How do you perceive the relationship between the two?

Bertrand Tavernier: I think it is difficult to split. I don't find them psychological, because for me the characters are very deeply rooted in and related to their social context. I don't believe, however, that the social context can explain everything. It's too easy sometimes to blame actions on a character's background or family: it's really a combination of society and personality. I think it was Henry James who said something about character being the product of a situation, and the situation the product of character, and it's true. I cannot conceive of a character completely cut off from any kind of context. It is the important element in all the films I've made—this relationship between the character and everything around the character.

Q&R: Do you feel you are always successful at doing that?

BT: I don't know; if I say yes, I sound pretentious. In *The Clockmaker* [*L'Horloger de Saint-Paul*], the evolution of the father was, I think, very believable. I was dealing with somebody who was moving only a little bit, one small step, yet for him it was enormous. It was difficult to show this without becoming didactic, without betraying the characterization. Even now, I wouldn't do it any differently. His evolution, the way he talks with his ˉson and accepts him, succeeds for me; it's the dynamic and organic movement of the film.

Q&R: In *Spoiled Children* [*Des Enfants gâtés*] the movements or changes were smaller, more minuscule.

BT: Yes, they are not large. In *The Clockmaker*, though, the change is enormous for the father; in his context, they are great. I always said that *The Clockmaker* was the story of a man who would not cross against a red light, and at the end in a courtroom, he is testifying for his son, affirming his loyalty to his son. What I like in *The Clockmaker* is that there is nothing heroic about the father. Some people say he is crazy not to have his son plead to a lesser crime than murder, so that his son will get only life or six years, but there he is fighting alongside his son, and I liked that. It was not an easy choice and not so glibly political; there is something ambiguous about it.

Q&R: What was the significance of the scene between the father and the son in prison when Noiret tells about punching an officer in the face in 1940?
BT: It was Aurenche (co-scriptwriter Jean Aurenche) who thought of that because he had actually seen it during the war. I added the stupid order to save a piano from a burning house, and Aurenche added that violent confrontation and I liked it. The incident had the kind of craziness, and absurdity, the kind of irony I've always liked. I don't know why, perhaps because people reveal things about themselves when they tell stories, perhaps because it's an image of myself, for instead of speaking directly, it's up to the audience to understand the point through the story. I feel uneasy speaking in the first person in my films, but feel more relaxed using a third-person voice, which also allows me the kind of dramatic confrontation which interests me.

Q&R: How did the politics emerge in *The Clockmaker*? Were they in the Simenon novel?
BT: I think they are mostly mine, but the novel supplied a basis for it. You know the novel takes place in upstate New York in the mid-fifties. The murder came from the fashionably anarchic attitude of the 1930s gangsters, the rebellion against law and order, the feeling they try to get in *Bloody Mama* and *Bonnie and Clyde*. But when scriptwriters Jean Aurenche, Pierre Bost, and I began work, we wanted the story to be more rooted in French society, and the political background became more and more important than it had been in the novel. In my first adaptation I had made the murdered man, who remains unknown in the book, a factory cop.

Q&R: The anarchist influence in the film seems very strong. The father's actions are opposed by his orthodox leftist friend.
BT: The friend is a Communist Party member and a strong unionist. He doesn't know how to deal with the situation, because in accordance with his beliefs, he cannot accept this young man, whose politics are so obscure and whose act of murder is a little like the gestures of the nineteenth-century anarchists. So there

is a conflict between him and the father, although the Communist Party member (Jacques Denis) is right when he reproaches the father for not being deeply interested in his son. What has always puzzled me is the tendency to make one of two characters totally right, and the other completely wrong; in this film the Communist has one or two points where he is right, and two or three where he is wrong.

Q&R: What about the peculiar relationship between the father and the detective in *The Clockmaker*?

BT: The impetus for their friendship comes mostly from the cop (Jean Rochefort). That character did not exist in the novel. The inspector is one of those types who have the need to see people who are more unhappy than themselves. The detective has not succeeded with his family, and here he sees a man who has everything he does not have. He's warm, seems to have a lot of friends, and doesn't have a difficult job, and I don't say that to be funny. It is difficult to be a policeman, a detective has a morally difficult job. I hate people who facilely make fun of cops. This detective sees a man for whom it is hard to believe there could be anything difficult happening between him and his children. However, it turns out that this man is in the middle of a horrible drama, something far worse than Rochefort and his family have gone through. The detective then must understand, and try to get warmth from his relationship with Noiret.

It's not very different from the relationship between Michel Piccoli and Christine Pascal in *Spoiled Children*. It's a fascination, a desire to understand why such a thing happened . . . perhaps, because he is relieved to see a man so different from him having such enormous problems. And the deeper he delves, the more interested he gets. When Rochefort and I talked about his last scene, he told me a lovely thing: "I want to play this scene exactly as if I was losing the first friend I had in the army." I think he got it; it's wonderful. The detective would also like the crime to be comprehensible. He would like it to fit in, to put a label on it. He cannot accept the possibility that maybe there is no real explanation or at least not a single explanation. As for the father, the clockmaker discovers that there comes a time when you have to be on one side of the barricades. Noiret cannot be on the same side as the cop and must leave him. Perhaps it's a bit unfair to the detective, but Noiret chooses to be closer to his son, so he destroys his friendship with the detective.

Q&R: What is your political position?

BT: I have been a Trotskyist for some time and still am in a way, I was always interested in politics even when it was not fashionable. I worked as a press agent, and I did a lot of work on the Blacklist. I met people who influenced me, like Abraham Polonsky, Dalton Trumbo, and Herbert Bieberman. I re-did the subtitles of *Salt* *of the Earth*, which I think was a very important film, and incredibly ahead of its time, especially about the women's movement. Equally incredible is the story of its production, which excuses the mistakes of its director. I was very fascinated by what you call the "liberal movement" in Hollywood—Joseph Losey, John Berry, and Carl Foreman—and how that movement was destroyed. Despite its limitations, there were good things in it, very important things which are sometimes too easily dismissed by leftists. It's too easy to say, "It's just a liberal film." If you make a Marxist film today, it is impossible to ignore the old Hollywood films simply because they are so good and so well-made. They reflect the American idealism of the thirties—despite their optimism, they reflect reality in terms of myth. Their films were rooted in the nation's spirit, even if sometimes in fact they are not true. They caught something which is difficult to catch, the state of mind, the collective unconscious. It is too easy to dismiss *Young Abe Lincoln* or *The Grapes of Wrath* by comparing them politically to today's film. As a filmmaker I know the fight led by Capra and Ford to get the freedom to do their own editing. If people like me can get to do the films they want, it's because of people like Renoir and Capra. It was a political fight against the Establishment for Ford to use all those long shots without a close-up. It's a very difficult thing to explain to an intellectual leftist who cannot see these men's strength, and understand their struggle.

Q&R: I think in America a lot of leftist criticism has gone beyond that sort of crude, vulgar response to the topical.

BT: We should go to some of the critics I admire, G. K. Chesterton and George Orwell, to learn how not to speak in slogans. It's so easy to dismiss John Ford by saying he's not a Marxist—you don't have to write another line. They used to say that Dickens was a less class-conscious writer than some contemporary Marxists—so what! It is interesting to see how progressive Dickens was for his own time. I've been raised as a Catholic, and I don't want to belong in a church, a little political church. I hate people who become teachers and cops, people who excommunicate. Zola once wrote, "You have to live with indignation," and though I know it's the classic artists' statement, I believe there are truths that go beyond party. Still, Trotsky wrote beautifully about art in *Literature and Revolution*, and when Lenin wrote about Jack London, it was wonderful. But sometimes the disciples are less impressive than their masters.

Q&R: Some lefties have criticized that the focus in *Let Joy Reign Supreme* [*Que La Fête commence*] is on the Regent rather than the peasants.

BT: When a film is about a subject, you must see if that subject is treated, not ask for another subject. If I had wanted to make a film about the peasants, I would have. I had a reason for making a film about the Regent: the first thing any critic must look for is the reason behind the film, and then whether it is well handled. I chose the Regent because I could easily approach some modern feelings and facts, some political ideas which fascinate me. I was interested in the Regent's character because he seemed unusual and dramatic and very modern. The Regent's story was one of a man who saw what he had to do very clearly, and because of the pressures on him and the nature of his character, was too weak to do it. It was a situation representative of the political conflicts in any transition period. You can find men like the Regent in pre-fascist as well as pre-revolutionary moments; you found them in the Weimar Republic and the 1905 Revolution in Russia.

That criticism is exactly as if somebody was making a film about the 1905 Revolution, and the first thing critics ask is, "Why didn't he show Lenin in 1917?" I did that, because I wanted to show the story of three men who tried to change the world around them—the reformer, the Regent; the cynical politician, the Abbé; and the crazy idealist, the Breton nobleman; and the girl who looks at them, and in a way judges them. The three men all have qualities, they have their reasons and they all do good things, but it's not enough. At the end I show people without names, unknown peasants, the people who are going to change the society. That is the story and structure of the film. If I make a film about the impossibility of change in those times, I must discuss the real power in that period. That's what drives me crazy: I've never seen a literary critic who suggests that Shakespeare should have written a play about the gravedigger and not Hamlet. It's so clichéd to say a film cannot be political unless it deals with gravediggers rather than princes.

Q&R: Are you politically active now?

BT: Yes, I think I am in my films. After showing *Spoiled Children* I held at least fifty discussions with public groups and tenant committees. In connection with *The Judge and the Assassin* [*Le Juge et l'assassin*], I conducted as many meetings with unions, the public the "Red" judges . . . I'm active in that way. I was active, of course, in the tenants' committee, since I prefer working in some local, exact, modest project—like actually dealing with the capitalists, by going over the land-lord's account books. It's no big thing, but that is the kind of political activity I prefer. Most of the time I'm active through films, not only the ones I make but the ones I try to help. I co-produced *La Question*, the first French film to deal with the torture of the French by the French in Algeria. I'm trying to help a young director who is preparing a film about a hospital where he worked, both as a surgeon, for five years, and as an orderly for two, so as to see the other side. That man is a Maoist, my assistant is a Communist, and though I have disagreements with the Communist, I am committed to helping all film people who are honest and interesting. The worst thing now is all the barriers between the left factions and movements; you have the Maoists who want to destroy the Trotskyists and they in turn want to destroy the Communists. I'm tired of leftists dismissing, with words like "horrible," the films of other leftists. One should keep some of the adjectives like "disgusting" for the real reactionary films. I'm interested in all kinds of political films—commercial and militant—and I feel the militant film director can learn from me, just as I can learn from his work.

Q&R: Your latest film, *Spoiled Children*, seems to deal both with the despoliation of Paris and, more importantly, with the gap between generations.

BT: I love cities—to walk in them and feel their essence—and the film was partially inspired by my son's remark that he felt oppressed about the impossibility to play in a great many places in the city. It struck me then how much of modern Paris is built by people who never live there. The theme of generational conflict is the basic one in *Spoiled Children*. The film began as the story of a man (Michel Piccoli) who was provoked by a young girl, a girl (Christine Pascal, who worked with me on the screenplay) who is closer to her own emotions, her fears and anguish, than the man. She is also more self-conscious, and willing to express and share her feelings. She has lost her job, and she's with a man who has everything. He has a job that he likes and a kind of solidity behind him, and she hasn't. I myself feel closer to Christine, I feel that at my age there is a need to be provoked and confronted.

A Conversation with Bertrand Tavernier

Françoise Audé, Jean-Pierre Jeancolas, and Paul-Louis Thirard / 1980

From *Positif*, no. 227 (February 1980). Reprinted by permission. Translated by T. Jefferson Kline.

Audé, Jeancolas, & Thirard: Here's an abrupt question: why is the film [*La Mort en direct/Death Watch*—Eds.] in English?

Bertrand Tavernier: When I read David Compton's book, which appeared as *The Incurable* in the Dimensions Collection and will be republished as *The Continuous Katherine Mortenhoe*, I immediately knew I wanted to adapt it for the screen. I never imagined it in any context other than an Anglo-Saxon one, as much because of the role of TV as because of the connection to death—and even more because of the language. For everything to do with science fiction, English is more condensed, less Cartesian language, with many more possibilities for expressing the fantastic. It's a less didactic language. I've been even more aware of this as I do the French version of the film: we have to use lengthy paraphrases. That was the major reason for using English. It wasn't to make an American movie to gain entry into the American market. If that had been my motivation I would have quickly abandoned the whole thing since the script would have been turned down by everyone, by the English and the Americans.

Q: Is this a project you've been wanting to do for a long time?

BT: A very long time. I was already thinking about it when I was filming *Le Juge et l'assassin* [*The Judge and the Assassin*]. I'd taken an option on the title. But after that it took a very, very long time. I tried to get Gaumont interested in the project by proposing that they do both *La Question* [*Torture*], and if *La Question* lost money, then they could get their money back on my second film, by taking my share. It was a little Don Quixotesque and, what's more, it didn't pan out . . . The script took us almost sixteen months to write. Almost two years to complete the project from the moment I first became interested in it.

Q: So it's a coincidence that the film is coming out at the moment that the two biggest French films are *Tess* and *Don Giovanni*.

BT: Totally coincidental. It was supposed to have been completed earlier, before anyone had thought about *Don Giovanni*. As for *Tess*, I don't know. They began shooting long before I did. But when I began work with Rayfiel, neither *Tess* nor *Don Giovanni* had been proposed. But then *Don Giovanni* isn't really a film in English. If things evolved during our work on the script and the *mise en scène*, it's less because of films like *Tess* or *Don Giovanni* than because of the impact of certain science-fiction films, in the style of *Star Wars* or *Close Encounters of the Third Kind*, and especially their derivatives.

When I set to work with Rayfiel (we'd finished the first draft of the scenario in 1978), we came up against the American companies. I brought the project to them naively, encouraged by their warm welcome: "We'd like to do a film with you! . . . Ah, [*L'Horloger de Saint-Paul*] *The Clockmaker*, *Que la fête commence* [*Let Joy Reign Supreme*], well, we wouldn't dare try such things here." Some of the young staff members, very dynamic people, invited us to dinner and we met people in the industry. That's the agreeable side of the Americans: you're more easily introduced to the president of Fox than to the least of the bureaucrats at Gaumont in Paris. The disagreeable side is that is when, six months later, none of the people you spoke to is still in the same job or in the same company. The guy who was at Fox is now at Columbia, the one at Columbia's gone to Orion . . . And then when you arrive with your project, it's a catastrophe. Someone at *Cahiers du cinéma* told me that the president of Orion, Mike Medavoy, had said he wanted to do a film with me . . . Mike Medvoy got hold of my screenplay. He sent a short letter to my agent in the States. Three lines: "Seems like this is about death and its conclusions aren't very clear." That's it! I couldn't understand. What could be clearer than the death of the heroine at the end? And these are people who claim they want to work with young European filmmakers. After a while, you figure out that the corruption of money is even worse than in France and that, as far as they're concerned, we're a bunch of Zulus. We're an underdeveloped country that they look upon with some sympathy. But when I tell them, "Since you like what I do, why not try to work together to do more of the same?" they react with cries of horror. I wouldn't last six months in the atmosphere in Los Angeles. It's suffocating! Suffocating! The pressure for money, which is already intense here, is about five hundred times worse there.

In France, the people in power, with all the snobbism we have here, with all their control, are nowhere near as arrogant as in the US where everyone goes about praising or condemning films they haven't even seen! At the time I was there, Boorman's *The Heretic* had just appeared. All the agents and the studio execs were competing to see who could massacre it the most completely and after three minutes it was obvious that none of them had seen it. When you mention such and such a scene, they'd answer, "No, I've haven't seen it, but everyone told me . . ." And I'm pretty sure that the same people who said good things about Boorman's *Deliverance* hadn't seen that either. It's an absolutely hideous atmosphere. In the few studios where some people were backing my script (people who were living in Europe, like Sandy Lieberson at Fox, but those people don't really have any say since all the decisions are made in LA), when I mentioned Romy Schneider and Harvey Keitel, they acted as if I'd just proposed to make a film starring my grandmother and my cleaning lady. Romy, they had no idea who she was, and didn't want to know. Harvey wasn't "sellable" on TV. Because, to make a film in the US, you have to have actors who've been in serials on TV. At Fox, they send you a piece of computer paper on which there are checkmarks for various categories. Everything is fine, except that "You have to have Robert De Niro and Jane Fonda." They called to tell me this . . . It's not hard to make a film like that. You open the phonebook and look up the numbers for Robert De Niro and Jane Fonda; the banks immediately give you $40 million. Anyone can make a film like that and, for me, that explains to a great extent the failure of "gadgetized" American films. There are no more real film people, no more real producers. You never meet people who get excited about a story, but young technocrats with their attaché cases who are into marketing.

Q: And so you think these difficulties aren't really about the austere nature of the script?

BT: On the contrary! They're very connected to the script! With Rayfiel, we met people who said "It's too cold!" We told ourselves we'd been idiots. We should have put: "This is a love scene" even if there wasn't a single word about love in it. We should have underlined in red all the moments that were moving, and in green all the sad one, so they'd notice. I arrived saying, "Look, I can make a film for five, six, seven times less than any of your films." I told them, to put them at ease, "I'll do it for Robert Redford's salary. If you lose, you lose nothing. If the film has a minimum of success, you can get your money from screenings in Europe, and you can make a TV channel take it. You can't tell me that Columbia and Fox, when they sell *Close Encounters of the Third Kind* to a TV channel, don't make them buy another ten films with it, so you can make up your losses that way." But there you're faced with completely illogical situations. They prefer to make a film like *The Sorcerer*, that cost $20 million that can be quickly recovered, so the risk is minimal. Ultimately, I might have gotten into the system if I'd accepted a proposal that had us taking Richard Gere, who's a good actor but was thirty times less appropriate for this film, than Harvey Keitel, but that would have meant a film that cost $8 or $9 million, a much more difficult amount to recover. The whole thing was extremely depressing.

As for England, the companies that I went to see . . . there practically aren't any now. There's Rank that's started making films again. We went to see them the day they'd decided that. They received us in an office where the paint wasn't dry yet, at Pinewood. We left them the script. They hesitated, then decided it was too intelligent for the British public. They wrote me this, and I still have the letter. Then we realized what Rank's policy was: to do remakes of their former successes. The other company, EMI, wanted American stars. We ended up realizing that England has completely sold out to the Americans. Once again, for them Romy Schneider and Harvey Keitel just didn't cut it. I only gave in once. Under pressure from Fox and some people I knew, I tried to approach Jane Fonda. I tried for four days at Cannes. I sent her three or four messages but not a sign of life. I was introduced first by Costa-Gavras and then by Sydney Pollack, who'd sent her a note on my behalf. I sent her some reviews of *The Clockmaker* that had appeared in the US. Nothing. Not even a word to say, "I'm busy, I can't see you." So I gave up. Afterwards I saw *Coming Home*. I don't know whether it was because I was treated by Fonda the way I'd been treated by the producers, like someone from the third world, whereas she responded right away when Herbert Ross proposed *California Suite*, but I found the film unspeakably bad and ended up glad I'd given up on her.

Q: Had you decided on Romy when you started the project?
BT: Right from the start. She first, and then pretty quickly Harvey. I didn't know him, but one day I invited him to lunch at a very good restaurant: Harvey's really a gourmet, which he discovered when he was filming *The Duellists*. The only French words he knows are "confit de canard" and "omelette aux cèpes" . . . When he entered the restaurant, I immediately saw the possibility of using him in a way no one had ever done before. I saw him as he is in life, and I wanted to work with him from that perspective and get as far away as possible from the neurotic roles he'd been given.

Q: It's curious, but we have the impression that you kept this aspect of him throughout the film—perhaps because of his previous roles.
BT: Well, we had to at times. Harvey is not an easy actor to work with: by that I mean that he's someone who works extremely hard at every stage of the film. We saw each other during the writing. He went to England to visit the author of the novel. We exchanged letters and phone calls for a year and a half. When I went to New York, or when he came to Paris, we would spend hours together talking about the character. For every phrase, for every word, he needs to know the character's motivation and what's behind it. It's true that sometimes you have to restrain

him; he's someone who's afraid to be alone in front of the camera. Where I had the most trouble was not in the violent scenes, but in the scenes where he isn't doing anything. He came to see me to ask, "Couldn't I be eating ice cream or playing with a ping pong ball?" I wanted to have him use a very childlike register, not at all mature. That was a direction he'd never been pushed in and films where you see him smiling are very rare, as you've noticed. He always wants to add something of his own: It's the Scorsese school, where they got used to improvising and bringing lots of ideas to their roles. You have to be constantly on your guard. Some of these ideas are no good and often he's aware of it. And sometimes there are some wonderful ones. His work on the film is exhausting for everyone, as much for his dresser as for the cameraman. But this work pays off, without doubt. I've spent evenings with him in front of a video player watching movies he'd made of blind people and then shots he'd taken of himself imitating them, trying to get his hand and eye movements right. And every night he'd ask me if it was good and if he was making progress. He wanted to be able to act the part of a blind person without any trick photography, special lenses or anything. When you spend every evening, every single evening for two weeks with him, you go crazy. But finally, you get one of those shots and it's amazing! And his work on the set created a very positive tension. When he had to get his shirt wet, he'd get it wet. When he had to bump into a wall, he'd bump into a wall. He knocked his head against a rock at one point. Ok, it's true that he didn't know the rock was there. But he didn't stop the take, and he told me later that he'd thought he was forty meters farther to the right.

Q: Let's come back to the production. How did you get started?
BT: First there was Planfilm and I have to give them credit: Henri Lassa and Adolph Viezzi read the project and they said, "Let's do it!" and financed the first steps on the screenplay. And then when things were falling apart for two years, they hung on. Drucker allowed me to finance David Rayfiel's script, and he charged me a fee that was much lower than what he usually got in the States. Those are the people who allowed me to get the project off the ground. Next we found a Lebanese producer, Gabriel Boustani, who took care of foreign sales and some German support, etc. And finally, Antenne 2 gave us some money. Of the five films I've made, this was the hardest to produce. Backbreaking work. Maybe also because of the year I'd lost with the Americans. Maybe because the French producers, at that point, were less confident about Romy because her most recent film, *Group Portrait with a Lady*, had been a failure. Yves Gasser, for example, who was interested in the project at one point, had said, "Okay, but without Romy." Finally when I decided on Glasgow, that was the final blow and seemed to make things especially precarious. But I was absolutely firm about Glasgow, and right up to the last minute, I had to fight like crazy for it. Boustani and the Germans, at a

certain point, agreed that I should shoot it in Berlin. They had a completely crazy scheme: do two weeks in Glasgow and then go shoot the interiors in Berlin. It was insane! The extras wouldn't have been the same, the architecture of the houses isn't at all the same . . . So I organized a commando operation in which I ended up getting Toscan [du Plantier] to finance the film on condition that I have absolute say in where we'd shoot. I have to say, Toscan took on the role of d'Artagnan and saved the enterprise.

But even the English, when I brought up Glasgow, threw up their hands. A very good guy, David Putnam, went completely crazy: "You're mad! You'll get massacred. They'll steal all your equipment. The last team from the BBC that worked there had nothing left two days after they arrived!" In their minds, they had to be imagining it would be like something midway between the suburbs of Naples and the idea of a team from South Africa shooting in Harlem wearing armbands in favor of apartheid. But things turned out wonderfully. We were welcomed admirably. The Scots are great francophiles. I even had to bone up on my history, because when we were looking for shooting sites, people would cite battles in which the French and the Scots fought side by side. I had to review the life of Marshall MacDonald and the history of James the Second. They welcomed us as if we were saving them from those bastard Englishmen. It's appalling to think that there's never been a film shot in Glasgow. We complain in France about the centralization on Paris, but I think it's worse in England. All the extras in my film are Scottish actors, people who work in theater. I interviewed about a hundred of them who work in theatrical troupes and some of them are first class. Well, none of these actors had been contacted by Rank when they shot *The Thirty-Nine Steps* in Scotland. They shot there for five weeks, with about twenty roles for locals, all of which were played by English actors who took on Scottish accents.

Q: This discussion of Glasgow leads us to ask you about your thoughts on décor and your thoughts on science fiction. You're opposed to the futurism of the traditional science-fiction film.

BT: I wanted to make a science-fiction film that was Victorian or Dickensian and that's why I chose Glasgow. Why do people who are making sci-fi always choose plastic towers? In this regard, the cinema is way behind literature. It's just as shocking as when Verneuil makes a film that takes place in the US and there are only towers. This is an absurd vision of America, and completely outmoded, even in film. For example, in *Three Days of the Condor*, the little CIA office is located in a house dating from the nineteenth century, and the hero rides around on a motor bike. Americans are necessarily guys who drive around in huge Cadillacs and live in towers. It's the same thing in my film. The Victorian houses in Glasgow will still be there in fifty years. That's the basic idea of the film: not to employ a kind of false futurism. Same for the clothes: it's not because the film is situated ten to fifteen years in the future that people should be dressed in togas. If you look at automatic styles over the last ten to fifteen years, there's been very little change. So making this decision allowed me to eliminate all the gadgets that usually encumber sci-fi films. I wanted to make a sci-fi film without any special effects in order to focus on the characters. My film is sci-fi before it begins, even before the titles. It's the same approach in the two historical films I made: I want people to forget they're watching a sci-fi film or a historical film. I want the film to address them directly.

Q: Aren't we meant to feel that the film is a projection of our society into a world after the crisis. Ten years after we run out of fuel, a Europe become a society of homeless people . . .
BT: We thought about that, particularly in our conversations with Tony Pratt, the set designer, who'd worked with Boorman on *Zardoz*. There was a special effect that would have taken us in that direction, but that I've never been able to do: I wanted to have moving sidewalks in the streets. You wouldn't have seen them but there would have been signs, railings, and notices like, "the moving sidewalk between such and such a street and another street is out of order." I'd also thought of having newspaper headlines, and so I talked to some futurologists who made some, on the price of a barrel of crude oil, for example or on Yasser Arafat. We had a whole series of them but it ended up feeling like a series of winks at the audience . . . And then, Harvey and Romy are the kind of beings who overshadow details like that. When they're there, they simply force you to change your mise en scène. The force they exert is such that a certain number of accessory details just end up getting tossed.

Q: But isn't it also a question of the script? Before Romy runs away, they're each ensconced in their own worlds where there might have been news headlines. But when they go underground, all you focus on is them. Society just disappears. It's the same logic that dictates that Romy doesn't watch TV anymore.
BT: Absolutely. That's one of the big problems of the script. I added a scene where she talks about this: in front of the fire, she asks how they continued to do the program after he ran away. And there, Harvey goes out on a limb, since with his tendency to be a bit suicidal, he proposed that he should go and see, and it's she who refuses. This scene avoided lots of explanations. But to come back to the first part of your question, there were two or three scenes we dropped. After the moment when we learn that she's dying, I'd planned to place a machine near the bus stop on which you could read the newspapers: you put in a coin and the headlines appeared. But I cut it after we'd done the shoot to avoid having any kind of gadgets in the film. After that, all the inserts I tried to stick in, all the trick shots

just seemed totally artificial and literary in relation to the character: in essence all you want to see is her, confronted with the most naked feeling that she has of death. All the rest of them just seemed shoddy. Whether she's walking next to a newsstand doesn't matter at all. There was a scene, after she'd learned that she was dying, where she entered a bistro, and was approached by a guy whom she sent packing in a very funny way. We originally thought that, after such a touching moment, a scene that was practically out of an American comedy wouldn't be so bad. But it wasn't right. Romy's body, her way of moving, simply eliminated all these artificial add-ons. I had to follow her every move. In the same way, I'd planned to have Harvey cut out the sound with his watch. There was supposed to be a connection between sound and image. But that didn't work either. Oddly enough, the more we tried to be realistic, the more the film looked like a James Bond film. So we ended up focusing on feelings rather than gimmicks. The only one we kept from Compton's novel was the book-writing machine. I believe that Compton, who's a very perceptive writer, got the idea from his own job of rewriting and condensing texts for *Readers Digest*. I'm quite sure that's where he got the idea. We kept the idea, but changed its meaning. We wanted, at the moment she's dying, to have her struggling against the machine and hoping to beat it. This is an integral part of her character: her revolt against the robotization of life is even one of the reasons for her death. Rayfiel wrote a really terrific thing: when she interrogates the machine and it answers, "yes."

Q: Is Harvey's character's revolt less complete than Romy's?
BT: He's more childish, less mature as a character. He's very sensitive, very intelligent, very professional, and very good at his job, but completely eaten up by his work, and he has a child's reactions at times. At the end it's not so much a realization of what's at stake, but a huge wave of romantic disgust that overcomes him. But when he says, "They're going to fix me," he's like a kid who's just been injured in a soccer match, who's bleeding and who says, "I'm ok!" Next to Tracey his wife, he's also very childlike. His revolt is much deeper than Romy's.

Q: And will he recover his sight?
BT: Oh, surely not! Compton, Rayfiel, and I are in complete agreement on that . . . I didn't want his condition to become an audiovisual symbol, I was much more interested in the character of Keitel as a "filmmaker." The over-insistence on feeling and the question of how we deal with feelings was really what interested me, even if I do fiction film and he's doing a kind of documentary, not to say *cinéma vérité*; in the scene in the pub, Keitel said, "Vincent behaved in an honest way, he didn't falsify things with his editing, we could see Katherine as beautiful, ugly, piteous, etc., and yet we didn't really see her, and yet she really wasn't there, and it's

as if you took a series of images of a person, it wouldn't be the continuity of that person." That's the sense of the English title of the book *The Continuous Katherine Mortenhoe*—a mysterious notion, this idea of "continuity" and the impossibility of "restoring" the person, if you filmed her without stopping . . . *Cinéma vérité* or not, that's not the issue: it's a question of morality vis-à-vis emotion. It's a film that posed incredible problems the entire time; emotional problems, moral problems: we had to film each scene differently, and not film as though Roddy were filming, had to change point of view and when it was the same point of view, that was supposed to indicate his culpability. That led to a certain number of difficult choices, for example, never see death, never show Katherine dead. In the first draft, we showed the stretcher with a sheet covering her body; but when we were shooting, we realized that, with Max von Sydow on the doorstep, Harry Dean Stanton couldn't get through the door; it was impossible. So it was during the shooting, we completely changed the ending: no one entered the house. But it's a film in which, in practically every shot, I had to ask questions as a director that the character, Roddy, didn't ask. Romy was extremely helpful in all of this. She took a very moral approach to the role; she worked hard to prevent the character from becoming too pathetic or tearful—or too psychological. Thanks to her, I think I avoided having the film be a denunciation of what Roddy was doing. So is the end symbolic? I don't know. Perhaps, in reality, it's a way of saying that the film is an enormous flashback from a present we never see. It's the story, that, later, some evening she tells her ex-husband. It's a narrative device that I don't believe has been used before . . . it ties things up with Tracey, Roddy's wife, the character who's there at the beginning of the film.

Q: Max von Sydow's house creates a complete change in the tonality of the décor. It's a preserved space. Is it a way of maintaining humanism?

BT: It's a bit that . . . but not absolutely, because that would privilege it too much. There's something else, though. It's the only time that I felt like using warm, golden colors. I didn't want Katherine's gesture to be a gesture of despair or defeat. And then there's something else: it's as if, all of a sudden, you see things from Katherine's point of view. Before that, literally everything is seen from Roddy's point of view, he's the emotional link between the scenes and the spectator. And now, Roddy is blind: Katherine begins to see, to be seen, to exist in her own right. And also, this ending is romantic, it wraps up a long love scene in which no one speaks of love so it had to communicate at one and the same time, the comfort of the place, Katherine's past, and the reasons she left it behind. The present and the past mingled in every gesture. Everything that was strong and captivating in Gerald, and how all that became suffocating for Katherine, why she had to leave. So the tone of the scene is different from the rest of the film: it's the only time that a character is wearing a light color, and we were especially lucky because those were the only two days of sun that we had during the entire production . . . We wanted to give the entire emotional background of the characters here. It's not a symbol, like the "book people" in *Farenheit 451*.

Q: Yes, but it's reassuring and familiar.

BT: Yes, it put the spectators at ease and renews their confidence. If you feel this immense love, then the final break is stronger. The ending had to be almost happy: which makes Katherine's decision all the more powerful. That came from the script: in the novel it's more muted since she doesn't die voluntarily.

Q: Was she really manipulated? She wasn't really sick?

BT: Of course. She's doubtless a bit sick at the beginning, but her sickness is knowingly aggravated, for the needs of the broadcast, which had to conclude with a happy ending; I had to struggle with this broadcast, and bring us to the opposite of a happy ending though the cure of her disease. Katherine's gesture is also the break between Roddy's broadcast and me, as the film director.

Q: Is it punitive?

BT: No, there's a lot of pride in her act, as though she has to beat the machine. In a first draft of the script, it was more explicit, and she said, "I don't want to be a 'miraculous' survivor," etc., and then we preferred not to psychologize and I think it was better, especially thanks to Romy. It was also a way to destroy the broadcast and the people who were manipulating her. Such a program would not be possible in French society as we know it today, but could exist in England or the States. *Life Line* produced by Rank Xerox, is a kind of medical soap opera with real doctors and real operations . . . The advertising for the program was: "Will this baby survive this heart transplant?" And it was all real with real operations and real deaths.

Q: Isn't the idea of suicide a little too ordinary?

BT: It was Compton's suggestion and we kept it. She didn't just take sleeping pills, she took an overdose of the medicine they were giving her and so she uses their weapon against them. Frankly, I don't see what alternatives there might have been. We'd showed the script to Theodore Sturgeon, who loves the book, and he suggested that she leap off a cliff. Other than that we didn't have a cliff handy, it seemed a little too Verdi an ending.

Q: What about the episode with the musician?

BT: I wrote that myself . . . and then David continued it and wrote this scene that Losey likes better, in which they talk about lions and things that have no meaning.

It's real David Rayfiel, his poetry. There are still some lines in the dialogue whose meaning continues to feel very mysterious to me. At the same time, it didn't ever bother the actors—it was great for them. Then every sentence, as in what Rayfiel writes, there's always a hidden meaning, it's exalting for the actors. So this very calculated, very literary dialogue ended up being easy for them. The particular poetic references in the film are Wallace Stevens, who is quoted a lot, and also Willa Cather, whose novel *My Antonia* is cited frequently in Douglas Sirk's film *The Tarnished Angels*. David has a quote from Cather posted over his typewriter: "Whenever what you're reading escapes all precise meaning, it's a sign of the miracle of creativity." And it's this type of dialogue (Rayfiel greatly admires Pinter) in which people say one thing and mean something else that I wanted for this film, and that's why I wanted to work with Rayfiel. I noticed this phenomenon in *Jeremiah Johnson*, and in *Three Days of the Condor* there was a phrase of Redford's that Pollack cited in an interview in *Positif*: "I can't remember yesterday and today it's raining."

Q: How is that rendered in French?
BT: For the French version I was enormously helped by Etienne Périer, who speaks English admirably well, and who found lots of nuances . . . But it's horribly difficult! The word "stuff" for example, is pronounced fifteen times in the film, and each time with a different meaning . . . And then there's the concision of the language! We had to use more words or periphrases. For a phrase like, "What do you do at night?—I daydream," Périer put the best equivalence he could in the subtitles: "*Je rêve éveillé*" [*I have waking dreams*] still loses a lot . . . There are many repetitions of things in the dialogue, things you come back to.

Q: In the opening scenes, there are two distinct social strata: the people who live in the town center and those who live outside.
BT: This is very hard to get across in French, the idea of "downtown"—even the cops from the suburbs are looked down on and are very conscious of being inferior. That's an idea you find in the book. In fact I think it's an error to think that only people who are "politicized," socially conscious, are aware of this class division. It's very widespread in their daily lives. I discussed this a lot with the actors from a group known as 7/84 (which stands for the fact that 7 percent of the people control 84 percent of the wealth). They said they'd often encountered this kind of reflex from cops from the suburbs . . . *Metropolis*? Sure, it's sci-fi! Fritz Lang anticipated this phenomenon in a very symbolic way. Here it's more realistic. He saw it from a more political perspective; here it's just a fact. A fact, however, that is mostly missing from sci-fi films: you almost never see poor people in them.

Q: Sci-fi novels are way ahead of the cinema.

BT: Yes! Take John Brunner's *Stand on Zanzibar* or *The Squares of the City* or Norman Spinrads' *Bug Jack Barron* that are based on this division and also on a meditation on the audio-visual. But it's missing from sci-fi films. Which is one of the reasons I chose Glasgow. It's a city that, architecturally, posed the problem very well. No need to explain it in words, you could feel it immediately. The ghettos in Glasgow are horrifying, and there are two or three things I decided not to show because it would have been too much! People would have thought it was constructed like the Berlin ruins in *Group Portrait with a Lady*. Of course there's the opposite excess: people who use sci-fi; people who use sci-fi to exploit the theme that everything's gone wrong. Everything is horrible and ugly. That a cliché as well. So I wanted both these run-down exteriors and the Victorian interiors, that create a sense of security. Very warm. And then you go outside and fifty yards away you see the slums. Glasgow is like that! You're constantly assailed by these contrasts. But it's true in New York as well, and in lots of modern cities . . . I couldn't think of a better city where you got this visualization so quickly and in addition a city that could be entirely caught on Cinemascope! Those Mcintosh buildings that are so hard to frame. I know of no place where the contrasts can be found in such density.

Q: When he's arrested, she arrives, meets a woman, it's all very mysterious. "Everybody is moving in this building." It reminds one of Welles's *The Trial*.
BT: I didn't think of that. But that's included in the scenes "in parenthesis" that don't have any direct relationship with the plot, that could have been cut, that aren't narrative. There are a lot of these in the film: there's also the meeting with the girl in the bar . . . It's in these lost moments, in these empty moments that you can catch things. There's also maybe something in common between this scene, with the girl in the bar, and this sort of need to communicate, which is also, ultimately, the goal of the TV broadcast . . . There are these aborted contacts, like the one with the father . . . Real communication happens only at the end, in the moment of death. In the structure of the film there are a lot of monologues, people who tell stories, and all of these stories, to some degree (and we only saw this when we were editing, so it wasn't premeditated) these moments where two people try to get closer, take us ever closer to something stronger, more intense, where something might happen, but doesn't, and happens only at the end. I spent a long time trying to decide whom to dedicate the film to: I thought of three directors, Delmer Daves, out of friendship and because of the crane shots, of landscapes, of moment towards the landscapes; then there was Tourneur, for the mixing of the fantastic in daily life, for his work in fantastic cinema that I felt very, very close to, and finally Douglas Sirk, because of those bursts of happiness that you find occasionally in his work, which wound, which abort, but sometimes which succeed. Three filmmakers I've thought so much about.

A Conversation with Bertrand Tavernier

Dominique Maillet / 1984

From *Cinématographe,* no. 100 (May 1984). Reprinted by permission. Translated by T. Jefferson Kline.

Dominique Maillet: When and why did you create your own production company?

Bertrand Tavernier: I created "Little Bear" after *Le Juge et l'assassin* [*The Judge and the Assassin*] in order to make *Des Enfants gâtés* [*Spoiled Children*], because I realized that I'd already done the job of co-producer on my films. On *L'Horloger de Saint-Paul* [*The Clockmaker*], for example, I contacted Raymond Danon, the producer, only after I'd completed the screenplay, negotiated permission from Simenon, and signed contracts with the actors and a distributor as well as a circuit of distribution! For *Que La Fête commence* [*Let Joy Reign Supreme*] I accompanied the producer Michèle de Broca to all the discussions (and even found money at the Mérieux Institute when the film was in danger of falling through). So I finally said to myself, "Why not become co-producer—which is what most of my colleagues do—since we've already done so much of the work before we contact the producer. This work can be considered a certain percentage saved and it can be spent on the production itself instead of on a payment to a third party. In the case of *The Clockmaker*, that represented an entire year's work! And also, being co-producer gives you rights on the film. Because if the rights of the author are guaranteed in France—numerous countries probably envy us our law of 1957—they aren't so good when it comes to the material rights protecting works of art. This is something I verified later at the Cinémathèque, by calculating how many amateur filmmakers—which is one of the strengths and great dramas of French cinema—never took care of ensuring that their film stock was conserved properly. When I was at the Nickelodeon, I discovered how difficult it was to find copies or negatives of certain films. Those of Edmond T. Gréville, for example! I think that as early as my first or second contract I had a clause that gave me a copy of the film along with my salary. Every filmmaker should do this! So I created "Little Bear" for all these reasons. Thanks to this corporation, I've guaranteed myself a certain number of liberties. I had access, theoretically, to all the accounts concerning my film, to all the figures on foreign sales. But sadly it's a clause that isn't always respected. We continue to try to establish transparency on this issue of foreign sales.

DM: Who's on the board of your company?

BT: I founded it with some friends: Philippe Noiret, Laurent Heynemann—and our company was also founded so that he could make *La Question* [*Torture*]—and Philippe Sarde. But Noiret used the company only for *Rue du pied de grue*, and Philippe Sarde practically never, except for some music for the film *Coup de Torchon* [*Clean Slate*], which I paid for. As for Laurent Heynemann, he never uses it, though I have no idea why. In some cases, it helped me to find money to fund films, and it guarantees that for the future, I'll be paid for every sale or use of my film on TV. It was this capital that helped me finance *Mississippi Blues* and the television series that will be based on it, *Pays d'Octobre* [*October Country*].

DM: That was financed mostly by government funding, no?

BT: Yes, plus a little money that was lying around in our company. Which also allowed me to finance one or two scripts of some friends or, in some cases, to provide money to filmmakers who were having problems writing . . .

DM: So why didn't you create "Little Bear" right away as soon as you made *The Clockmaker*?

BT: Because I wasn't in a strong enough position. For example, at that time, Danon refused me any percentage. And since I'd been trying for fourteen months to get the project going, I gave in. I took a hundred thousand francs [$20,000] as a salary, and I did the film. It seems to me that maybe I did get some percentage after three hundred thousand tickets in Paris. The film reached something like 296,000 tickets . . . So when Denis Chateau heard about it later, he said, "I should have extended the run for a few weeks in a smaller theater!" That way I would have earned ten thousand dollars more! On the other hand Michèle de Broca immediately gave me a percentage of the profits on *Let Joy Reign Supreme*. She's a very rigorous producer; as soon as a sale is made, as, for example, to Australian TV, eight to ten thousand dollars arrives. These are terrific little pleasures. But people aren't always so honest, and sometimes you have to send them requests by registered mail. And even if they aren't dishonest, you have to ask sixty times for your share and it's exhausting. What we should have is what the SRF (Society of Film Directors) and the SACD (Society of Dramatic Authors and Composers) have requested: a percentage of gate receipts that is controlled by an independent agency. The producers have an astonishing objection to this idea; they say, "Oh that's going to alienate the authors from the producers!" But the only thing that alienates an author from a producer is when the producer doesn't pay! Moreover, since these calculations are based on profits made after the film is released, oftentimes directors and producers are no longer working together. Because these percentages only come due three months later. And since distribution and TV broadcasting have had such an impact, it's time actors and directors got a fixed percentage of the distribution monies. Because the distribution people have become stronger than the producers.

DM: So you have the impression that, today, becoming a producer is the only way to acquire a minimum of freedom?

BT: No, but it helps! At the same time, it's a lot of work running a production company: there are board meetings, paperwork . . . There are people who just aren't made for such work. But we need to own the rights to our films to be able to survive. When the subject of authors' rights comes up, you always think there's big money involved, but it's only a marginal piece of our financial success. At the SRF they did the math: on average, film directors produced a film every five years. That's the general average, but let's say that for most of us, you need a film every three years to survive. While I was working on *La Mort en direct* [*Death Watch*], I was able to hold on financially thanks to the money I was making from *Spoiled Children*. And I'd hear people around me saying, "I have to make this film to pay my taxes. I have to shoot it at all costs." So they end up accepting scripts that maybe they wouldn't take otherwise.

DM: Why is making a film today so difficult? Is it the production costs?

BT: Yes, costs have risen enormously, for sure! So, from time to time, they tell you, "It's because interest rates are so high!" But when the rates go down, the costs of the film don't come down. Salaries have gone up, which they should do, but the stars' salaries are way up.

DM: But aren't the producers partly responsible?

BT: Enormously! There are things to say about the technicians' salaries as well. It's all part of the cost of living. But that Panavision's costs should be set to the price of the dollar is annoying. That's American imperialism for you! And where producers are responsible is in the signing of high-cost stars in order to get films noticed right away and to run up the distribution figures. But the price of certain stars just doesn't fit with the possibilities of the French market. The producers are doing their job when they hire big stars. There's no discussion, no bargaining, they just want to have a "name" and they give in to whatever the stars ask for. But when it comes to the visual side of the film, they start haggling with the decorator: "What?

You need how many weeks to prepare?" Or else they refuse to shoot in a studio. As much as I'm not keen on returning to the studio at all costs, I'm nevertheless sorry that films that could benefit from studio shooting have to be shot in very disagreeable circumstances. It's just that producers don't begin by imagining the visual aspects of the film. This didn't use to be true with the "old" producers, like Mnouchkine or Dancigers . . . Today, for a certain number of films, when you get to the question of the shooting team, suddenly there's no more money! Or even when there is, they try to keep expenses to a ridiculously low amount after having spent a fortune on the stars. They seem to forget that a film is also a visual experience.

DM: Do you believe the situation is so different now?

BT: It's quite simple actually: it's due to the fact that the majority of people who wield power now are in distribution and don't have any experience as producers. For example, there is enough attention paid to close readings of screenplays, to what is important and what isn't. Some of the people in power are just investors and think only about their investments. There are others who make real efforts but who don't necessarily have the experience or the way of gaining experience about these things. This is also a situation which can help the authors and directors, who may end up having more freedom, since there are fewer tyrannical producers. On the other hand there are directors who need more support and more contacts. At the AMLF, for example, I discovered some amazing people. You can tell they're interested! But they themselves tell me, "We're not trained to be producers!" At the same time, they're strong people who should be moving up. We need a different approach. In France there's no respect for authors, except for the few that are known. When they're starting out, people can't get their work read but in the mass of scripts I get, there are some that are first-rate. I have the impression that back in the day, it didn't use to be like that!

DM: So would it be an exaggeration to say that today the real producers are the distributors?

BT: The distributors are very, very important. It's a question of financial power. Because a large number of producers are less creative than they are talented managers. The producers feel at a disadvantage in their dealings with distributors and investors; they just don't have the power to impose certain films or certain ideas. Power has changed camps and the people who have it now are less creative than they used to be.

DM: You're bothered by the lack of contacts . . .

BT: In the big companies like Gaumont, UGC, or Parafrance, there aren't many, despite the individual efforts that are made. I have the impression that at a certain period, in Deutchsmeister's time, for example, there were people you could talk to. People like Lassa or Viezzi, who would pay attention to the script. And they'd also follow the entire process of production and distribution, whereas today, once the work is shot and edited, they abandon the film to the distributors as one might abandon a child to the DCF. People like Silberman, Mnouchkine, and others like Robert Dorfmann would arrive at the distributor's office on Monday saying, "Excuse me, but here . . ." Gaumont and UGC can't prevent a film from being shown in a certain movie theater without getting permission from the distributor. Lassa and Viezzi had the advantage of having been in distribution before. Though they might be reproached for lacking a bit of craziness and taste for risk-taking.

DM: What were your own relationships with your producers? Raymond Danon, for example, who wasn't initially so interested in *The Clockmaker*.

BT: I've remained good friends with Danon because he played the game and was always very correct in his dealings with me. He's not a cinema fanatic, but he's among those people who are admirable supporters and know how to build a business. He didn't come to see the rushes; it didn't interest him too much. But he came to see the finished film, to see if it corresponded to the screenplay. Once we began shooting there were never any problems with him. Nor with Sarde! I didn't have a close relationship with Danon, but as soon as he placed his confidence in us, things well very well. He's got a very honorable prize-list of films! When we did *The Judge and the Assassin*, we didn't agree on my percentage of the take, so there was a lawsuit and I won—that's just part of the rules of the game. Two days afterwards, our relationship was just like it had been before! I've never really had difficulties with producers, maybe because I've always kept my films within the budget.

DM: You never had arguments about the editing?

BT: Once with Michèle de Broca, who wanted to cut *Let Joy Reign Supreme* down to under two hours. The three weeks preceding the release of the film were very rough. For a moment we stopped speaking to each other, and at one point I got way too violent with her, which I regret. Because she trusted me. At one point I said to her, "Look, I made this film for myself, for my wife Colo, and for one or two other people and that's it! From now on no one lays another finger on it!" She sent a bunch of people to pressure me and I was getting phone calls late at night . . . But there were two people who really helped me: Tati and Pascale Jardin, who called me after they'd seen the film. Michèle de Broca and I made our peace after the film came out. And then there was Danon who, when *Le Juge et l'assassin* [*The Judge and the Assassin*] was released said, "I want my name in bigger letters!" Which was logical. There was no reason . . . As for Gabriel Boustani, the Lebanese producer of *Death Watch*, he said only one thing: "You can't really see the publicity of Seiko watches very well!!!" With *A Sunday in the Country*, Alain Sarde was really great. He said, "Even if I lose money on this film, I'm proud to have produced it!" Where I sometimes get irritated is when producers lose money for lack of human contact. People should put in their bills: "charges added for lack of human contact." After *The Clockmaker* I begged Danon to call Noiret: "Noiret did you a huge favor, he gave up half of his salary, so call him, send him a case of champagne." Not only did he not do it, but when we began *The Judge and the Assassin*, he asked him to make another sacrifice on his salary. Noiret replied, "If it's Danon who's asking, tell him I'll take another $2 million!" So I got penalized for Danon's behavior and it ended up costing the equivalent of two days' shooting costs, or a crane . . . The producer ought to have the same rapport with his director that the director has with his actors. And then people like Sarde and Terzian and the distributors like UGC or AMLF ought to have reading committees, so that the scripts get read in a timely fashion and don't end up on someone's desk for six months. At the moment I'm working with Irwin Winkler. As soon as there's the least problem with the scenario, he comes to me and talks about it, rereads the pages in question and sends notes, and gives encouragement when necessary. He's present without being oppressive. Philip Kaufman, as well as Martin Scorsese and Pollack told me, "He's a terrific help!" At times we need not to hide our fears and frustrations. When Sarde got enthusiastic about the rushes for *Une Semaine de vacances* [*A Week's Vacation*], it made me very happy. One day he said to me, "Careful! There's a scene that isn't working . . ." So I asked him, "May I redo it?" "Right away!" He made his decision on the spot. You don't always get to work with people like that.

DM: Not always or not often?

BT: I said not always because I've become accustomed to putting up with it. For *The Clockmaker* we were really alone. At one point Noiret even sent a telegram to the production company: "Do you know anything about making a film?" Ralph Baum, the production director immediately went to look at the rushes and fired off another telegram: "I've seen the rushes. Everything's fine, you can recognize all the actors!"

DM: You're one of a kind, since in fact, ever since *The Clockmaker* you've had the power in your camp.

BT: I wanted to utilize this power to go further. At the time I'd offered my services as a "consultant" to Sussfeld at UGC and Toscan du Plantier at Gaumont. Because I do get enthusiastic, I like a good fight! I wanted to bring them projects, and if one of them worked out, I'd get a cut or a percentage. My idea was to do what Altman does, which is to get films going on around him, and not necessarily films he'd be like to do. But there must be ego problems for some of these people who are afraid someone else will get credit for the project. Me, I don't give a damn. In my interviews I always say if some other director has given me a hand. I don't think it diminishes me! I was the one who brought *Diabolo Menthe* [*Peppermint Soda*] to Gaumont, and the same for *The Trace* and now with *Stress*, the film that Bertucelli is currently shooting. I've arranged for meetings between screenwriters, authors and directors. Lots of work that I've done in my spare time. Maybe there are not enough producers? Since distributors think only about their profits, maybe we need a European-wide system of advances on receipts that would sponsor quality films like the one we have in France?

Conversation with Bertrand Tavernier

Michel Ciment, Jean-Pierre Jeancolas, Isabelle Jordan, and Paul-Louis Thirard / 1984

From *Positif*, no. 279 (May 1984). Reprinted by permission. Translated by T. Jefferson Kline.

Q: What is striking about your work is that you don't settle into a kind of trademark image, but rather that every one of your films is a discovery, an exploration. What's your sense of this?

Bertrand Tavernier: I seem to need to make each film *against* the previous one while at the same time drawing lessons from my work on the earlier one. It also comes from the desire to go in another direction. Plus I feel and immense passion for a thousand different things and need to express them. For example I'd like to come back to historical films and make a film about the Middle Ages. *Coup de torchon [Clean Slate]* was done in an ironic and grotesque mode. It couldn't be farther from *Un Dimanche à la campagne [A Sunday in the Country]*. In the same way, *Clean Slate* was a significant departure from *Une Semaine de vacances [A Week's Vacation]*. And yet I believe that there are many connections between these three films, especially in my exploration of mise en scène, in the use of camera movement where I was determined to integrate the characters into their milieu. I wanted the camera work to be melodic and not strategic. It was beginning with *Death Watch* that I wanted to really work this out concretely.

I have the impression in my films that the décor is present without being symbolic, that it's organically linked to my actors. There's been a lot of discussion about the Ardèche countryside in *Le Juge et l'assassin [The Judge and the Assassin]*. But there are only fourteen minutes of exterior shots in the two hours and five minutes of the film. And yet you get a very strong sense of the open air. Likewise, Glasgow is very present in *La Mort en direct [Death Watch]* whereas there are very few shots of the city as such.

In *Clean Slate*, I also had the pleasure of working with a Steadicam. And while I'm on this point, I want to clarify something. Michel Chion, writing about *Clean Slate* in *Cahiers du cinéma*, said that the Steadicam "eliminated the use of the off-screen." Chabrol and I were discussing this sentence the other day and we agreed that it will be a long time before anyone can explain what he might have meant. I suppose that given one's dispositions about a filmmaker or a film, you can prove just about anything. It's true that the images are not stable in *Clean Slate*, but we knew that. I adopted this approach because it immediately provided the maximum distance from the films I was referring to directly: the French colonial films of the thirties. They were entirely based, as we see in the excerpt I've cited from *Alerte en Méditerrannée* [*SOS Mediterranean*] on the use of symmetry and the diagonal axis on the screen. Every shot had a very clear center, whether Pierre Fresnay or a bugle. You can find the same thing in the films of Duvivier, De Baroncelli, Christian-Jacque. The notion of composition is always observed. What interested me with the Steadicam was precisely that there's no center, that it communicates to the viewer this sense of floating. Other than the fact that it permitted me a great deal of ease with my actors—which wouldn't have been possible with a lot of complicated tracking shots, especially given the conditions in Africa—it also distanced me, given the texture of the image, from prewar films which, by the way, *Clean Slate* has a very close connection to: Noiret's character, for example, could have been played by Harry Baur; and it also created a link with Renoir's camera work and his tracking shots, which the technicians of the time considered too unstable. What's more the Steadicam helped recreated the world of Jim Thompson, where you never feel like you're on solid ground, but always in a minefield.

Q: It's crazy, but a very sly craziness.
BT: Right! You never know whether it's put on or real. You find this disequilibrium even in characters who don't speak in the first person, but are described by someone who's not considered to be crazy. Thompson expresses this in italicized sentences that directly contradict what was just said, and by abrupt breaks in tone. So the Steadicam corresponded to a narrative necessity as well as the audience's relationship to the characters, rather than simply a taste for experimentation!

Q: The feminine characters in Thompson's novel seem to represent three different levels of consciousness. How did you express this by your use of the Steadicam?
BT: The character of the teacher is, for example, rarely shot with the Steadicam. She could be said to represent the superego. When she's walking with Cordier, however she's shot with the Steadicam. The same when she leaves the movie theater. But in the apartment, she's seen in fixed shots. As for Cordier, we frequently used the Steadicam, to the point where my editor, when Noiret enters the Hotel de la Poste and finds Guy Marchand, edited it in shot-counter-shot. He didn't

want to have a pan where the camera would make a sort of waltz movement and then return to Marchand. I wanted it because I felt it anticipated what was going to happen in this scene where there's a complete reversal in the plot. But we didn't go about it in a theoretical way. The fight scenes, for example, were filmed with a hand-held camera because things are so clear at that moment. I was very touched by two different reactions during the shooting. One was Fuller's who told Irène Skobline, "Your character really works because normally a teacher dressed in white who gets on a train turns me off; it's *Dodge City* with Olivia de Havilland and Errol Flynn, or *The Virginian* with Gary Cooper and Mary Brian, which inspired *Dodge City*. But there was a moment when I really felt for your character: it was in the train when Philippe Noiret sits down and stretches his legs in such a way that you have to move yours to the side and sit in a very uncomfortable position. Now that's mise en scène!" And I was also moved by the reaction of Genet, with whom I'd discussed a film project, and who told me that *Clean Slate* portrayed the most beautiful theme in the world: martyrdom by abjection, which was a religious paradox that made it the first chestertonian film.

Q: After having done this visual work on *Clean Slate* how did you go about working on *A Sunday in the Country*?

BT: I told Bruno de Keyzer, who was doing his first film as cinematographer, and Jean Harnois, the framer, that I didn't want any movement of the camera that was purely functional. They had to use the camera to amplify such and such an action or emotion. On the other hand, when the characters were walking, they should be shot in a fixed shot or a pan. The only exception—because we absolutely had to—was when they were walking down the street toward the church. Before beginning the shoot, I showed them a film that was in appearance as far as possible from what we were trying to do: Robert Altman's *Come Back to the Five and Dime, Jimmie Dean* because I thought the framing in that film was prodigious. Altman had told me that he'd planned to cut all of the pans out of the film since he had several cameras. But since the pans come at very moving moments he kept them all. At first Jean Harnois was doing camera movements I didn't like. We did retakes and from then on, everything worked marvelously well. Frequently I'd give him a take just to sort things out; that's how we shot the entire scene of the meal where the camera takes different faces, and also the scene in the kitchen with Monique Chaumette and the little girl. There again there was camera movement we should have interrupted but ended up keeping. The idea was to have movements that relate the characters to their environment and at the same time to the music, and thus to give the film a sort of musical pulse. Moreover, very often we'd listen to the music of Fauré before beginning a shoot just to get the tempo.

Q: Why did you change your team for this film?

BT: Well, there just comes a moment when you feel the need to do so. It wasn't directed against Glenn, who brought me an enormous amount of ideas, but I just needed a different atmosphere. Glenn ended up knowing me so well that he began anticipating certain of my desires; when in fact, however confusedly, I would have wanted to go in another direction. So I needed another kind of psychological relationship, more human, and also another work rhythm. After the very aggressive rhythm of Glenn's team, that gets you to the end without your realizing it, after his morale boosts, I found a team that worked quietly and was prodigiously attentive since they didn't yet know me. They forced me to explain things, and allowed me to feel my way. If I ever work with Glenn again, which I'll no doubt do, it will be with a different set of signals. Although we had great fun, I really needed some serenity to do this film. What's more, despite the limited budget (a little over a million dollars) it's with *Clean Slate* that I did the most careful preparation: lab tests, lighting, makeup. And I owe a lot to Yvonne Sassinot de Nesles (who'd worked on *Swann in Love* and whom Schlöndorff had recommended to me), because, with the modest budget we had, she created miracles: the costumes and the decors were all made as a function of lighting and photography, and allowed us to complete the shoot in thirty-three days.

Q: What kind of problems were posed by this single block of time?

BT: Problems of lighting mostly. We had to be checking the weather reports hourly. Moreover, the procedure we'd settled on (eliminating the bleaching bath which attenuates all the colors, and pulls the tonality more toward ochres and golds and a monochromatic feel) made the reds, blacks, and whites more intense. As soon as the light began to fade a little it was night, so we ended up having only four or five hours of real shooting a day. Plus in the Vexin region, the weather changes every half-hour. The problem was to arrive at a continuity of inspiration despite all these atmospheric changes.

Q: And yet you interrupted the flow voluntarily with fades to black.

BT: Yes, and they're all done with the camera. I hate those editing tricks that you see thirty seconds before. The last shot of *Clean Slate*, for example bothers me because it's too green in relation to what precedes it. I think we should try to return to all those photographic discoveries of the artisanal geniuses of prewar film, who made so many discoveries in both photography and décor that many of the technological improvements have caused us to forget. Even with today's cameras we don't seem to be able to get the same effects they got.

Q: *A Sunday in the Country* might have been titled "Portrait of an Old Man as a Second Rate Artist."

BT: Ah, I like that a lot since it was, effectively, the subject of the film. Pierre Bost's book took a more ironic approach to the character. That corresponded no doubt to the attitude Bost and many people of his generation had toward painters. But now many of these artists have been rediscovered and are appreciated, like Gervex and Morin.

Q: Whose paintings do we see on the walls?

BT: Several different painters. Some belong to the Lyonnaise school and I found their canvases at the Gallery Lutrin, that is run by a friend of Bernard Chardère named Gauzit. Notably, there's a painting that represents a little locomotive, painted by Besson, an artist who'd just been discovered during an exhibition of his work in Lyon. In the atelier, the portraits of Sabine and the other characters were painted specially by Jean-Pierre Zingg. The others come from the workshop of a painter named Ravanne, who worked between 1880 and 1920; someone who lived near where we were shooting brought them to us. What interested me was that he had painted the entire region and its light under the influence of impressionism.

Q: We wondered, as we read Pierre Bost's book, how you managed to treat this entire meditation on painting that, in the novel, is a voice "off" that accompanies the old man as he readies himself for the day. From that point of view, the invention of the scene of the tavern was entirely convincing, and all the more so since, by placing it near the end of the film, you valorize all the discourse on art.

BT: This was an area where I was not in agreement with Bost, who, I thought, judged the character too quickly, already in the first ten pages of the book. Knowing Pierre as I do, I thought he would have agreed with this change. He was a man of extraordinary modesty, and I thought that the novel was, in some way, a self-portrait. He thought of himself as a novelist and playwright who, despite some indisputable successes—plays staged by Louis Jouvet, the discovery of people like Queneau, Giono, Marcel Aymé—was little known. Through a kind of protestant modesty, he'd treated himself ironically, including the physical traits that mirror Bost's own. He'd been liberated by the Germans because of his "terrifying emaciation." So he put himself in a "secondary" role, and I enjoyed portraying him. I don't know if the word "secondary" is right, but I think he saw himself as having, in a sense, missed the boat, not sure if he could have really belonged to the movement, not really knowing very well . . . and that touched me.

Q: Which movement?
BT: Impressionism!

Q: We were talking about Bost's biography . . .
BT: I think Bost's problem was to have been very successful in film where he was well known. Soupault, in his dialogue with Aurenche, said that Bost was an amazing novelist; and, "Excuse me, my dear friend," he said to Aurenche, "he was more or less a failure in film." So Bost had this image of being a failure in literature, because being a screenwriter is really a fifth wheel on the carriage. And then there's the matter of my own tastes . . . even if he'd been more known, I would have wanted to continue, in his memory, this kind of battle that Rissient and I had had in the past to bring to light such and such a filmmaker, whom we claimed was more interesting than many who were known.

Q: What about the reference to the Old Testament?
BT: Ah, Moses. I found that very touching. We reworked Bost's text a bit where he speaks so magnificently about death, and kept the ideas as they were, even if we changed the text a bit. There was this sentence that I found absolutely splendid and that I kept: my wife and co-scenarist, Colo, and I had fascinating discussions with Louis Ducreux who didn't want to play it that way and said, "That is protestant talk. I don't see it like that . . ." Colo fought to keep it and we had long discussions about the sentence "One could die more cheaply," on its meaning. I found it very beautiful and not easily explainable. And at the same time, I understand it very well, I feel it completely. So that's why the allusion to Moses. It was very important to me. I'd had the idea of moving it to the last third of the film, Colo had the idea of the tavern; there was something I missed in the book: the father constantly told his daughter he'd take her there and he never took her there. When I read the book for the first time, I was convinced he'd taken her; but then when I re-read it to adapt it, I thought, he doesn't take her . . . I'd already written a short resumée in which he took her, and so already added scenes to the book that weren't there.

Q: It enriches all of the characters, and increases the sympathy we have for them. In the novel it's frustrating that she leaves with so little emotion, without there being any real contact.
BT: Yes, I wanted more contact; I also wanted to change this very austere side of Bost that comes through in the book. The book is a literary miracle, with a very deeply French side, rooted in the real, coupled with a slightly aristocratic manner, and I wanted the characters to be closer to each other, especially Irene. Most of the work of adaptation went into her character. We gave her lots of scenes that

aren't in the book, and even in scenes that are there, she displays a different attitude. So we used Irene and her brother to try to get to something more emotional, which for me was very hazily limned in the novel and in Bost's personality. Some of the things he said to me really affected me deeply, but he'd say them in such a detached way. I remember that we saw him right after his wife died, and he said something I put in *Que La Fête commence* [*Let Joy Reign Supreme*]; the first sentence spoken by the Regent: "I don't feel sadness yet, and I'm taking advantage of this to get some work done." That's Bost through and through; he died of grief five or six months later.

Q: How did you choose Ducreux?
BT: There's a terrific casting director in France named Dominique Besnehard. We were talking one day about all the old men that we'll need to bring to film and actors who could play them. He mentioned Ducreux, and I said, "Ducreux! I see him every Thursday morning at the Authors' Society, where he presides in conflicts over authors' rights." And I didn't see how . . . the only thing that struck me was that I always had the impression he was drifting off to sleep; he never said anything. Would he be capable of acting? I'd also seen him at the theater in a play called *A Man Is Waiting*, the play Losey adapted in *Time without Pity* where he was playing the role that Michael Redgrave interpreted in the film. He impressed me a lot. He'd adapted several plays by Emlyn William. So I went up to him and spoke to him about the Authors' Society and he confessed, "I never say a word because I don't want to be put on a commission!"

Q: That's easy to understand!
BT: And I noticed he has, in fact, a remarkably sharp mind, and that he'd followed all the arguments, the votes, the speeches and that he'd been mentally completely present. I told him I was thinking of asking him to play a role, and as soon as I entered his apartment, he showed me his collection of paintings. He was the character! We talked about painters he'd known and I invited him to my place where, the minute she saw him, Colo said, "That's him!" And he contributed so much. His past experiences as an artist. He's a man of intense culture, an ostentatious erudition, which leads to gestures, little reactions, a certain behavior. The painting he's supposed to have painted when he was younger is a painting in his collection.

Q: Are the shots of the past meant to be rigorously subjective? The children, for example, don't seem to have the same age difference in the past as they do in the present.
BT: The mother doesn't change: the shots of the past are entirely subjective, but never from the perspective of the same person: the picnic comes from the son's

memories, who sees the last image he had of his mother when she was relatively old; these flashbacks interested me; they don't exist in the novel. There's one I particularly like which slips like a letter into the mailbox, no one asks any questions, and yet it's done in a single shot: when you see him with his wife, she says to him, "Leave off your reading, it's so much more pleasant to chat." The camera pulls back, it's a very beautiful phrase that Colo had written; so we pull back and there's a pan on the door, which lights up. We go in and there he is at table with Michel Aumont and the décor has completely changed, and it's all done so easily that no one has ever asked me, "How did you do that?" It was a hyper-complicated shot and, indeed, I wasn't interested in doing realistic flashbacks. I think they feel fake. So we went with visions and images and the age of the characters in them is unrealistic. But what interested me was that each character had some, and each was different from the others. There's even one that's a "flash-forward" to when he's dead.

Q: In the adaptation, you added the sequence at the tavern; it pushes the film into a sociological dimension that is not in the novel. It becomes a bit plebeian. The fisherman and the other characters there all look like they belong to another world.

BT: At a certain moment I wanted to take the film out of itself, to go elsewhere. There's the station of course, and their walk back to the station, but I needed something stronger. And this also relates to the painters of that period who were asking themselves: doesn't painting escape in some sense into dream? And then, I like parties and dances. My assistant, when he heard the waltz, said, "There we go, back to *Clean Slate!*" Okay, it resembles the waltz in that film, but it's not the same composer, it was arranged by Sarde. And I think these moments of solitude between people at a party or at a dance are very beautiful. I wouldn't have thought in terms of "plebeian" but I liked it that just as night is falling, with the last light of the sun, this man suddenly has a vision of something else, of people who behave differently, who move differently. Perhaps it comes out of the world that he painted in the beginning in the canvas of the acrobat . . . When the others let them dance all by themselves, I added a shot at the end where we see Milo and Tiffany watching them indifferently, but I almost added some other shots of people watching them. It seemed to me that the simple fact of the other people letting them dance was a form of respect; Colo wrote that someone said, "You'll see, she's going to break his heart."

It's a party and it's something he should have painted, but he's not indifferent to it. He expresses it in the painting of the acrobat, it's true, but in the tavern, I'm not so sure. But there is a connection between the two of them and she makes him feel that it's perhaps this that he should have continued to paint. What strikes us in his paintings is the absence of people. She calls it his atelier period, but she's not being fair.

Q: He paints ateliers and she tips him back into the world of Renoir.
BT: She's very angry at her mother. This was the only subject of discussion between Ducreux and me; in this scene he's afraid. He said, "I'm going to look like a failure." Very coquettish. He's the one who added the bow tie to his costume. It's not in the text. He worked very hard on the physical aspect of his character. He wanted to get as far as possible from Bost's description. He hated the Windsor tie. The impression of being a dauber. "I had my suits tailored in England," he said. Ducreux is a fanatic admirer of Caillebotte, he told me: "But do you know how he dressed, Caillebotte?" he asked. "I don't want to be dressed like Sacha Guitry playing a painter."

Q: The other original additions to Bost's novel are the two little girls . . .
BT: Ah, yes. That was my idea that Colo subsequently enriched. I don't know why I put them there. It's linked to several things, Ducreux's relationship with death. He's the only one that sees them. I wanted there to be some curious and inexplicable element, some correspondences. There are also some in the relationship between Irene and Mireille, the little girl. Notably the scene, which isn't in the novel either, where she reads her palm and tells her she's going to die. I wanted to create an eerie climate around the characters of Irene and Mireille, a whole phantasmatic world.

Q: We'd like to come back to the question of photography. On the one hand, Monsieur Ladmiral quotes ironically a phrase Degas used to describe Eugène Carrière: "His model moved." On the other hand, he speaks of photography as if it were something he's just discovered.
BT: He doesn't speak of it as a recent invention. Simply, photography hasn't become established yet. The photo he rejects is the one that isn't blurred. He's a painter, and he's telling himself that photography is going to replace painting. The painters asked themselves about the relationship between their art and photography and wondered whether one wasn't going to replace the other. Later the same questions were going to be debated about cinema and the theater. Monsieur Ladmiral speaks about photography in relation to his own vocation.

Q: In many of your films there's a relation to the paternal image, and strong father images.
BT: It's true that family relations are very important in all my films. In *A Week's Vacation* I added a moment with the parents, with Dasté. I noted that in my films

there are a lot of characters who are widowers, or alone. Or abandoned, like Dasté in his room on the second floor. There are the Clockmaker, the Regent, who's not a widower but might as well be. Noiret isn't married in *The Judge and the Assassin*. And again in a strange situation, at the very least, in *Clean Slate*. The only one I didn't feel was successful was in *Spoiled Children*: where the character is too abstract. This solitude, these strange family relationships seem to attract me more and more. *The Lost Sister* begins with the death of the father.

Q: And in *Death Watch*?
BT: The paternal figure that we've been waiting for so long finally arrives at the end, it's Max von Sydow.

Q: The décor in which you shot *Soupault*, the long sinister corridor that punctuates the film, is again the setting of an old abandoned man.
BT: *Soupault* helped me a lot to compose the character of Monsieur Ladmiral. I had a very rich affective relationship with Soupault, a very strong connection. Things were said about old age and death. His way of looking at his work, the somewhat egotistical harshness of old men can be very moving. Maybe it's because I made a documentary about Soupault that I wanted to shoot the scene at the tavern. It's an extension of the way Soupault talks about death, when he talks about himself and considers he's a failure, when he says. "I'm a failure like Lautréamont and Rimbaud were failures." That's very beautiful, like the moment he says in the Ursulines hall, "They're re-issuing my books, but it's only because they know I'm going to die." That's pretty amazing, no? Both playful and touching.

Q: It's a new thing in your work to alternate between fiction films and documentaries.
BT: I've wanted to for a long time, but didn't dare. I just went ahead and discovered how amazing it was to shoot the film on Soupault. I was so happy doing it that though we were asked to do a fifty-two-minute film, we produced one that was three hours long. Initially it was Danielle Delorme's idea. When I met Soupault I had the idea of having him do a dialogue with Aurenche to minimize the idea that it was an interview: just a discussion between two old men. But suddenly Soupault says to Aurenche, "But you were too young . . ." That's astonishing, no? And from time to time they had these sumptuous disagreements, like the one about Aragon. We had to edit it down a lot but there's still a lot there. Some things we couldn't keep, for example the moment when Soupault is talking about Proust. We could easily edit back in an hour of very useable things. We must have shot about twelve hours.

Q: In the same way the film about Soupault prepared Ducreux and *A Sunday in the Country*, you might say that the *Pays d'Octobre* [*October Country*] continued *Clean Slate*.

BT: Completely! I'd wanted to make *October Country* to go see Jim Thompson's characters in their own country, to get a sense of the people in the South and hear them speak. And when I heard them speak, I had my dialogues . . . When you read southern literature a bit more deeply, you realize there's an enormous connection between people like Thompson, and people like Faulkner or Eudora Welty. Welty is a sublime writer: you've got to read *Delta Wedding*, which Michel Gresset is translating, and all her essays. This trip was really to rediscover roots and I have the impression that in all my films, I'm looking for certain characters' roots. *October Country* is a sort of double film. Initially it was to be a film about Faulkner. And then one day, with Bob Parrish, we realized that we were collecting bushels of anecdotes about Faulkner and we wondered if it was really important to show a bunch of people saying things like Faulkner thought that the rat is the most intelligent animal . . . And so we went looking for something else. We did some shooting in Oxford. For three reasons: first because it was Faulkner's town—he describes the town and the land for a hundred miles around in all his books, Lafayette County, and also because it's James Meredith's town, and finally because there was this terrific guy there named William Ferris, the director of the Center for the Study of Southern Culture, which is doing fantastic research. He took us to dozens of places that it would have taken us three or four months to discover by ourselves. He got us to meet lots of people . . . Because in the South it's very difficult to get interviews. One of the rare people we'd actually lined up an interview with, Son Thomas, was away in Germany when we arrived. We filmed his uncle, his neighbors, and that's how we got the sequence with a bunch of unemployed guys playing the blues in a cabin, a completely improvised sequence. The film evolved little by little and gradually refocused around a few themes: religion, for example. It seemed to us, to Bob and me, that there was an extraordinary revolution going on in the South. There isn't a person who doesn't talk to you about the past and their profound desire to see things change. The South is making more efforts and is changing faster than the Union states. This was explained to us by a sociologist named Steve Milner, who pointed out that work in the South today is better than in Chicago, where the city is polarized around the fact that there's a black mayor. In the South, the change in the social fabric by the right to vote for black people and their election to some local positions is astonishing. So *October Country* began with the idea that we wanted to explore two themes: Faulkner and the relationship between Parrish's childhood and the South of today. But little by little these two themes disappeared.

Q: Did you choose Parrish because he's from the South?

BT: For that and because he's a friend. Parrish is a child of the South, and, thanks to him, we had an easy time meeting lots of people. As soon as he said, "I was born in Georgia," we were on solid ground and people would open up. When Marcel Ophuls came to see the film, I asked him if I should use a French voice-over when they were speaking and he said, "Absolutely not! You have an incredible quality of sound here, all the accents are different, so you shouldn't cover them with another voice!" And he told me that what struck him was the absence of any condescension vis-à-vis the people we shot. When the French go to film in America, they almost always have this sense of superiority: "We, Frenchmen, who are arriving in America . . ." It's true that Bob and I and our entire team had wonderful contacts with everyone we met. Little by little the team was integrated into the film.

Q: You make them intervene directly in the film. So the French discover the South not only through their camera, but in their relationships with the people around them.

BT: That was Bob Parrish's idea. From the start he had a second camera and he was filming the French. It was his idea to have a game of baseball, for example. But Parrish is a man frightfully troubled by self-doubt, and right away when we started editing, he wanted to cut most of his ideas. I had a hell of a time keeping them. He wanted to cut shots that evoked his childhood, and redo most of his work. But to answer your question: yes, I wanted the team in the film. I'd done a bit of this in the Soupault film, but not enough.

Q: Your documentaries are more in the first person than your fiction films.

BT: I have the impression of being prodigiously subjective in *A Sunday in the Country* and in *A Week's Vacation*. I so identify with my characters . . . In order to speak about myself I need a mask, so it's easier. In the character of the Regent there are many aspects of myself . . . But, how shall I say? When it's about me, it's hard to situate the subjective things, because I have so many centers of interest. It's easier to see in a filmmaker who's autobiographical.

Q: You mean monomaniacal?

BT: Oh, I wouldn't say monomaniacal. But simple that he's always recounting episodes of his own life. In Cocteau's *Difficulty of Being*, there are some beautiful things about this. People reproached him for not being personal because, he said, he had too many interests, too many passions. People in France have trouble admitting that you can talk about yourself in a historical film. We have an image of an autobiographical film: a man who recounts his childhood, or his sexual misadventures, or his military service. But the idea that you could completely identify with a person from an earlier century to explore him and explore the world around him . . . I feel more personally involved in *Let Joy Reign Supreme* than in *Spoiled Children* where I'm telling a story, the story of the tenants, that happened to me, personally. After *The Clockmaker* Bost told me something I'll never forget: "You said something more personal about yourself by using Simenon's novel and by using us as screenwriters than if you'd written it yourself. We pulled things out of you, we forced you to put them in the film, things you would have censored if you'd been alone."

Q: In the published filmography in the pressbook of *A Sunday in the Country* they skip directly from *Clean Slate* to your last film. Does that mean that you consider documentaries as secondary films?

BT: No, that's a mistake. I'm very happy with both experiences, *Soupault* and the South. I haven't established any hierarchy. There are things in *Soupault* that are among the best things I've done, like the last half-hour where he begins to really open up, or certain moments of anger, for example, when he gets furious at Dali: "I hope he croaks and the sooner the better!" I have the impression that the work on this film helped me progress. All my recent films, in fact, have been the occasions for great enrichment on both a human and emotional level. I felt greatly enriched by my contacts with Soupault and Aurenche. As well as people I met in Senegal for *Clean Slate*. I was enriched by a conversation I had with an old African man about religion and death during a tea ceremony. I'm sure those moments can be felt in the film. But à propos of work we put into a film, I was really shocked recently to read comments by Godard and Pialat, when they vomited on the technicians and the technical crews, saying, "They're people who don't want to do anything! All they think about is money." I find that scandalous! I think the technical crews inevitably reflect the film's director. You read articles on the way films were shot before the war, that describe the tech crews as "terrorized" and you read another story about Renoir, and there, you see crews where everyone was happy and having fun. Dalio reported that they had a great time when Renoir was filming. Personally, I can't work without a strong relationship with my crew. I need for myself and for those around me a happy atmosphere. I'm not saying that that's the only way to work. I wouldn't dream of saying Pialat is an idiot because he works in a coflictual atmosphere full of arguments. He's the kind of person who likes to work in the midst of drama, accusations and horror . . . Although in *A Nos Amours* [*To Our Loves*], where the shooting went less badly than usual, there are some delightful scenes. Today, Godard is also a tortured man, even if back when he was making *Les Carabiniers* [*The Soldiers*] or *Pierrot le fou*, he worked in a more relaxed atmosphere. I believe that today, no director should make generalizations about how to work based on his own experience. Such theories are all too often self-serving. To come back to Louis Ducreux, he told me about a conversation he'd had with Pagnol, when he was younger. Pagnol asked him what he thought of his theories about the cinema. Ducreux answered, "I think they're good for you, just for you." And Pagnol answered, "Well who do you think I invented them for?"

Q: You have now adapted four films from novels and made four original films. Is there a difference?
BT: None. Both are just as difficult and just as personal. The scenario with David Rayfiel is an original scenario that doesn't yet have a title. I'd love to steal the title of another scenario he hasn't yet sold, *Welcome home! Well done!* It's the story of a jazz musician who comes back to Paris to die. My other project *The Lost Sister*[1] is taken from an eleven-page short story. It's the story of a woman who finds herself alone with her child in a village in the American West or in Canada, it depends on where the funding comes from . . . and who meets her cousin, who was raised by the Indians and who's just been brought back but who has become completely Indian. It's the relationship between these two women, who have no common language and who are going to become very close, and one of them is going to do something which will spark a huge revolt. Colo is also writing something on the Middle Ages, that I've read forty pages of, and that I am very interested in doing. But no, in general I don't see any difference between an original film and an adapted one. It was as difficult to work on *Let Joy Reign Supreme*, where we started from an original screenplay, as it was to work with the Simenon novel.

Q: The two films you made from "contemporary" screenplays seem less successful than the others, as if plunging into the past or projecting into the future gave you some necessary distance.
BT: *Des Enfants gâtés* [*Spoiled Children*], I grant you, was not very successful. It's a film where I didn't get enough distance. I lost the sense of charm to be found in it, and that's my fault. But I don't agree about *A Week's Vacation*, which is one of my films I'm proudest of and wouldn't change a thing. On *Spoiled Children*, I made some mistakes. And also it was shot in Paris, so it didn't feel like an adventure. I need a sense of adventure to shoot a film, to be cut off from my daily routines. Fictional characters so invade me that I need documentaries to regain a sense of reality. To make a fiction film is to go away . . . and not return.

Note

1. This film was never made.

Painting Pictures: An Interview with Bertrand Tavernier

Dan Yakir / 1984

From *Film Comment*, October 1984. Reprinted by permission of the author.

Dan Yakir: What attracted you to *A Sunday in the Country* [*Un Dimanche à la campagne*]?

Bertrand Tavernier: For a long time, I've been looking for a film that has no plot twist, which I consider mostly theatrical, but moves along by virtue of its characters. I wanted to make a film that would be based entirely on feelings. A film where emotions could reach a peak simply because a young woman leaves her father a bit early on a Sunday afternoon—that's the only dramatic moment in the film. I found it irresistible. The film is based on a short novel by Pierre Bost, the last thing he wrote. It wasn't successful, although people like Audiberti and Raymond Queneau liked it. I liked its style, which resembled that of the *Nouvelle Revue Française*: intelligent and poignant without any concession to fashion. Razor-sharp. I was taken by phrases such as "All sorrows resemble each other." I found in it moments of profound truth. For example, Monsieur Ladmiral won't ask his daughter if she has a lover, and she won't say it either, so as not to hurt him. Both know they have reason to lie about it. I like these little moments.

DY: Tell me about your collaboration with the veteran screenwriters Pierre Bost and Jean Aurenche.

BT: With Bost I worked only on *The Clockmaker* [*L'Horloger de Saint-Paul*]—he was already sick at the time. He was a journalist who liked to say that he knew all about human stupidity. There was something strong and rigorous about him. His approach was as lean as his physique. In fact, he was so lean that the Germans freed him from prison in 1940 for being in a pitiful state. He was the son of a Protestant minister, whose poor parents were forced to rent out rooms. Among the lodgers was Joseph Conrad's son, whom Bost met in his adolescence. He was a real man of letters whose output was great. By contrast, Aurenche wrote very little—some poems and one play with Jean Anouilh. He was mostly a screenwriter, and prior to that also a director and author of commercials, which he made with friends like Jacques Prévert and Max Ernst. Some were photographed by Marcel Carné and Yves Allegret; I show one of them in *Coup de torchon* [*Clean Slate*].

DY: You are credited as having saved the reputation of certain auteurs of the *ancienne vague*, such as Aurenche and Bost.
BT: The New Wave had destroyed people unjustly. Truffaut's famous attack singled out Aurenche's script for *Les orgueilleux* [*The Proud and the Beautiful*], in which a point is made verbally when the hero decides to cross the word "tenderness" out of the telegram. He unfairly compared a dialogue scene to a visual one in Hitchcock's *Under Capricorn*, where Michael Wilding waves his jacket by the window for Ingrid Bergman to see. It was a vicious comparison. The fault was not in the writing—Hitchcock or Scorsese would have made that scene well with the same dialogue—but in the mise en scène. By the same token, I wondered if the credit for Hitchcock's scene should have been given to the screenwriter. Truffaut later wrote Bost a letter, which I read, in which he stated that he didn't believe a word of what he himself had written. He said he was a young critic who had to get ahead and therefore wrote controversial articles. Two weeks after he published his attack, he wrote Bost. "I admire you greatly. I really meant to attack Aurenche, not you." Bost never showed the letter to Aurenche. Twenty years later, when I read it, I asked him why he never published it. He responded, "I didn't want to use the same methods Truffaut used." Truffaut, who's a wonderful director, was right about several points: about the way some films were shot, about the production system. But I reject all labels and categories. To lump so many directors as the "*tradition de la qualité*" or the "New Wave" or now "*la nouvelle qualité française*" is the best way to ignore the individuality of each filmmaker. I'd say that the definition of "*tradition de la qualité*" applies when academism stands in the way of expressing emotions. But in certain films by Allegret, Jean Delannoy, Julien Duvivier, and most of Claude Autant-Lara's, I do recognize the auteur's personality. Sometimes it's likable and sometimes it isn't, but it's there. Many of Autant-Lara's films minus Aurenche and Bost weren't great. These are intermittent auteurs, but films like Duvivier's *Panique* [*Panic*], or *Le temps des assassins* or Autant-Lara's *En cas de malheur* [*Love Is My Profession*] are simply great. I took Aurenche and Bost not as a reaction against the New Wave, but as people who wrote in a modern way without auteurist words, unlike Henri Jeanson and Charles Spaak.

DY: You've worked with Isabelle Huppert, Nathalie Baye, Christine Pascal. Perhaps there's a Tavernier heroine. . . .

BT: That's my type . . . When I was young, I was attracted to Janet Leigh and Rhonda Fleming. Now I like thin, child-women with small breasts. The opposite of the Playboy type. And they're good actresses. Isabelle finds her own pace, makes her own music. But like Romy Schneider, a director has to find her rhythm and calculate his mise en scène around it. She needs long takes. In *Heaven's Gate*, she didn't come out all that great, because her scenes were heavily edited to help Kris Kristofferson. But let her do a four-minute scene and she'll reach great heights! Nathalie can do many things she hasn't done yet. She moves better than any actress I've worked with, maybe because she was a dancer. Her gestures are terrific; she has great control over her body. She can be both sexy and exuberant. Up to Isabelle in *Coup de torchon*, my heroines moved very slowly. But Isabelle played very quickly, as did Sabine Azéma in *A Sunday in the Country*. I was told, "You made her play like Truffaut's heroines." Actors like to work with me, because I'm a good public—I like to be astonished. When you seek to surprise, you discover wonderful things. And I too want to surprise them. It's so much fun: on *A Sunday in the Country*, we laughed like crazy much of the time. Maybe this is because I was influenced by a director like Jean-Pierre Melville, who was very authoritarian, very hard. I suffered a lot because of that and vowed not to do the same. He discouraged me, said I was a terrible assistant director. I once sent him to see Fritz Lang's *Moonfleet*, which he hated, and as a punishment, he ordered that nobody speak to me for two days.

DY: What kind of visual decisions did you make on *A Sunday in the Country*?
BT: I wanted it to be close to an impressionist painting, to have a great depth of field with colors but no filters or reflectors. Just as the cinematography in *A Week's Vacation* [*Une Semaine de vacances*] wasn't realistic—Nathalie Baye's apartment is lit in most of the daytime scenes as if it were night—I wanted to find an unrealistic tone of color for *A Sunday in the Country*. I tried to recreate the monochromatic quality of Louis Lumiere. I left all the silver on the film. I had to avoid all the vivid reds because they became black. There's no blue in the film and all the green and red hues are pale. But the yellows are enhanced, as are the blacks and whites. Sabine is a white shock arriving at the country house. I wanted to break the cinematic grammar by her arrival: it's like taking out an ax, so to speak. The roses in the garden seem natural but are, in fact, very pale. Someone said, "You found the lighting of [composer] Gabriel Fauré." I wanted a lighting that had the splendor of a moment before death.

DY: And the music?
BT: We did some of the complicated camera movements with Fauré's music on the set—even moments that weren't meant to be made to music. When I write my

scripts, I always have the tone of the music I want in my head. I don't start writing before I have it. I always knew that Duhamel's music for *Death Watch* would be similar to what he wrote for *Pierrot le fou*. Made of chords. From the outset, I thought of Eddy Mitchell's song for *Coup de torchon*.

DY: Has *A Sunday in the Country* been influenced by Bergman's *Wild Strawberries* or by Renoir's films?

BT: I've never seen *Wild Strawberries*, although I admire Bergman a lot. When I prepared *Sunday*, I didn't watch any of Renoir's films. I was inspired by Leo McCarey's *Make Way for Tomorrow*. I also screened for my camera operator *Come Back to the Five and Dime, Jimmy Dean*, because I felt the camera movements there were completely musical and beautifully inventive. I was also influenced by Joseph Losey's *The Go-Between* in terms of image composition, camera movements, and the way of seeing things. But I still can't escape Renoir: you put people in a tavern with dance and music and his name comes up. It bothered Louis Ducreux, who played the painter and is a great connoisseur of painting. He said, "Why do they speak of Renoir? The colors of the film have nothing to do with the colors of his paintings." And I believe Renoir the filmmaker had a different tone. But, with all modesty, I do think he would have liked the film.

A Conversation with Bertrand Tavernier on 'Round Midnight

Michael Henry / 1986

From *Positif*, no. 307 (September 1986). Reprinted by permission. Translated by T. Jefferson Kline.

Michael Henry: *Autour de Minuit* [*'Round Midnight*] is the story of a black American jazzman, living in Paris at the end of the fifties.
Bertrand Tavernier: I want, first of all, to clarify that this is not just a film "about jazz." It's also a film about two men brought together by their love of music. These two friends could have been painters, for example. Their exchanges would have been different, but their affective relationship would have been fundamentally identical. David Rayfiel and I first thought of making the story about two musicians and for a long time, struggled to create a credible link between these two characters. But it was extremely thorny, since musicians are so enigmatic. They only really communicate when they're playing together. I watched them during the filming: their exchanges were more concise and more cryptic than a dialogue by Pinter.

MH: What kind of work relationships did they have?
BT: Herbie Hancock told me that when he was playing with Miles Davis, they tried to outdo each other. Every night they'd try to improvise something new and always go further with it. They had the sense that they were "risking their lives" in each confrontation. It was exhausting and agonizing. Their art is very different from that of traditional musicians, who work from detailed scores. They must constantly invent new developments and new forms of expression. Bobby Hutcherson improvised on the set a few of these "conversations" to explain the element of permanent risk in which these jazzmen live, plunging ever further into the unknown.

MH: Why did you choose as your protagonists a French writer and an American jazzman?

BT: It was Francis Paudras who furnished me with the key to the film. He told me: "You can't build a plot on two musicians because their relationship won't be dramatic enough. The music is their only and unique connection." So David Rayfiel and I decided to make the connection between a musician and a non-musician. At first we thought of using a story by James Jones about the exile of a musician who'd been blacklisted, who'd frequented numerous other jazzmen, including Django Reinhardt. But the theme of blacklisting threatened to take over and consume our idea. It was at that point that Francis Paudras told me about his connection to Bud Powell. Some nights, when he was short of money, Francis went to listen to Bud through the ventilator of one of the nightclubs and would sit there for hours, even when it was raining heavily. When he told me this, I knew I had the subject for the film.

MH: At what point was Dexter Gordon chosen to play the role of Dale Turner?

BT: We were already 50 percent of the way through our first draft, when Francis had the idea of showing me films he'd done on different jazz musicians. I looked at all the ones he had of tenor sax players, including one on Dexter. It was a revelation and I was particularly struck by the way he used his hands. People find that he has a strange walk, but he moves to the rhythms of bebop! After having watched Dexter on the screen, I couldn't imagine using any other actor than him. Irwin Winkler and I had immediately agreed to use a musician and not an actor trying to pass for a musician. There is no actor in the world I admire more than Robert De Niro, but it's really clear from watching *New York, New York* that we're not watching a professional musician. He doesn't follow the tempo, and almost never reacts at the right moment.

MH: So how did you pick up Dexter Gordon's trail?

BT: It was really difficult. Francis Paudras had suggested we use him, but he'd disappeared two years previously, and some people thought he'd died. That's when I got a call from Henri Renaud, director of the jazz department at CBS and a very talented pianist. (He introduced cool jazz in France and performed with Clifford Brown). Henri told me he'd just talked to Dexter, who'd returned to New York. I took the first plane over and asked for a meeting. When I saw Dexter I was overwhelmed by his presence. You would have thought that from one minute to the next he was going to collapse and die right in front of you. I'd never had such a powerful impression. When I began presenting the project to him, I became worried by the fact that he took two or three minutes before answering each of my questions. I thought he might be distracted, that he couldn't understand my accent, or that he thought I was a weirdo. But then suddenly, he'd say something funny and very sharp-witted. So this meeting was decisive for me. It allowed me to see Dale Turner's character in a new light. David Rayfiel, however, had only sporadic encounters with Dexter and didn't seem to want much more than that. He likes to have the freedom to create without letting reality get in the way, and produces his best work in a kind of sober lyricism. There's an exchange in the film that is pure David Rayfiel:

> Francis: Dale, were you happy in Paris?
> Dale: (After a pause) Very beautiful city.

This dialogue was so poignant that I had to shoot it in a medium long shot, since a close-up would have been redundant and invasive.

MH: What did the musicians teach you during your work on the film?
BT: Well, David was always referring to the artists of the thirties that he'd met and I would talk about bebop. They're two completely distinct styles. When we couldn't agree, we'd each write our own version and submit it to the musicians. They usually chose my version over his, especially Dexter. Before we started shooting, I conducted a long interview with Dexter on video. I got him to talk for ninety minutes about his life, about Paris, about Bud Powell, who was the original model for the Dale character. I took a lot of elements from this interview and a couple of ideas for the scenario. On set, Dexter also made up all sorts of lines, like "Happiness is a moistened Rico reed." Or this question he asked Bérangère: "Do you like basketball?" David had written something else that was good, but Dexter wanted this touch of the incongruous: "What's more foreign to the preoccupations of a fragile little French girl than basketball?" he pointed out. It's one of the best lines of the film and I decided to use it during the shoot. A phrase you hear in several different scenes ends up by having a special resonance. I treated the dialogue as if it were a jazz score, allowing the actors lots of space for improvisation. In this way Wayne Shorter made up numerous lines right on the set. I discovered that he was a very knowledgeable cinephile, and had memorized whole scenes of various films. I made him tell the story of *The Red Shoes* to Davoud during a rehearsal, and he gave us a hilarious imitation of Anton Walbrook.

MH: What elements did you take from the lives of Bud Powell and Lester Young?
BT: Certain scenes are borrowed from Lester's life, but we didn't try to reproduce his personal language. The military references belong to the stories of Gordon and Lester Young, and reflect the experience of most of the jazz musicians of the period. Military service was a traumatizing experience for them, the worst of

their lives. Those who were accustomed to playing in large cities, suddenly found themselves in a segregated system. Dexter described for me that shock he felt in the period. Without the intervention of a Jewish doctor who took him under his protection, this experience would have been a catastrophe.

MH: To what extent does the relationship between Francis (François Cluzet) and Dale Turner (Dexter Gordon) reflect that between Bud Powell and Francis Paudras?

BT: The connection between Dale and Francis is inspired, *grosso modo* from that between Bud Powell and Francis Paudras, but we invented many details, for example, the story of Francis's wife. Our problem was to make Francis understand that we weren't telling the story of the pianist, Bud Powell, but that of a fictitious saxophonist named Dale Turner. And that Dexter wasn't Bud . . . Moreover Bud had been in a much more critical state than Dale. Sometimes he couldn't say more than five or six words a week and didn't open his mouth for days at a time. The way Dexter expresses himself was more like Lester Young, especially in his use of certain terms and odd nicknames. Notably the sobriquet "Lady" which he bestows on his friends. Lester Young was also in the habit of dong this. He invented expressions that have now become part of every day language, like "The Big Apple" to designate New York. Dexter is situated somewhere between Lester Young and John Coltrane. He's got a sense of humor and has easier relations with people than Bud did.

MH: Did you also borrow elements from the life of Dexter Gordon?

BT: A few. For example there's a scene where a French doctor asks him if he's had sexual relations. In the original scenario, Dale answered, as Bud had, that he'd stopped all sexual activity since his internment. Dexter, who's always been a great Don Juan, wanted to change this detail. He also added numerous other lines, including two in Danish, since he'd lived several years in Denmark. He's also the one who added some references to Manet ("Manet sounds like bebop") and to Debussy. One day he improvised a long monologue on his father. We were shooting a very nice scene, written by David Rayfiel, during which Dexter noticed on the other side of the courtyard, a little French girl practicing her cello. She was making a lot of mistakes, which had inspired Dexter to comment: "That must be a girl!" So he went to see and said, "Easy does it, relax!!" And to set a good example, he played a few notes on his sax, and then began talking to her about music, even though she didn't understand English. Dexter than launched into a long improvisation about his father, who was one of the first black doctors in LA. Dexter still remembered that he'd taken him to his first Duke Ellington concert, when he was only four years old. And while he was telling this story, he burst into tears. It was the first time in years that he'd talked about his father. But we didn't keep this scene in the editing. It was too much of a tear-jerker.

MH: Is the parallelism between the two girls, Bérangère and Chan, inspired from reality or did you put it in to make the story symmetrical?
BT: Francis Paudras didn't have a daughter. It was my ex-wife Colo who invented the character of Bérangère to emphasize the fragile, slightly dark side of Francis. The character of Chan was invented very spontaneously. Most jazz musicians have been married at one time or another and then have abandoned their children to whom they often dedicate their compositions.

MH: How did Dexter conceive his role and what responsibilities did it entail for him to play a jazz musician?
BT: One evening he said to me, "Do you know why this film is so hard for me? It's because I have to be responsible to both Charlie Parker and Lester Young, who never got the chance to be in the movies. I have to make them live through me." He'd tacked up on the wall of his dressing room two large photos of Duke Ellington and Lester that he contemplated before going on the set. At the end of the shoot, he said "Lady Bertrand, how long will it take me to get over this film?" It was very moving. The last time I called him in Mexico, he said, "Lady Bertrand, your film still haunts me."

MH: How did he adapt to the conditions of filming in a French studio?
BT: He found it very exhausting. He's sixty-two and suffers from diabetes. But I never had any problems with him. He totally knew his part, and he was always keyed in to everything that was happening on the set. He was always aware of where the camera was, and knew how to best situate himself in the lighting and what gesture to make to establish continuity. I directed him by using musical metaphors: "Now do that in another tempo!" and he'd react immediately. It was prodigious to watch. The hardest part was getting him to the studio and waiting 'til he was ready. Every gesture required a half-hour, whether it was drinking a glass of water or lighting a cigarette. Despite our modest budget, I had to do the shoot much more slowly than usual, but he found this pace much too demanding and complained of not having enough time. He insisted on taking a two-hour nap every day, which forced us to change our schedule. And occasionally he identified a bit too much with his character and went on some binges worthy of Dale Turner.

MH: How did François Cluzet and Dexter Gordon get along?
BT: François held Dexter in great esteem, and was so impressed by him that he frequently imitated him. He was interested in jazz long before he got involved in

the film, and very carefully prepared for his role. He bought all Dexter's albums and listened to them all day long. He was completely fascinated by Dexter. In the beginning, Warner had proposed Christophe Lambert, but I wanted a more fragile, more interior actor. We had to avoid making Francis too much of a boy-scout and bring out the selfish and childish side of his personality. Francis is a hollow character and lives by proxy and yet it's through Dexter that he will succeed in remaking his life. François had to walk a very fine line. Most often he simply acted "in reaction" to Dexter. He had to carry this giant on his shoulders, which was no mean affair. François brought something very powerful to his role. He knew how to convey that Francis was as much at risk as Dale and that in saving Dale he was also saving himself.

MH: Did you identify with Francis?

BT: Completely. Especially his passionate and destructive sides. This identification was absolutely necessary to allow me to approach this subject, which otherwise, given its cultural roots, would have felt entirely foreign to me. With Francis's character I felt I was in unknown territory. The scene in the offices of Warner in Paris had an almost autobiographical side, since I once worked as a press agent for this corporation. Irwin Winkler was supposed to play the American producer, but at the last minute, he had to go to New York, so it was my friend Philippe Noiret who stepped in to play it.

MH: How did you acquire this passion for jazz?

BT: When I was a student in high school, I played the drums. Very badly, but I was able to produce a fairly faithful rendition of "Tin Roof Blues" which I'm sure I couldn't manage today. So I got into jazz when I was thirteen. At that time I bought all of Bud Powell's records. For me the three great revelations of my adolescence were Sidney Bechet, Louis Armstrong, and John Ford. There are, by the way, lots of resemblances among them, especially the last two. They were criticized for their excessive sentimentality. Wrongly, in my view. It's through them that I discovered film and jazz. I learned lots of things like that. After having listened to their records, I would study up on the lives of the musicians. *The Grapes of Wrath* led me to study the New Deal, and *Stagecoach* inspired me to read up on the conquest of the West. For me, these films were a constant incentive to learn more, to get to the bottom of things.

MH: Did you frequent jazz clubs at that time?

BT: I went to the Blue Note and to La Huchette occasionally, but since I was broke, it wasn't often. I was able to buy inexpensive recordings through the Jazz Guild. I remember having seen Gerry Mulligan, Duke Ellington, and Miles Davis when he came to Paris in 1958 to do the music for Louis Malle's *Ascenseur pour l'échafaud* [*Elevator to the Gallows*].

MH: Herbie Hancock was very impressed by the way you integrated the music into the story. When did you begin to choose the pieces?

BT: I had selected pretty much all of the music of the film before we began shooting, with the exceptions of Herbie's compositions and the piece by Thelonius Monk (that Dexter wanted to play in the sequence of Birdland) and "Now Is the Time." I wanted a mix of ballads and famous compositions by Dexter ("Tivoli," "Society Red") with pieces that were less well known ("The Peacocks," "Fair Weather" that had never been recorded). I had Herbie listen to Bud Powell's version of "Autumn in New York" to give him the tempo and atmosphere that I wanted. So when Herbie got involved in the preparations for the film, the musical structure was already in place.

MH: To what extent did you remain faithful to the specific sounds of the fifties?

BT: Herbie Hancock and Dexter Gordon thought that we shouldn't try to stick exactly to the sound of 1959. We wanted to keep in the fabric of the film musical concepts of the period, while, at times, integrating some harmonies that were a bit more modern. If we'd wanted to keep strictly to the music of '59, we would have used their records.

MH: What did Herbie Hancock add to the film?

BT: He wrote four original compositions: a song by Lonette McKee; "I Love a Party" (which was cut during editing); "Still Times" that's used several times in the film, notably during the sequence of the silent montage of "Bérangère's Nightmare" that's played by Freddie Hubbard in the scene in which Francis is going back to his apartment; and "Chan's Song" that you hear at the end of the film. I also asked Herbie to sit down at the piano after an entire day's shoot and play another version of "Bérangère's Nightmare" with John McLaughlin, Pierre Michelot, and Billy Higgins. We used this in the scene where Francis is running through the streets.

MH: Did Dexter Gordon also influence your choices?

BT: His influence was considerable. He didn't miss a thing. For "As Time Goes By" Herbie had written a marvelous arrangement but it was a bit strange and complex. Dexter didn't go along with it. He explained: "This is the first time that Dale would have been playing with these musicians so he wouldn't have used such an arrangement. Later, maybe, but not the first evening. The first time he'd just play the melody. When a musician arrives in a new group it takes him two or three days to get in synch with them." So in that case Dexter simplified the orchestrations. But later, he went along with some arrangements that were much more sophisticated than that one, like "Tivoli" where the trumpet has to harmonize with the soprano sax. Originally, Herbie had wanted to be accompanied by Ron Carter and Tony Williams for the sequences at the Blue Note. But Dexter told us: "To be faithful to the context of the period, you need a French bass player. In 1959 you'd have never seen three blacks in one rhythmic section. There would have been at least one white guy." So he recommended Billy Higgins to be the drummer, which was an excellent idea. And since he wanted a bass player "who he could get along with," I suggested Pierre Michelot. That's how Ron Carter and Tony Williams found themselves in the sequences at Birdland, at the end of the film. From the point of view of the musical progression, it was perfect.

MH: What do you think of the way jazz has been represented in Hollywood films?
BT: The majority of films are really bad, though there are a few that offer some historical interest like when you see Fats Waller or Duke Ellington. But in general, the musicians are reduced to being mere amusement, or even clowns. When great musicians like Cab Calloway and Louis Armstrong are represented in the Betty Boop animated films, it's always in the most grotesque way, for example when Betty Boop is being chased by a group of cannibals. I remember, on the other hand, Jack Webb's *Pete Kelly's Blues*, which gave a decent representation of the New Orleans style. And there were a few interesting New York indie films like *The Connection* and *The Cool World*.

MH: Talk to us about *Jammin' the Blues*, the 1945 classic . . .
BT: In the film, Barney Kessel, who's the only white guy in Lester Young's band, is always backlit so that you can't tell what color he is. At that time you could have a film where whites were playing with blacks. Over time, they began mixing races in the orchestras, thanks, in particular, to people like Benny Goodman. Dexter Gordon compares him to Martin Luther King Jr. Goodman was the first big band leader to put an end to segregation. He deserves a lot of credit. And yet, when they played in Carnegie Hall, his black musicians didn't join the rest of the orchestra. They played in a separate quartet. Today the situation isn't much better. When we were shooting a scene at La Guardia in New York, a group of porters came over to greet Dexter. Some of them had played with him, others had listened to him at clubs years before.

MH: Has the situation for black musicians changed over the years?
BT: For a very long time, they were exploited to death. That's what we wanted to

show in the film. Dexter had just recorded a fabulous record that was going to be re-released by Savoy. He'd composed eight of the twelve pieces, and for that he got six hundred dollars, but no rights to royalties. Herbie told me that, in the fifties, people like Donald Byrd began to warn musicians never to give up rights to their compositions. Herbie Hancock, Miles Davis, and the other musicians of the new generation were such easy prey. For his first album at Blue Note, Herbie refused to give up the rights to his music. Among the songs was "Watermelon Man" which became a great success (and you hear it in the film). Dexter is trying today to re-gain rights to his music. Bud Powell and the other musicians of the period didn't get more than a hundred dollars for each composition. They were kept outside the system and had no control over things. It's enough to read Charlie Parker's letters to realize how bad it was.

MH: *'Round Midnight* seems to be the first film to describe the spirit of jazz and account for its universal appeal.
BT: It was bebop that gave America its true musical geniuses. They were the heirs of Debussy, Fauré, Bartok, and Ravel. They created a form of music that's never been recuperated or bastardized by the system. Blues was. Broadway appropriated Duke Ellington by producing a white version of *Sophisticated Ladies*. But they've never been able to falsify bebop. It was a fundmentally free form. Thelonius Monk said that to understand bebop was to understand the very essence of liberty. I'd tried to render that in the structure of the film: no complicated plot, nor reversals of situations, but a fluid and free construction, with voice-overs, ellipses, flashes forward, and musical themes all interpenetrating one another. Dizzy Gillespie said of bebop: "It's the most serious music that American has produced, and a bunch of people died to make it happen." Bud Powell once remarked, "Bebop is a very lighthearted name for such a demanding form of music."

MH: How did your collaboration with Irwin Winkler go?
BT: Irwin brought his support, his warmth, and his vivacity. He was always there when I needed him and never pressured me. He gave me ideas and was always attentive to mine. It was his idea to edit in "As Time Goes By" and "Society Red" when Francis kneels down in the rain next to the air vent of the Blue Note.

MH: The first connection between Dale and Francis was made during a long, purely musical sequence. Were such long sessions common at that time?
BT: I filmed Dexter Gordon in two sets at the Blue Note to illustrate what the life of a musician was really like. These guys typically played three or four sets every night, and didn't quit until it was practically dawn. That required a prodigious

amount of concentration. I always want to scream when I see a singer in a movie get up on stage, sing her number, bow and go off to chat with a client. In reality, these girls sang ten numbers a night.

MH: Did the film give an accurate representation of the Blue Note?

BT: Yes, the replication is extremely precise. The bass player, Pierre Michelot, who played for seven years in this nightclub, found it accurate in every detail, including the wooden beams. He regularly bumped his head on them back in the day, and banged into them twice on the set! But our goal wasn't to make a museum piece. I shot in a studio to produce a kind of dreamy and slightly unbalanced décor.

MH: The Parisian and New York hotels where Dale is staying have the same sordid look and give us an impression of solitude.

BT: That's exactly what I was looking for. Alexandre Trauner told me that the most difficult work for a set designer is to imagine a hotel room, because they're such anonymous spaces. He really succeeded in giving the film this feeling of solitude. The mistake in *Paris Blues* was to depict the jazz musicians as if they were tourists and to show them visiting Sacré-Coeur and other major sights in the capital. The jazzmen spend their time in hotel rooms, and I wanted to evoke as faithfully as possible their feelings of confinement. When Dale eventually leaves his room, it's like a rebirth. That's why water has such a presence in the three long sequences outside, along the Seine, by the East River, and on the beach in Normandy. In each of these scenes I wanted a completely open space magnified through Cinemascope.

MH: You worked out a very precise chromatic scale for the ensemble of the film.

BT: I tried to eliminate a number of colors and only used a very restricted tonality for each scene. Trauner is always saying that in the studio you have to begin by eliminating everything you don't want: so creation begins by subtraction. So we made a very precise list of forms and colors, emphasizing blue-gray, which gives a kind of smoky atmosphere. Trauner painted everything with cold colors and was particularly satisfied with the work done by Bruno de Keyzer, who took a lot of risks by using a minimalist approach to lighting, quite the opposite of *Un Dimanche à la campagne* [*A Sunday in the Country*].

MH: Between that film and '*Round Midnight* there's an interesting contrast, but also certain similarities.

BT: They're two films that take place at a pivotal time in the evolution of their respective arts, two films that avoid big plot reversals, and two films about families. It's only recently that I realized that most of my films are about families.

MH: You hired John Berry to play the part of the owner of the Blue Note, and Martin Scorsese as the owner of Birdland. Why do you use these two directors?

BT: We thought about Alan King to play the owner of the Blue Note, but he turned us down, because he would have had to improvise the majority of his lines. Then I thought of John Berry whom I've known for a long time. He's an amazing actor with exceptional presence. I knew he'd have no difficulties with the script and that he'd be very helpful in other ways. He worked out well because he's great at improv. If you don't stop him he can go ten minutes without taking a breath. He brought some very funny ideas to the set and picked up with remarkable presence of mind every time one of his partners improvised a line. As for Birdland, I wanted an actor with the completely opposite temperament. That's why I thought of Martin Scorsese. I owed him big time since it was he that introduced me to Irwin Winkler.

All the Colors: Bertrand Tavernier Talks about 'Round Midnight

Michael Dempsey / 1987

From *Film Quarterly* 40, no. 3 (Spring 1987). Reprinted by permission.

With *'Round Midnight* [*Autour de Minuit*], Bertrand Tavernier has made a fiction feature about jazz musicians without false picturesque details or corkscrewy melodramatic plotting. Meandering and eddying like the curls and backflows of a developing jazz improvisation, the film chronicles the West Bank Parisian existence that so many black American jazzmen, fighting homegrown racism, poverty, and neglect, took up during, and after World War II and throughout the 1950s. Instead of the floating party presented in *Paris Blues*, all glamorous romances, tempestuous artist crises, and the usual tourist attractions, or *Les Liaisons Dangereuses*, which (to quote Pauline Kael) "uses jazz and Negroes and sex all mixed together in a cheap and sensational way that, I assume, is exotic for the French," *'Round Midnight* shows these expatriates existing in a continuous orbit between the stages of tiny boîtes like the legendary Blue Note and a series of drab, characterless hotels. In these clubs, they swim in their self-generated seas of sounds usually lost even as they loft forth, except in the dimming memories of each night's small bands of aficionados or on an occasional bootleg recording. In the hotels, they sit torpidly, drink, cook southern-style when they can find the ingredients, exchange occasional gnomic remarks, wait out the leaden hours until the next set.

Tavernier and David Rayfiel (a frequent collaborator, not always screen-credited, of Sydney Pollack and the co-writer of Tavernier's *Death Watch*) have fictionalized material mainly from the experiences of bebop pianist, Bud Powell, who eventually succumbed to the stresses of the life, and commercial artist Francis Paudras, whose love of jazz led him to befriend Powell and at least slow down his decline. Their protagonist is tenor saxophonist Dale Turner (played by real-life jazz veteran Dexter Gordon), but the trajectory remains the same: a late-in-the-day re-flowering of music and humanity before the final fall.

The movie's grip and eloquence arise chiefly from Gordon's mesmerizing presence—lolling walk that continually threatens to send his 6' 5" frame tottering to earth like a felled tree; a gluey, sandpapery voice whose range of low rasps speaks every instant of both a longing for release and a mulish determination to hang on some more. Taking his cue from this poetic hulk, Tavernier keeps exposition about his past to a minimum, focusing on the tones and cross-currents of the moment instead. For instance, he never spells out the relationship Dale once had with much younger, dazzlingly beautiful singer Darcy Lee (Lonette McKee) but, rather, concentrates on the heady outpourings of regret-tinged but perfect happiness that burst radiantly from their scenes (one of them a rendition of George and Ira Gershwin's "How Long Has This Been Going On?").

François Cluzet (who manages to resemble both the young François Truffaut and Robert De Niro) is also riveting as the starry-eyed self-appointed keeper of Dale's flame. Under his ministrations, as Paudras has done, Dale escapes, at least for an unexpected time, his prison of depression, alcoholism, and heroin, finding fresh outlets for the courtly, lyrical side of his nature, not to mention some fellow feeling, the renewal of his composing, and a few decent paydays. But the film also shows how Francis's passion for jazz makes him inattentive to his vulnerable young daughter Bérangère (Gabrielle Haker) and piercingly cruel to his estranged wife Sylvie (actress-writer-director Christine Pascal, another frequent Tavernier collaborator, particularly on *Spoiled Children* [*Des Enfants gâtés*]).

'*Round Midnight* works to present what Dale calls "all the colors" of jazz yet remains intent upon nuances of sorrow and human weakness that not even perfect creative fulfillment can assuage indefinitely. This element surfaces most poetically when François, his daughter, and Dale visit the seaside and the film stunningly cuts from its heretofore cramped spaces to aerated vistas of sky, beach, and ocean. Lying back and gazing upward, Dale slowly croaks, "It's funny how the world is inside of nothing. Your heart and soul are inside of you! Babies are inside of their mother. The fish are in the water. But the world is inside of nothing." The film, finally, is a tribute to the commingled gaiety and sadness of all attempts to fill up that void.

'*Round Midnight* reportedly began its road to the screen when Martin Scorsese introduced Tavernier and producer Irwin Winkler, whose credits include (along with Scorsese's *New York, New York* and *Raging Bull*) the *Rocky* films, *The Gambler*, and *The Right Stuff*. Warner Bros. put up the budget of approximately $3 million, partly at the behest, one story has it, of Clint Eastwood, who is a jazz enthusiast. Scorsese closed the circle by portraying the owner of a New York club where Dale Turner plays out his last days, adding his own distinctive brand of motormouth New York spritz to the movie's array of notes. What follows comes from an interview done (in English) on October 15, 1986, when Tavernier was in Los Angeles on a promotional visit.

Michael Dempsey: A note runs through the movie: beauty is connected with pain. The usual idea is that a vision of beauty is a barrier against pain. Here it is not, and not because the music is neglected or there are no financial rewards for those who play the jazz. It's that playing the jazz itself causes them pain at the same time that it gives them ecstasy.

Bertrand Tavernier: Yes, exactly, exactly. And sometimes adoring jazz, understanding it deeply causes the same thing.

MD: What is Francis's real nature? In particular, what is his condition at the end of the movie, when he is watching films of his friend, that he shot, and it's several years later? I had the impression that he might be lost and unable to recover himself.

BT: Francis for me is a very important character. First, because he allows the audience to approach Dale Turner in an impressionistic way. So sometimes without even realizing it, the audience sees Dale from his point of view, from his emotions. And I think you are projecting Francis's emotions or reactions upon Dale. For me, it's not only a balance, but I think that a lot of people don't realize that without Francis the emotion would never be the same. And the other thing about Francis is—I wanted the character to have some dark side. I didn't want to tell just the story of a friendship, just the story about someone rescuing another. I wanted to show the selfish side of people who want to save the world. And I wanted to show that sometimes the communication was difficult, and sometimes are they even really communicating, Dale and Francis? In the last scene with Francis, I wanted him to be partly the cause of Dale's death, unconsciously. By taking him to his parents, to Lyons, taking him in his family, he makes Dale aware, very aware, that he is an exile, that he is cut from his roots, and he provokes that need to come back. I even had a line, a thing which I shot, just before the Lyons concert. Francis was saying, "I think I should not have had him brought back to New York." And I felt it was too much of an explanation, so I cut it. The last scene between Francis and his daughter was improvised on the set. When she says, "I'm going out," and then she comes back. I wanted to show that at the same time that he was maybe more mature, he was left with all those memories, and he had never completely thought of her: And I wanted to show that, in a way, Berangère was more mature than he, was helping him. It's true that Francis has made a step towards her, he went to her. But he's still caught in a story. And she comes to him. I wanted that. She comes to him to give him tenderness, to tell him that it's not over. I mean, Dale is still alive. The image is still there. The sound is still there. It's why I wanted the voice-over of

Dale at the last scene. The lines were not in the script. At the end of the shoot, I went to the studio with Dexter, and I made him talk about certain things, some of which I used at the end in the sound track. And then . . . I had written something which he had told me one day. "I hope that one day there will be . . ."

MD: . . . the parks and streets named after great jazz musicians.
BT: He did it. He recorded it. And I suddenly asked him, without preparing it, I said to him, "What about Dale Turner?" And he looked at me, surprised, but immediately he said, "Maybe a street called Dale Turner." And I said, "My God, I will cut my questions," and I had the ending.

MD: One reason it's perfect is because when he's saying, "I hope we'll all live long enough" to see that, he himself is no longer with us.
BT: Yes, yes, yes.

MD: In addition to which, we still don't have those streets and those parks.
BT: Yes. This is exactly the problem which I wanted to get at. In a way, I can relate to the passion of Francis. When I was a press agent I had the same relationship that he has with Dale Turner, I had it with people like John Ford. When I took care of John Ford, when we had him come into Paris. In those first days—not at the end, he was perfect at the end—but those first days he was really drinking a lot. To the point that we had to sleep in the same hotel room to take care of him. So when Francis Paudras told me the story of his relationship with Bud, I could very, very, very much relate to that. I had lived several times that innocence. The scene when Francis tells Dale how much he loves him and he loves his music, and Dale says, "Do you have enough money to buy me another beer?"—it's based on one of the meetings between Bud and Francis. But at the same time, I experienced the same thing with Ford. When I told John Ford how much I love his work and had been talking about *The Sun Shines Bright*, *She Wore a Yellow Ribbon*, *My Darling Clementine*, *The Searchers*, *Young Mr. Lincoln*, we were talking a little like Francis in the picture, and he said, "Do you think I could get a B & B [Benedictine and brandy]?" "My God," we said . . . We had the same reaction as Francis—surprise, disappointment, and it was very easy for me to relate to that kind of emotion. Francis has a very French, romantic, naive, and passionate attitude toward Dale. He loves him, and he respects him. And Dale always has a way of cutting him. And I liked that.

MD: There are moments when you just want to come out and say it. You don't want to be oblique or subtle.
BT: Yes, exactly, exactly that, sure. And Francis Paudras several times told me that he had had the same experience with Bill Evans. One day he was with him in a car,

and he had, like, three minutes to communicate something. You can not be oblique in those moments. And, too, it's not the way of the character to be oblique. The people who love the films, they will go directly to somebody and say, "I love your work." So I had a big discussion with David Rayfiel about that. David is a wonderful oblique writer. But sometimes not everybody has to be oblique. David is great for making a love scene where people say "I love you" in talking about matches and . . . I don't know, the grass or things like that. He wrote beautiful scenes like that. But maybe there is a moment, sometimes, where the people have to say, "I love you." David would even have a problem writing a scene with somebody asking for eggs and bacon. He would like to find a subtle way. And I found the same thing with the scene with the wife [when Francis tries to borrow money from Sylvie to move himself, Berangère, and Dale into a roomier apartment]. David was thinking that the scene was telling the audience that Dale is great. And I was saying, "No, David, it's a very violent scene." It's somebody who is so childish and immature that he is telling the woman whom I think he still loves that he has been inspired by her. So he hurts her all the time during that scene. And I think the scene is very, very, very important because it brings out the dark side of the character. Which I think doesn't make him less likable or interesting.

MD: In a way, it ties in with what Dale says: "Music is my life, music is my love, and it's twenty-four hours a day. That's a heavy sentence to face. It's like something that will not turn off and will not let go of you."
BT: Yes and I think it's completely true of all the jazz musicians of the period, completely true. Maybe that story of friendship and passion is more related to the jazz musicians. I don't know that anything like that happened in rock-and-roll. Maybe because the other kind of music is more the music of the establishment. It's a music where people are making lots of money, where in jazz, the people were not making lots of money. They were outside of the system. And I still think that the bebop is the only part of the American music which has never been recuperated, swallowed up by the system. I mean, Broadway has used the blues, has used Fats Waller, Duke Ellington. They took everything.

MD: The way the numbers are shot, there are rest periods in the middle of them with little bits of byplay and behavior between the musicians. Instead of playing, Dale will sit and rest for a minute, or he'll look at a drink and try to get it, and there will be looks passing back and forth between them. Rock-and-roll wouldn't allow for such a thing. I thought that was one of the most effective aspects of the film.
BT: We were determining a certain number of [camera] positions because we never knew where we were going in the numbers because jazz is so much an

improvisation. So we had like, twelve positions, and when I was watching the numbers, I was behind the grip and the operator, and I was saying [whispers] "5 . . . 4 . . . 3 . . . 2 . . ." And we were constantly moving.

MD: Were you shooting with only one camera?

BT: Two cameras. And I always said that I wanted to use the movement. So they were trying to make the movements smooth and fast. And then suddenly I would say, "Pan on the drummer, on Billy . . ." And I wanted to get a lot of shots of the people listening. There is, I think, a wonderful shot of Billy Higgins doing "Body and Soul." You see that he is listening to Dale. And you see that he is thinking a lot of things: "Well, Dale may be a little bit out of shape. I hope he will make it, but he went into a kind of adventurous course. Will he go until the end? What kind of note is he going to hit? I *want* him to play that." You feel that he wants to help, that he's interested, surprised, pleased, and at the same time that he would like to be there to *help*. So he's changing his drums, he's thinking of something else, and he's waiting for the note. We were able to get those kinds of scenes because we recorded live.

MD: I want to ask a couple of things about the audience. For example, the shot of the man who seems to be surreptitiously recording the sets . . .

BT: That's the real Francis Paudras. I mean, certain jazz fans did record the music during a set, and it's how a lot of pirate records appeared. And the bad side is that sometimes the musicians were not paid. The good side [is that] certain records got moments which were incredible, the moments that sometimes you don't get in an album, where somebody in a club suddenly has a wonderful night and a wonderful solo. And I wanted to show that because I've seen that all the time, people recording. And sometimes with bad sound. I mean, you have an album of Lester [Young] or Charlie Parker where you hear the forks, you hear more the noise of the club than the music. But still some of them are very interesting. The audience, well . . . we chose only jazz fans. I mean, some people came from the South of France to be in the movie. We had a teacher who took his holiday to be there at Epinay, the studio, for two weeks during the shooting. We had some musicians. We had the wife and the daughter of Charlie Parker in the crowd. I had the son of Kenny Clarke. I had some jazz critics. I had people who were at the Blue Note at the time. And I wanted them to listen, to really listen, to the music. And when they do things, mark the tempo, that they are right. Because a lot of times in movies, they will be either overdoing or completely out of tempo, out of the beat. So I wanted that to be very precise and noticed. I mean, the extras in some of the films about jazz are absolutely dreadful. I mean, the way they act. They are moving and acting and pretending to be excited, overdoing it like nobody does in a club. In clubs like the Blue Note, people were not dancing; they were listening. In *Paris Blues*, you see people dancing to New Orleans music, Dixieland music, but not to bebop. And they never know what is the style of the music. So they are mixing Ellington, Armstrong, swing, New Orleans. So the musicians always refer to the music but never to a style, never to a real thing. I mean, I never knew what kind of music Paul Newman was writing in *Paris Blues*, or Sidney Poitier. Was it Dixieland? Was it an Ellington type of arrangement? Was it Stan Kenton? He says, "I would like to try to write a piece of important music."

MD: Which means nothing.
BT: Nothing. It's absurd.

MD: At one point, you pan from Francis to a very beautiful woman, who's also listening very intently. If this were another kind of movie, their eyes would meet, and something would start to develop between them, and this would be woven into an elaborate plot that would become involved with the jazz and the musicians and everything.
BT: [Laughs] No, I wanted that kind of thing where nothing happens, just people listening. Because I've noticed, especially people who are the real fans, they don't communicate. They are there; they are lost. Especially in that number, which was very emotional, "Body and Soul." I felt it was much more moving that way.

MD: The musicians seem to be in their own individual world, yet still attentive to the other musicians. But they're not that concerned with playing directly to the audience.
BT: Yeah, because if they are well together, they immediately admit that the audience will get it. It's very, very strange, the relationship between the bebop musicians and [audiences]. Except a few people like Dizzy Gillespie, who really try to have a lot of fun with the audience. Bobby [Hutcherson, who plays in the film's Blue Note band] told me a wonderful story. It explained the attitude of the musicians: George Coleman was always practicing his own scales, and he was repeating them on the stage. And Miles [Davis] got very angry and said, "I don't want you to discover something alone. You have to share that with the audience, and you have to discover it when the audience is there, not when you are alone." And that's very important. You have to discover things when the others are there and the audience is there. It's a real confrontation. And in a way, they are closer to some classical musicians. They think the audience is mature enough to be able to catch that. But at the same time, they were demanding, and they were challenging each other.

MD: A question has arisen a few times: "Dexter Gordon is really playing himself, isn't he?" It doesn't seem to me that he is. I was struck by the way when he was trying to get his money directly he says, "I've been straight enough to play my axe . . . and sweetly." That's incredible, and it's obviously acting.

BT: Yes, it is. The word "sweetly" was something he added. First, I think a lot of the great actors and stars bring a lot of themselves to the part. I don't mean their ideas or that but their way of speaking or behaving. I mean. Cooper, Wayne, Bogart—they have their way of delivering the lines. Jean Gabin. In a way, Dexter is like that, and he has a way of speaking which is very special. The other thing is Dexter was never, never somebody who could be controlled as easily as Dale Turner. He was always a charmer, always a ladies' man. He had certain moments of his life which are similar to Dale Turner's. He had downs, he had moments where he would destroy himself, he had a lot of things like that.

MD: He lived that hotel room life?

BT: Yes, he had that, but you cannot imagine Dexter being locked up in a room like that or anybody controlling Dexter. I know that. We spent fifteen, sixteen weeks together, and it's very, very difficult to control him. We had once or twice some problems with him. I mean, he has his own mind, he knows what he's doing, he has a way of imposing what he wants, which is not Dale Turner. In the other way, Dexter is very, very sharp, very intelligent, and he's acting in life all the time. Like in the scene that you mentioned. I had a big argument with him, a big discussion, because he wanted to slap Sandra Reeves-Phillips, the woman playing Buttercup [a jazz singer who serves as a kind of den mother to the musicians]. He said, "I have to take revenge on her. I have to knock her down." And I had one hour of discussion with him trying to show that it was not in line with the character. And he said, "Yes, but me, I would slap her." I said, "You don't need it." When I was arguing, I said to him, "Dexter, do you think that Gary Cooper would hit a woman?" And he thought for a while, and he said, "No." And it's how I got the scene. The whole idea of the character is based on something that Thelonious Monk said at the end of his life, when he was asked to play at Carnegie and was being given a lot of money, and he turned that down, and he said "It's too late. I'm tired of trying to convince people."

MD: When Dale says to the psychiatrist, "I'd really like to rest. I'm tired of everything except the music," I thought that he meant, "I'd like to rest permanently. I'd like to die, I wish I could be tired of the music, too."

BT: Yes, that was the idea. And that is something in the character which is not at all in Dexter. Not at all. Because Dexter is a survivor. Dexter is somebody who is surprising everybody by the way he's coming back all the time. The biggest fight

I had with any actor in my life was with François Cluzet, because François was so much in admiration for Dexter when we had those two or three crises. Which were difficult but, after all, I think they even helped the film, and they are nothing compared to the moments of pleasure and happiness and great emotion that we had on the set. But there was one moment when Dexter was really completely exhausted, and the film was bringing back bad memories, and he was in bad shape. And François was so distressed that he was doing the same thing. François started to drink. We began to be worried because François was so much in his part, and a lot of people of the crew began to say, "When he will be in New York and the characters have to separate, that will be very, very difficult. I don't know if we're going to be able to get him back." And I had a one-hour fight on the street. He kept saying, "This is the greatest love story, which I'm living" and "The man is dying in front of me." I said, "Look, Dexter is not dying, Dexter is a survivor, Dexter in four years from now will be recording a new album, and *you* will be in the gutter." After all that, François was absolutely perfect and great.

But the film was incredibly emotional to shoot, because the frontier between life and fiction was always completely thin. At the same time, at certain moments we were in fiction, and suddenly we were getting right into life. And at certain moments when we were thinking, "Oh, this is life," Dexter had a way of playing an action or having a line which put us back where we started, making a movie. He had an incredible aptitude for that, which I have seen only with some great, great actors, like Philippe Noiret. We shot the scene when he wants to get paid, and then about two or three weeks after, we did the shot where he has been paid and he waves the wallet. And suddenly, I heard during the take, "I have been paid direct, like anybody." He has used the line which he has said [in the earlier scene] without telling me. That was a very good dramatic effect. I would have liked to have written that line, and so would David. That's very, very good thinking. He has an incredible memory: And he's a little bit like Robert Mitchum. He seems always a little bit away, dozing, his eyes closed, away from the scene in which he is, and then suddenly he will surprise you, because three months later he will tell you exactly what happened during the scene. And that's the way he survived, I think, the way he protected himself, because I talked to people who knew him and said he was exactly like that twenty years ago, exactly.

MD: None of the characters expresses any racism; they don't even seem to be thinking of it. Was this characteristic of French society in general or just this particular world?

BT: I think it's completely true. It was very true of what was around the jazz musicians at that time in France. James Baldwin even wrote that there is racism in France, but you don't have any racism on the Left Bank. If I had put the story in '49 or '50, I could have shown Lester or Don Byas arriving in France and being surprised (that was told to me by several witnesses) that they could go in by the main door. The problem was that in '59 [when the film is set] I could not make such a statement. The other thing is, I talked to a lot, *a lot*, of musicians about Lester, and they were never mentioning [racism], never. Sometimes Lester was talking about it, like I have in the film where Dale talks to the camera about the Army. But never with self-pity, with some humor in it. It was not part of their discussion. Maybe because they knew it too much and didn't have to talk about it. The only thing that Lester said was that he had done *D. B. Blues, Detention Barracks Blues*, and that was his revenge upon those racists. I used one or two lines which are typically Lester. At the beginning, when Dale says, "No cold eyes in Paris," that means no racists in Paris. But there was no more than that. In a way, for me, it's stronger. I had thought of putting in some lines. I even recorded Dexter speaking about his first tour in the South in the forties, when he arrived in a city in the South for the first time, and the driver asked somebody where is the colored bar. He said it was a shock for him, because he was from Los Angeles and his father was a doctor. When I tried to get that in the film, that looked like, "OK, I forgot to speak about it. I'm bringing in a few lines about it." I hate to have scenes where a character is explaining to another character something that the other character should know. Like, "You can come now through the main door." They know it. I'm sure that Dale Turner has come several times to Paris. He knows it. In '59, everybody knew it. In a lot of films, you have explanations which are designed for the audience but not for the character. We tried to avoid that. And again—this is something, important—I think the same way that in the jazz the notes that the people don't play are as important as the notes that they play, the lines which are not there are as important as the lines which are there.

MD: I want to bring up a possible relationship between Dale Turner and the painter in *A Sunday in the Country* [*Un Dimanche à la campagne*]. It's the only film I've seen about an artist who may be a failure and seems to consider himself one, partly because his work has gone out of fashion, but also because he feels that he has become a perfectly competent sort of painter but not one of the great people who blaze new frontiers. This seems like another example of the link between pain and beauty.

BT: I think the two characters are very much related, although they are the opposites. One didn't dare enough, maybe, and the other went maybe too far. In fact, the emotions are exactly the same, the fears are the same. If you were not bold enough, or even if you were very brave or innovative, you always have the same fear, you always have the same obsession that maybe you didn't go far enough, maybe you could have done it better than you did only part of what you should have done. They are two films which are based on, I would say, a musical storyline. I asked Bruno de Keyzer to do a photography which would be closer to the film noir, closer to the work of people like John Allan. The color, the design, the mood is the opposite. [But] the way that the camera is trying to work in it, to move to build certain emotions, for me is exactly the same. Whether the camera is trying to move for me is always related with music and with the emotion of the character more than with the movement of the character.

MD: It seems as though, contrary to some other movies about jazz, you can't really make a jazz film and also have an elaborate plot. You must get rid of the plot so you can fill all that space up with details that are analogous to what the musicians create with the music.

BT: Exactly. And I think because the life and the emotion of the musicians are a challenge, in a sense, to plots. They have a life which is so based on emotion that any conventional storyline is reducing the emotion, is reducing the true spirit. You have to be completely free in terms of writing and directing, completely free. For instance, for me, a film like *Children of a Lesser God*, which everybody seems to admire very much, has a very conventional plot. Very, very old-fashioned. I mean, it's like an old-fashioned play of the thirties a little brought up to date. Well-acted, very well-acted.

MD: David Rayfiel did some work on *Out of Africa*, a $30 some-odd million big studio prestige Academy Award winner that does not have a plot.

BT: Yeah. It's true, but I mean, that's great. It's one of the qualities of David some-times. *Jeremiah Johnson*, which he wrote lots for, has the same quality. Very often, people I think are making a mistake between plot and story, between what should be synopses of the plot and what is really in the film. And that very strong belief in some American critics and even in part of the audience, in which they approach the screenplay as a stage play. And very often I've heard things like, "In this film you don't have the third act." Or "The first act is brilliant." In the films which I admire, from *The Grapes of Wrath* to *The Sun Shines Bright*, *My Darling Clementine*, *The Rules of the Game* [*La Règle du jeu*], *La Grande Illusion*, *Casque d'Or*, *The Life and Death of Colonel Blimp*—I can name a thousand films—I wonder, "Where are the acts?" I mean, if they were asking me, I would *never* know it. But even in the teaching in schools . . . I mean, I've been to Sundance, and I've heard a lot of writ-ers talking about that: "You don't have a first act." Where is the first act? I don't know. [But] it's not only now. I think it's a very old belief which is never true. I mean, you would never have Michael Powell, never have Jean Renoir, Jean Gremil-lon, Jean Vigo talking about acts. Or [Luigi] Comencini. Never. Never. They would talk in terms of fluidity. They would talk in terms of construction. And sometimes

I've seen certain critics, puzzled by films by [Maurice] Pialat, [Jacques] Doillon, or by *A Week's Vacation* because they don't see a construction, which means a real progression where people go from A to B to C to D. I still believe very much for me that film is very, very close to music, and it should have the same construction, with counterpoint, with a melody which has a counterpoint behind, or a variation. Like a fugue. The films which are done like a kind of chronicle, like a series of moments—like Dos Passos, let's say—with breakings, different stories, getting them together . . . a little less now, but they seem to puzzle a lot of people. They say, "There is not much of a plot." I know that on *A Week's Vacation* I worked very, very hard, and I think in its genre that screenplay and that film are completely, completely successful. And I think that a person who would talk about not finding a plot there, they do not see what the film is about. They do not understand that you can have things which are giving you the impression that you are seeing moments of the life of somebody or a series of emotions. I mean, a construction closer to impressionism, closer to music than to a stage play.

On the other hand, I have found always that a lot of plays admired in this country—let's say Arthur Miller—are deadly boring because they are so staged, so built, and so obsessed by construction that I see the mechanics but I don't see any inspiration, any language. I mean, Tennessee Willliams is much more interesting than Arthur Miller even if the plays sometimes are not so well built. They are built through poetry, through language, through lyricism, where Arthur Miller is like having two ideas which are repeated over and over, for five or six hours. In fact—it's true of France, too—you have a certain type of critic or audience who like the screenplay to give the impression that they are intelligent and that they have understood certain deep things about subjects which are important. And they feel, "My god, I'm quite bright." I mean, a lot of films have that kind of attitude. I like films that puzzle you a little bit. I like *Leo the Last* by [John] Boorman, where you don't know what to make out of it. I think it's a super masterpiece, it's a great, great film. I like *Badlands*, which I think is a very important film. At the same time, when I see a film like *The Color of Money*, I say, "My God, I would like one day to be able to do that kind of very, very beautiful demonstration of what direction is about." The good films at the same time they inspire you and they make you feel very, very modest. I know that certain directors say that it's depressing to see a film which is great because you feel that you will never do it. I don't feel at all like that. Yesterday, after seeing *The Color of Money*, I immediately wanted to start to work on a film set again and try to see if I could do as well in certain things.

John Ford and the Red-Skins: An Interview with Bertrand Tavernier

Eric Derobert and Michel Sineux / 1989

From *Positif,* no. 343 (September 1989). Reprinted by permission. Translated by
T. Jefferson Kline.

Derobert & Sineux: *La Passion Béatrice* [*Beatrice*] and *La Vie et rien d'autre* [*Life and Nothing But*] have in common a fairly erratic construction, as though we're feeling our way along multiple paths that keep converging.
Bertrand Tavernier: Well, this tendency has been there from my first films. In *Que la Fête commence* [*Let Joy Reign Supreme*], for example, the construction of the film reveals influences which I feel from jazz music and from certain novels (Dumas, Hugo, Balzac): a taste for parentheses, and circuitous paths. You can see [this] more systematically since *Une Semaine de vacances* [*A Week's Vacation*]. I wanted to struggle against the plot. In *La Mort en direct* [*Death Watch*] there were three or four points in the story that I didn't know how to deal with. So *Un Dimanche à la campagne* [*A Sunday in the Country*] was based on a single dramatic event: a young woman is going to leave a family reunion sooner than expected because she gets a phone call. In this film, there's a story but no plot. This is also a reaction against the screenplay as Americans envision it, which often unfolds in "acts," which I've never understood very well, even in their own films. But you don't see this in the great filmmakers like John Ford. In *Autour de Minuit* [*'Round Midnight*] I had the same desire to get rid of this. And that's what I immediately liked in *Beatrice*. The writing was very free, detached from any dramatic contingencies of plot.

In the opening scenes of almost all my films you have to feel your way along uncertainly. I'm a great believer in this because it's a reaction to films where, within five minutes, you can guess the outcome and there are no more surprises, where all you see is the filmmaker's technique. What I'm looking for is the kind of surprise you find in Renoir's films: in *La Règle du jeu* [*Rules of the Game*] for example where critics of the time complained that it took you forty minutes to figure out what the film was about. That's amazing—as long as the film is interesting! With Colo Tavernier it was easy, since she has a very free style of writing and my role is to add "road signs" to the plot. It's a very poetic kind of writing, structured like a dream with a series of images rather than something very organized. With Jean Cosmos, who's a playwright, and who wrote a lot for TV, but had never written for the cinema, it was different. He's made numerous adaptations of plays, from Shakespeare to Brecht, and including *A Thousand Clowns*, *The Life and Death of King John*, and *Saint Joan of the Stockyards*, all of which I adored. With Cosmos I had to undo the plot that was often too tightly constructed. What he wrote was too elaborated, too precise: the relationship between the two women, the discovery of the proof . . . So my work was to make the obvious more mysterious, so that the turns in the plot wouldn't be treated in a theatrical manner. In one of the last versions, Irene finds the ring. So I told him: "We won't see this happen, it'll just be mentioned in the dialogue." I just want to focus on the emotions and not be caught up in the folds of a calculated narrative, which worked at a time when films were constructed along codified genres. But when you break free of genres, then very calculated plots become too heavy. I preferred a structure that was more evasive, based more on counterpoint. My editor was always laughing when he saw me trying to create flash-forwards to break up the narrative, since very often it didn't work at all. I would shoot them, try to edit them in and then discard them. I think it's in *A Sunday in the Country* that I succeeded in this for the first time: you go from past to present without seeming to notice.

D&S: In *Life and Nothing But*, I had the impression there was no contradiction between the fact that we were seeing a genre film and the film's freedom of structure. In the romantic register where it's situated, there's a point of departure—the meeting of the two characters—there will also be a point of arrival. The freedom would then be in the twists and turns that will link this point of departure to the point of arrival.

BT: For me, romantic is not a genre. Moreover, when you take account of the very small number of films that have been made about this period and this particular theme, I don't know if we can even speak of a genre. That said, we knew that the minute we made these two characters meet, we were creating a relationship that could have existed in American comedy, but were turned upside down by the awful background against which they evolved. At the outset, we said, "They could be Katharine Hepburn and Cary Grant . . ." As for the twists and turns you mentioned, they weren't planned, they just evolved organically. In the first version, written by Jean Cosmos, we wanted so much to get away from this predictable ending that they ended up separating after a complete breakdown of the relationship. And then, we started over, following a habit I'd learned from Aurenche, which was to work without a scenario, or even a synopsis. At a certain point in the rewriting we said to ourselves: "But why should they split up?" It just evolved as if it had been dictated by the characters. We just felt that it had to happen—the spark between these two characters—but that at the same time, it couldn't happen right away. That's how I got the idea of the letter. It's something I like a lot, to extend a subject into the future by a few years, when some time has passed. That's Balzac, the ending of Une Affaire ténébreuse [A Shady Affair], which marked me for life. The novel is over, but you learn two or three years later how the things turned out in the end. There was also the fact that I identified very strongly with the character in Life and Nothing But; I felt that he was really not ready to make a declaration of love, and so he retreated from it. Marcel Ophuls, to whom I showed my first edit, and who agreed that the character resembled me a lot, told me that he didn't understand why things would end in a separation. From his point of view, the character should have "jumped" her in the car. And he suggested I show some shots where you'd see the car shaking. For him, Noiret was the most perfect personification of virility since Gabin.

D&S: What was the inspiration for the scenario?

BT: It was the number of soldiers who'd disappeared in the First World War, a statistic that astonished me: 350,000 people is enormous! And then, what does it mean to have disappeared? Let's imagine the story of a woman who's looking for her lost husband, who goes to a hospice at the battlefield. Something like Gogol's Dead Souls, but involving an unknown soldier. Jean Cosmos began research on this, and the first thing that struck us was the very short time that elapsed in the search for the unknown soldier. It had been discussed from 1916 to 1920, but between the decision and the execution there only a few days and our story was supposed to unfold during these three or four days. In the material that Jean Cosmos brought me, in the results of his research, there was an officer who was in charge of a bureau charged with the discovery and counting of the cadavers. So I knew immediately that he would be my main character. I also wanted to come back to Noiret, with whom I hadn't worked since Coup de torchon [Clean Slate]. I wanted to give him the role of an officer, while giving play to all that is free and anarchic in his personality. I also thought that talk of war and violence would have much greater force when spoken by someone who'd experienced it. And Noiret was personally involved, since he had memories of his father who'd fought at Verdun. In the film he used props that belonged to him: the cane, which had belonged to a solider from Grenoble, and the medals he wore, that his father had earned.

D&S: How many versions of the script were there?

BT: A lot. Jean Cosmos is a very rare person, who really knows popular trades. He's an extremely hard worker. He wrote everything by hand in magnificent calligraphy, and he'd use an eraser. He's very organized. If I wasn't satisfied with a scene, he'd correct it in three minutes. And we did this throughout the writing, right through the shooting, when we were adding stories of the people we recruited from the area. For example, the photos we pinned up in the Café de Valentine belonged to the Mayor of Verdun, who told us that in his mother's café, people came in for twelve years following the war to give her photos. I worked almost by osmosis with Cosmos, who, when he's sure of himself, works a little like Prévert does. He creates characters and goes as far as suggesting who should play them. He knows the world of actors very well, as I do.

D&S: If you were to sum up the film in two lines, what would you say? Is it a "war film"?

BT: It's a "peace film," I think. It took a long time to get this film going because people were afraid of the subject. I encountered this problem a lot. We really didn't know how to sum up in a few words *A Sunday in the Country*, or *'Round Midnight* for *Pariscope*! For me, this is a love story: two women are looking for their husband and fiancé respectively while, in a parallel story, the government is trying to identify "the unknown soldier." Most of the TV channels refused to participate in the film, believing it would be too morbid. For me, it was supposed to be a film about hope, reconstruction, the living-dead who relearn how to live. Alain Corneau saw it as a bunch of somnambulists trying to relearn how to live and how to feel. The idea was certainly to speak of war by making a film about peace, of taking up a series of oppositions. I felt that the lyricism of the film would save it from despair, something like a mix of *Clean Slate* and *A Sunday in the Country*.

I was coming from a very dark film [*Beatrice*] whose failure had profoundly wounded me, especially since I feel it's the best thing I've done. What really bothered me was that the critics refused to consider the gambles and risks of such a film. They knew what risks I'd taken by accepting to forego any attempt at the pleasure that might have derived from such a story in which the characters are childlike, naïve, primitive, and incapable of any understanding of themselves, unable to get any distance on their feelings and who are risking their lives at every second like wild animals set free. Each of the characters is created as if s/he were a part of some global idea of the unconscious. On the other hand, this uncivilized side of the characters, the way they lived out their feelings at that time, impressed the historians. Jacques Le Goff wrote to me to tell me that I'd captured the spirit of the period. Some psychiatrists noted that the moments of violence were not perceived by the audience as moments of liberation, but rather as moments that were more oppressive than the rest. But that was just what troubled me during the shooting of the film: to avoid making it lyrical or like a Western. I also believe, deeply, that when we talk about the Middle Ages, people lose interest. Unless we present the period as a crime drama, as in *The Name of the Rose* which allows us to appreciate the context of the period.

D&S: Of all your films, [*Béatrice* is] the one where connections with our contemporary world are the least evident.

BT: Except the portrayal of religious feelings, and also all the fears we have now. In the US the film was perceived as very contemporary, tackling issues that are very thorny: the fear of God, sects, different beliefs, this sort of feeling about the end of the world and the emergence of a new moralism. Three or four American film critics discussed this aspect of the film. There's also the feeling the characters have about war, which feels very modern. Take for example a guy who's in Viet Nam feeling that he's defending a powerful cause. He's taken prisoner and comes back four years later to a small town in the Midwest or in the South of the US. In the state of violence he's stuck in, he's going to come back in total conflict with the values in America and rape his daughter. It's this same subject in *The Passion of Beatrice*, but given the weight of the decors and costumes, the audience is probably not going to see the connections with today. In films about other centuries, they're accustomed to looking for them. For the eighteenth century, for example, our scholarly education teaches us to see the period as a modern one, where everything was invented or anticipated. Every line in *Let Joy Reign Supreme* is immediately interpreted. It's true, however, that we slipped a bunch of contemporary phrases into Philippe d'Orléans's lines, quotes from De Gaulle, and things added by Aurenche or by me.

D&S: The Regency—that was Giscard d'Estaing.

BT: Yes, everybody was saying so! There was even a doctor Chirac that I didn't invent. But in *Beatrice*, the connections with the present weren't of a social nature but rather a metaphysical one. That said, the mayor of Puyvert—an amazing eighty-two-year-old living in the village where we shot the film—told us that we'd perfectly captured the mentality of people from there!

D&S: In *Beatrice*, a beautiful but wholly inhospitable nature must have repulsed the viewer: we really don't like time travel that leads to a place like this! In *Life and Nothing But*, we're in a kind of no man's land, but it's also a very inhospitable décor. Tell us about your work with Guy-Claude François, the production designer in these two films.

BT: Guy-Claude François originally designed the scenery for the *Théâtre du Soleil* and was recommended by the production director of *'Round Midnight* and *Beatrice*. In the theater he'd collaborated with Roger Coggio on Molière's *Les Fourberies de*

Scapin [*Scapin's Deceits*]. I immediately realized how sensitive and capable he was. On *Beatrice*, he began by talking to me about wood and the importance of wood, which was always what you saw first in the early castles. I was a bit haunted by the idea of the opening shots of the chateau, as you're arriving and I didn't want it to look like something made for TV, or provoke the feeling I had every time I watched films about history. He shared my ambitions, and I explained that the truth of the décor should not be naturalist, in the style of "folk arts," but that it must instead be linked to the feelings of the characters and that the characters should belong to their surroundings and be, as it were, "welded to the décor."

D&S: That they shouldn't be tenants . . .

BT: Yes, they shouldn't be tourists. And as soon as Guy-Claude talked to me about the idea of a tunnel as our entryway into the chateau, I knew he wasn't just a set designer but someone like Trauner, who understands the dramaturgy of the film and provides the means to express it. For *Beatrice* he created very precise structures with very short sight lines and rigorously kept to this same geometric figure throughout the film. As for the natural settings, he figured out how to adapt them to his other choices. It's he who built the magic tree that we planted, using dynamite, in a rock. When we'd finished the film, he sent me a letter to tell me that Bernard-Pierre Donnadieu gave the impression of being a part of this nature and that Julie Delpy began to see her skin taking on the grey color of the stones. His work was really unbelievable, and it's tragic that he didn't win a César award for production design when you see the inventiveness of his work. What's more, the people who visited the set didn't recognize any of it: it's because half to three-quarters of the décor was constructed, and I defy anyone who's watching the film to distinguish the natural from the artificial settings.

D&S: What about for *Life and Nothing But?*

BT: In that film the problems ended up being somewhat similar to those in *Beatrice*—problems of connecting the characters to the scenery, which was meant to imitate Losey's way of using scenery to extend the characters' feelings. We had to find a single idea that would succeed in translating the visuals of the period without it being uniquely realist or naturalist. So Jean Cosmos and I suggested to Guy-Claude that every scene should take place in spaces that had been originally designed for some entirely different purpose: In this ravaged country that had been turned upside down, the offices were in a theater; the hotel was in a factory; the church serves as a nightclub, and there are picnics on the battlefields. In this way we were able to express a lot of feelings and bring out an absurd, but sometimes comic side of things.

D&S: So this is an idea you gave to the production designer. It wasn't his . . .

BT: No, but he liked it immediately. In searching for our locations, he made some sketches that were so amazing that we ended up writing the scenes as a function of his drawings. His originality lay in his ability to reuse the same materials. Most of the time, that was, in fact, what the army had to do as they reconstructed barracks everywhere. So he used the same wooden structures in different places as if everything was a product of the corps of engineers. When you go from the theater to the factory, the decors are completely different, and yet they resemble each other because of the geometric spaces he created, as if they'd been built by the same people; in this case, a bunch of soldiers.

D&S: Which the mise en scène brings out by the use of a series of high-angle shots which emphasize the same geometric structures in each different set.

BT: Yes. It is, by the way, one of the films in which I used the most high-angle shots, because the sets in these hastily constructed buildings were involuntarily composed according to the same model, and seemed to require such visual figures.

D&S: If one did not know the entire story here, one's first reactions, knowing Guy-Claude François's origins as a set designer for the theater, would be to say that his designs are inspired by the idea of Wotan and Siegfried strolling through a twentieth-century factory.

BT: Yes, this factory, or rather these factories must have amused him, for we shot in four or five different ones, all of which were headed for demolition. It is, moreover, a monstrous idea to eradicate these masterpieces of industrial architecture. To shoot in places where the past isn't felt as the past contributed enormously to the spirit of the film. For the people who lived there, the history of these buildings was part of their daily life—they weren't museum pieces—and that helped our actors a lot. To come back to Guy-Claude, these settings permitted him to express the absurdity, the strangeness, and the disjointedness of the entire film. It was the same for the laundry room where we put the sheets; it was the only place where we could hang sheets in the entire factory, so we had the impression of imitating Planchon, giving a wink to his sets for *Tartuffe* or for *L'Avare* [*The Miser*]. And while I'm on the subject, I think we have a lot to learn in film from the use of lighting and set design in the theater. Twenty or twenty-five years ago, the influences worked in the opposite direction: theater sets were greatly influenced by film.

D&S: You've talked with us about Noiret, but you surely have plans to work with Sabine Azéma again?

BT: I'd love to, yes. When we started, she wasn't our choice, and then suddenly choosing her became top priority. What interested me was giving her another

image, of having her mature, of going beyond her girlish side, and making her
more of a woman as if she bloomed during the few days that the narration cov-
ers. In the scene of the laundry room, she is sublimely beautiful and mysterious,
reaching a register she'd never achieved before, of a woman discovering passion.
I knew I could rely on her for all the comic scenes, to which she brought her sense
of timing and an extraordinary vivacity. Noiret was completely won over. There
was a lot of electricity between them, like with Galabru and Noiret in *Le Juge et
l'assassin* [*The Judge and the Assassin*]. The theater scene, that we'd hoped to shoot
in two and half days was done in a single day. Everything was so evident and took
shape with unbelievable speed and force.

D&S: Noiret is always good. Sometimes he's exceptional as he was in this case. As
for Sabine Azéma, she sometimes plays at the limit of mannerism. You must have
directed her differently in *Life and Nothing But*, because she acts differently, with
extraordinary humor, yet, when she has to, with reserve.

BT: Well I upset her a little in the beginning. When she got to the set, she was
thrown into a milieu composed entirely of men—just as her character was—with
hundreds of supernumeraries and actors and I tried at first to stay out of her way.
But she's someone who really needs contacts and I could tell she was upset. That
was hard for me, but at the same time, I saw her losing herself, getting used to
her costume and her character. After that, as we gradually got into more involved
scenes, I got closer to her, a bit like the mise en scène of the film.

D&S: And by that you mean?

BT: I like to establish rules for myself right at the outset, rules not only for myself,
but applicable to the cameramen, the actors, and everyone else. On this film, the
guiding principle was John Ford. In the same way that the narrative was a reaction
to Hollywood films in which the theme is exposed in the first five minutes, the way
of framing was opposed to the gangrene of TV framing which are either ignored,
absent, monotonous, purely functional, and with no regard for the scenery, atmosphere, or wind. With my cinematographer, we watched *Stagecoach* which made
me want to work with a wide frame and a minimum of close-ups. And in the same
way that I took time to get close to Azéma, the camera took time to get close to
the actors. The first close-ups of Noiret didn't happen until the factory, when they
were eating dinner; before that, he's always filmed with other actors. On the other
hand, there are a great number of wide-angle shots that often last quite a long
time. The actors loved this, since it gave them the freedom to play expansively.
Noiret told me that it had been a very long time since he'd had this impression
of being able to move, to cross an entire set and talk to someone who was thirty
yards away. There's actually a great reluctance to do this: filmmakers tend to take

refuge in close-ups right away in a film. By contrast, Ford, working with a super-star like John Wayne didn't give us a close-up of him until the eightieth minute of *Stagecoach*; before that, Wayne never filmed closer up than in a medium long shot. This way of shooting was very helpful to the actors and gave them enough space to really act in; it also contributed to the "choral" structure of the film, mixing bunches of actors together, with dialogues in which people interrupt each other and/or speak at the same time.

D&S: All these wide-angle shots and high angle shots that you made in the factory contribute to a sense that these people are being crushed by industrialized society. Noiret's final retreat, trading his light blue military uniform for a green and brown costume that merges with the greenery around him, is also a retreat from history, which is a novelty in your films.

BT: There are a lot of new things in this film. It's the first film I've done in which someone says, "I love you." I'd never treated a love story so directly. Before, things were done more obliquely. But here I forced myself to do it. Some barriers must have fallen. Since nothing happens by chance, it's life and our experience that tell us we can attempt certain things. Never having done a film on a couple (for if the question of the couple arose, it was always broken), I felt that this was completely new in my filmmaking, and that this time the film was tending toward this type of story.

D&S: At first this couple is surprising, not to say improbable . . .

BT: I like improbable couples, oppositions. I've filmed a lot of them, moreover: Noiret–Galabru in *The Judge and the Assassin*, Dexter–Cluzet in *'Round Midnight*, and including Nathalie Baye–Gérard Lanvin in *A Week's Vacation*. At a given mo-ment, in *Life and Nothing But* someone suggested Deneuve. I have the impression she's one of those "Scenaristic" actresses whose destiny is in part inscribed in their own appearance in the film. If it had been Deneuve, the film would necessarily have finished in a break-up. There's also a sort of film director's ego at play, which consists in wanting at all costs to create new relationships between the actors. Noiret had already told me several times that he adored acting with Deneuve, who's an incredible actress and gives a lot of herself—a bit like Mitchum saying that he was never better than when he acted with Deborah Kerr. But I wanted, even if there were points of departure and of arrival that you could guess, to shuf-fle the cards and let Azéma shuffle the cards. And she did so with a high degree of honesty, in the sense that she never tried to improve, or make the image of her character more sympathetic or touching at the beginning of the film. She really played the game, able at times to seem very dry and hard, without any attempt at protecting her image as an actress, the same way Julie Delpy does in *Beatrice*, who never tried to seduce her audience, which is extremely rare for a young actress. But Noiret doesn't make any attempt to charm his audience either: you can shoot him from behind. It's what I asked of him in the scene where he's talking to Alice (Pascale Vignai), and he told me he was completely fine with it.

D&S: From behind he's almost as powerful as Brando.

BT: It was Gabin who said you should always use your mug sparingly. There are two sorts of actors, he explained, the prolos and the Red-Skins: Always be a Red-Skin!

Journey into Light

Patrick McGilligan / 1992

From *Film Comment* 28, no. 2 (March–April 1992). Copyright © 1992 by Patrick McGilligan. Used by permission of the Film Society of Lincoln Center/Film Comment Magazine & Patrick McGilligan.

Patrick McGilligan: What led you to undertake such a massive revision of the '69 edition of your book [*50 Ans de Cinéma Americain/50 Years of American Cinema*]?
Bertrand Tavernier: For a long time, now and then, we were approached to do another edition, adding just a few pages more. One day the proposition looked serious and we started thinking about doing a slightly bigger book—but not much bigger. If we had known that it would become that book, we never would have agreed to do another edition.

PM: How long did the work take you?
BT: Three years. We decided there were three ways to proceed: Either we were going to keep the original text, in some cases, providing we saw nothing to change. Or we were going to keep the text of the '69 edition and comment on it—saying we had been right or wrong [in our initial critiques]. Or we were going to start from scratch in some cases, especially about many directors whom, in 1969, we knew very little—Borzage, Leisen, Curtiz, etc. Plus, we decided that directors like Lang, Hawks, Hitchcock, or Chaplin—who are much covered elsewhere—did not need overly long essays; it was sometimes easier to condense what we were thinking about them, than in the case of some directors where you have to study less the ensemble of work than a series of films that are all different. Let's say, for instance, Sidney Lumet—he practically needs to be discussed film by film; whereas with Fritz Lang or Chaplin, it's possible to see their work thematically. We decided— and it was a fatal decision in terms of the amount of work—to see all the important films again, and all the films recently rediscovered: for example, in Chaplin's case, the films unearthed by Kevin Brownlow in *The Unknown Chaplin*. The first option, in the end, we nearly always rejected—because we always found new things

to write about. Sometimes our original perspective had been right, but even so, the essays, which were very short in the first edition—one or two pages—grew to twenty, thirty, forty pages. Slowly we got carried away by ourselves. We wrote it in the same way as we did the first one; Jean-Pierre was in New York and I was in Paris. That meant several hundred letters, practically a long phone call every night. It was a labor of love. I didn't take any money to write it, and I left the advance from the publisher to Jean-Pierre, who needed it more.

PM: This summer ['91] in Paris we talked about certain directors who had risen in your estimation, in the intervening years since the '69 edition, while others had fallen or been diminished. Who is the American director who perhaps rose highest in your pantheon?

BT: First, I must say it feels strange to comment on a book of opinions and essays. It is like commenting on one's own commentary. But there are certain people whom we more or less condemned, too quickly or wrongly. Like Robert Aldrich. We said that his career was coming to a dead end, and I think that was a mistake. We were not the only ones; everybody in the world was writing that. Aldrich always had that certain moment where people thought he had lost everything, and he was always rising again like a phoenix. Just after we finished the '69 edition Aldrich did some of his best work—at least one of his best films, which is *Ulzana's Raid* ('72), a stunning Western. And I think we were wrong in saying *The Dirty Dozen* ('67) was the antithesis of, let's say, *Attack!* ('56). In reappraising him, I think Aldrich never betrayed his political ideas and positions. Sometimes his direction weakens the original ambition, makes the films look ambiguous; but on the whole he is one of the few directors who never changed politically. Just look at the complete version of *Twilight's Last Gleaming* ('77)! I myself wrote most of the text about Aldrich—and the words that came to mind when I was writing about him were "forcefulness" and "consistency." That was one case. I cannot say which man climbed the highest. One would be Jacques Tourneur. . . .

PM: Why?

BT: His direction, his style, consists of a very mysterious mixing between a very elaborate lighting and a soundtrack very different from the average American film. Tourneur was always making the actors speak very low, in a subdued way, which you can only appreciate in good prints and not in a dubbed version. Some of the films we wrote about in the '69 edition we saw in bad prints, sometimes dubbed, which always hurt the films; and in the case of directors like Tourneur, really destroyed the films. You need to see Tourneur's work, especially, in good prints. Then you have the case of someone like Gregory La Cava. Some of his films were real discoveries . . . especially in the thirties. The same with Michael Curtiz. And

William Wellman: *Heroes for Sale* ('33), *Wild Boys of the Road* ('33), *Other Men's Women* ('31) . . . real discoveries. When we wrote about Wellman the first time, we were primarily looking at his films of the forties. On the other hand, there were films we had praised too much, like *The Adventures of Hajji Baba* (Don Weis, '54), which was a cult film in France. We became a little more dubious about it. Or there were directors we praised a lot, like Tay Garnett. Later on, we saw most of his films—some are good—but when we had seen only a few of them, the totality of the work seemed [as if it must be] more interesting than it is; judging by *Her Man* ('30) or *One Way Passage* ('32), you might think you would find the same values in thirty or forty other Tay Garnett films, but that's not the case. The same could be said of [Frank] Tashlin, George Sidney, or the last films directed by Jerry Lewis or Hitchcock, which were overrated in France. Sometimes we overrated part of the work of a director because we did not know the other part. When we wrote that the best work of Allan Dwan were those films he made with producer Benedict Bogeaus, his last films, it was not true. Some are quite remarkable, and I still like them very much—*Silver Lode* ('54) and *Tennessee's Partner* ('55). But when you see some of the films Dwan did in the silent days, with Gloria Swanson, they are even more interesting. I could name a lot of directors like that . . . whose best period was sometimes unknown, even to us.

Take Douglas Sirk: This time around we had more reservations about some of his melodramas that people love now—*Written on the Wind* ('56), *Imitation of Life* ('59). Especially as compared to certain films of John Stahl. In the new book, now that Sirk is a director very much admired by everybody, we expressed reservations about, for instance, the treatment of the black characters in *Imitation of Life*—especially as compared to Stahl's version ('34). Stahl was better. Stahl was, in a way, more modern and less paternalistic. (Jean-Pierre wrote most of that essay.) And we had fresh reservations about Dorothy Malone [in *Written on the Wind*] . . . she's not very good . . . you cannot call that acting. At the same time, we were laudatory about a film of Sirk's like *A Scandal in Paris* ('46), which is completely unknown and is a small masterpiece. The direction is as brilliant; but for one thing, the screenplay, by Ellis St. Joseph, is better; the dialogue is terrific; the black-and-white photography is by [Eugen] Schfftan; the acting—George Sanders in particular—is better; and the cynical aspect of the film makes it something more original. Some of those melodramas of Sirk's are not only very well made but very personal. Yet when you see the work he did with students in Germany [in the seventies], three little films—Fassbinder acts in one of them—based on material by Schnitzler and Tennessee Williams . . . these films are absolutely wonderful. And you wonder if Sirk had been given better material than Fannie Hurst or a better actor than Rock Hudson, maybe he would have done better films. There are certain films that are good in spite of the material, the actors, the kind of film it is, the studio. . . . Then you have certain other films, like *A Scandal in Paris* or *There's Always Tomorrow* ('56), that are simply good.

PM: Were there other people like Robert Aldrich whom you were unfair to, in the first edition?

BT: We were very unfair to the directors who had been the target of the French critics of the fifties, [critics] who, in order to promote Hawks, Hitchcock, Fuller, and Anthony Mann, violently attacked some directors respected by the Hollywood establishment and the American critics. Already in the '69 edition we were more open-minded, but still very unfair to somebody like Fred Zinnemann. It took us a while to discover a film like *Act of Violence* ('49) . . . and *The Men* ('50) is quite an interesting film. Making some of the films Zinnemann made at a certain time was very, very brave. Becoming a director myself, I began to appreciate more the difficulty of some films. Even if the result is imperfect, the fact that certain films are made implies such energy and real courage. About Mitchell Leisen we were too severe. I remember the [Leisen] essay in the '69 edition was not too long, because we had only seen three or four of his films. Jean-Pierre, in the intervening twenty years, has seen practically all of his films. So his essay on Mitchell Leisen turned out to be very long. The same for Frank Borzage, Curtiz, Wellman, and others. [Still,] we did not change our minds on a lot of directors. On the contrary, we reaffirmed our views on people like Anthony Mann, Delmer Daves, Billy Wilder. . . .

PM: Did meeting the filmmakers, interviewing them, sometimes help you in revising your opinions of their work?

BT: Yes. And not only meeting the people, but reading things too. In America, certainly, a lot of books exist now that did not exist in the sixties. Suddenly we had a lot of new information—people talking about unknown films and filmmakers. It's true, meeting different directors and screenwriters helped change our minds—but we tried not to, just because we liked somebody personally, always to find their films interesting.

PM: Sometimes you couldn't help it?

BT: Yes. [Laughs.]

PM: You told me that sometimes you did not like the people, either, and that that reinforced a negative view. My impression is that you detested Howard Hawks. . . .

BT: No, no, I liked him. You felt that he was forceful, a real auteur, someone who controlled all of his films. What I did not like was his politics. By meeting and talking with Hawks, I understood why I liked some of his comedies so much, and other films like *To Have and Have Not* ('44) and *The Big Sleep* ('46); but could also see very well why certain ideological things in his films did not please me. Because Hawks was very conservative, very right-wing. He wanted to make a film about Vietnam, and he told us he wanted to take some of the scenes deleted from *Sergeant York* ('41) and put them into his Vietnam film. That was frightening. It's good for him that he never made that film.

PM: Do your political preferences lead you overboard in certain directions—in terms of praise, or condemnation?

BT: We try very much not to be led by our politics. Someone very right-wing can make a wonderful film. But, for instance, in *Rio Bravo* ('59), I can't help feeling the Mexicans are caricatured and treated in a way I don't like. Someone who was not a left-wing director—Henry Hathaway—treated them better in *Garden of Evil* ('54), more respectfully. Not to mention a beautiful Western like *The Wonderful Country* ('54) by Robert Parrish. We try to study films in terms of content, so we have to deal with politics; but we try not to repeat the mistakes of certain French critics who condemned certain films just for political reasons.

PM: At the beginning of your career as a film critic, you were perhaps less considerate. . . .

BT: Yes, but I was always fighting with *Positif*, which condemned Fuller. They were calling his films fascist, which they were not. I saw that as completely mad. I think a lot of political labels put on some directors were very European, and had nothing to do with the real content of the movies. In France a lot of films were labeled progressive just because they were pro-Indian. John Wayne became pro-Indian, suddenly, in *Hondo* (John Farrow, '53). . . . The politics of the American cinema is not just a matter of left and right as defined by a European point of view. What we say in the book is that you can distinguish a liberal director (or writer) by his attitude towards certain notions, certain myths, which are very important to Hollywood films: Nature, Individualism, the Group, Civilization. . . . In the basic American ideology, the first two are usually very positive and redeeming, with Biblical implications of a Lost Paradise. On the other hand, the Group and Civilization contain elements of threat, danger, and corruption—of mobs, lynching posses, urban decay, the mad scientist, corrupt newspapermen. You can even link Nature and Individualism with the West, the other two with the East, and come up with an interesting ideological map of the American cinema. You would discover that *Taxi Driver* (Scorsese, '76) and Murnau's *Sunrise* ('27) have much the same content, as do *Apocalypse Now* (Coppola, '79) and much of Griffith. Add to that the American attitude towards the intellectual ([intellectuals] are, most of the time, a real threat) and The Other (another race, another country). . . .

In a film like *The Purple Plain* ('54) by Robert Parrish—which I saw again a few days ago—the attitude toward the Burmese culture is so respectful; the people are dealt with such respect, not only not making fun, but never patronizing. Politics is not only whether a film is pro-war or anti-war, but something that is more deeply felt. If you draw the lines this way, you can see that [John] Ford is not a reactionary director, as Georges Sadoul, a French Communist historian, said so often. For Ford is a director obsessed by collectivity and by group, and not by the hero, the individual, against the rest of the world.

PM: I remember that this summer you compared meeting Hawks to Raoul Walsh, and that you also compared Hawks's films to Walsh's, saying that in your view Walsh had risen in stature, and that there was much yet to be discovered in the body of his work. You surprised me by saying that Walsh may be the superior director.

BT: I don't like to state that. Jean-Pierre and I tried not to construct a hierarchy. I can say Walsh is a wider director; his interests were wide, and he had moments when he could do a nearly metaphysical Western like *Pursued* ('47) that Hawks would never have dared to deal with. On the other hand, Walsh was never able to do anything as controlled as *To Have and Have Not* and some of Hawks's comedies. Hawks is a great director, but narrow; he always did the same three or four films. There are people who have a narrow vision of the world, and Hawks is one. You don't feel the world in a Hawks film. You don't feel the world as you do in a Walsh film. Hawks was limited. He understood a certain type of person, a type of hero, a type of action—not job, action. From that range, he made masterpieces. Sometimes he was a genius. But Walsh did some daring things—very, very early. Walsh is handicapped by his legend. When I met him I discovered he was much more literate than people think he was. People put him down as a very good action and man's director. It's much more than that. Walsh was sometimes able to experiment. Certain films of his, like *The Regeneration* from 1915, are stunning. It's a film ten, fifteen years ahead of its time. It anticipates Stroheim. Martin Scorsese told me when he saw it that if he was shooting in the Bowery he would not change one shot of that film.

When they would give Walsh something to experiment with, he was immediately ready. Walsh was at ease with the sets, which were very avant-garde, of William Cameron Menzies in *The Thief of Baghdad* ('24). He could do *The Big Trail* ('30) in 70mm. He made an interesting habit of the diagonal—a geometric figure he used a lot—in the framing, in the camera movement, in the way people moved through the space. We wrote a great deal in the book about that, his filmic texture and pacing, which we compare to Count Basie or Max Roach.

I also insist that Walsh is a woman's director. Most of the time the actresses are terrific in his films; even the intermediate actresses, like Virginia Mayo, who is absolutely stunning in *White Heat* ('49); and when he was working with Ida Lupino, Olivia de Havilland, or Anna Nilsson, the results were flamboyant and expressed a vision that was truly romantic.

PM: Becoming a director, you mentioned, has somewhat altered your perspective as a critic. Do you find that, in the elapsed time since the '69 edition, you have become more or less tolerant as a critic?

BT: More tolerant for certain things—like real ambition and the difficulty of setting up certain kinds of productions. You suddenly appreciate the struggle it must have been for certain directors to keep their integrity, sometimes. To protect their work.

And less tolerant of certain things. For instance, as young film buffs we were very enamored of people like Dorothy Malone or Rhonda Fleming, that kind of actress. The bad acting of certain films I became less tolerant of. I became less tolerant of the portrayal of minorities [in many films]. In a way it's a function of growing older as well as becoming a film director—I became more irritated at the way [other] races were portrayed. Really angry sometimes.

As a director, I grew to admire someone like [John] Huston very much, especially during the last part of his career. At a moment when practically every director past a certain age was repeating himself, doing exactly what they had been doing—sometimes better, most of the time worse. . . . I mean Hawks with *El Dorado* ('67) and *Rio Lobo* ('70), even Hitchcock—in Huston's case you have somebody whose last fifteen years included some of his best films, maybe. At least his most intellectually audacious projects: *Wise Blood* ('79), *Fat City* ('72), *The Man Who Would Be King* ('75), *The Dead* ('87), even *Under the Volcano* ('84). It's an incredible body of work. Huston's a unique case in the history of the cinema. To end up your career with *The Dead*! Huston was more daring at the end of his life than when he was starting.

When it came to certain directors I was, for some time, too much under the influence of people like Truffaut. The worst thing for a critic is a lack of a real curiosity, and following the general fashion. We did not investigate enough, ten, twenty years ago, about some directors. For instance, we let somebody like Anatole Litvak die without ever meeting him—and he lived in Paris! Litvak is somebody whose films I've since discovered from the thirties and forties, as well as his documentaries for Capra: Litvak made the best of the "Why We Fight" series. But in the sixties, Truffaut, in order to boost *Bonjour Tristesse* (Otto Preminger, '58), which he loved, knocked other directors who had adapted Francoise Sagan. One of them was Litvak [*Goodbye Again* ('61)]. And stupidly, we followed Truffaut. Because Litvak's last films were bad, we refused to investigate his career. And his career had started in Russia; then he went to Germany and France, where he made masterpieces in the thirties like *Coeur de Lilas* ('32) [*Lilac*]—which contains scenes and a use of sound as imaginative as Renoir—as well as interesting films like *L'Equipage* ('35) [*Flight into Darkness*], which seems to me less dated than *The Dawn Patrol* (Hawks, '30). So the lack of not being open, being prejudiced, is the worst thing. Film history has suffered a lot from that. In Huston's case, it's true, I was a little like Truffaut—aloof about Huston. I admired some of his films, but I remember being aloof about *Red Badge of Courage* ('51) and some others. When I see *Red Badge of Courage* today, I realize it was not an easy film to do. There are shots in it that now, I say to myself, "My God, I wish I could do that!"

PM: Is there an irreconcilable gap between a film critic like you and one who has never been a filmmaker?

BT: Sometimes the critics are a little bluffed by superficial things, which they think are difficult, and they don't see the really difficult things, which are sometimes the most obvious. There is not a gap, but maybe I wouldn't make the mistake, like some critics who, when speaking of the style of Bresson, say he never moved the camera. It makes me laugh. Bresson moves the camera all the time—you just don't notice it, because he moves with the characters; you have at least thirty or forty tracking shots in a Bresson film, which is a lot for someone whom a lot of critics describe as a kind of French Ozu. You see a lot of technical mistakes like that from critics, technical mistakes that are also mistakes of reading the films.

Even as a film buff, I hated clans—chapelle—a group of critics thinking all the same. Neither Jean-Pierre nor I belonged to any group. And now it is even more infuriating to see young French critics repeat the opinions of Truffaut, Rivette, and Godard, without taking into consideration the discoveries made since that time—the books, the essays, published in America, England, Italy. Since I became a director I have become even less tolerant of that way of thinking.

Very few directors have made the transition from being a film critic. Truffaut did, and he became more tolerant. You can see it clearly in his book about Hitchcock—that he used his experience as a director in his questioning.

PM: Do you mean that sometimes a critic is beguiled by the superficial, but doesn't understand the real obstacles facing the filmmaker?

BT: Yes—but I mean a lot of other things too. As a young critic, I could often identify the responsibility for the visual look of a film, and whether it was much more the cameraman than the director, for example. Don't ask me how! It was instinctual. I could see that a director's style would completely change with another cameraman, while other critics were praising the work of the director. In our '69 edition we often specified that the visual talent came from the cameraman. Then, later on, we met the actor, writer, or director involved, and found out that what we had written was true. It is important to identify, in a film, who or what is the *driving force*.

PM: Not only the cameraman, but the scriptwriter, often.

BT: Already, in the first edition, I think we were the first in the world to have a dictionary of screenwriters. *Film Comment* was second, and quoted us very often at that time. Frequently we spoke of the writer when we wrote about certain directors, although we made mistakes at that time, even in that category. We overrated certain people, we underrated some.

For example, we were more lucid on the subject of Philip Yordan than [our colleagues were]—because we said it seemed that Yordan had not written a great number of "his" screenplays. And, I wonder why, in '69 we included essays on Jo Eisinger, Martin Rackin, Daniel B. Ullman, Gerald Drayson Adams, or John Twist—which have been taken out of the new edition. We overrated people like Clair Huffaker (whatever happened to him?), and even Burt Kennedy. At the time we said Kennedy was one of the most brilliant screenwriters; he is gifted, but I think now I would tone down the adjectives.

PM: So you try to strike a balance in your discussion of a director's oeuvre—incorporating the contributions of cameramen and writers?

BT: In even our longest essays about directors, we always make a point of quoting the writers and what part they played, and so on. In our text about Raoul Walsh, we mention the parts played by certain screenwriters in his career: one of the weaknesses of Walsh is that he used and trusted somebody like [screenwriter] John Twist too much. I don't know why Walsh used Twist on his last two films, when he could have employed better screenwriters. In fact I do know—it's because John Twist loved to womanize with him. . . . But Twist's writing weakens some of Walsh's films, from *Colorado Territory* ('49) to *A Distant Trumpet* ('64).

When we talked to Henry Hathaway, he said the screenwriters he preferred working with, whom he found the most talented, were Grover Jones and Wendell Mayes. We tried to mention, therefore, in our essay on Hathaway, what these people brought to his films; or what Ben Hecht brought to the films he worked on for Hathaway. We even mention that the last act of *Kiss of Death* ('47) was rewritten by Philip Yordan—it was Hathaway who told us that—which has never been mentioned elsewhere, not even in your book, *Backstory*.

PM: In the US, Henry King and Hathaway are given a certain amount of respect, but it seems that in reappraising them you have more than respect—quite a bit of admiration for them.

BT: Yes. I found that sometimes they were very interesting, and sometimes on a level that people have very rarely spoken about. The fact that *A Fable* by William Faulkner is dedicated to Hathaway is a sign of something. Hathaway told me in an interview that he really tried to originate only two projects in his life: One was *A Fable*, which he asked Faulkner to write as a screenplay—the idea of the coming of Christ during the First World War. Faulkner wrote it as a novel and sent it to Hathaway ten years later. The second project was a remake of *Of Human Bondage* with Montgomery Clift and Marilyn Monroe—which was, in the early fifties, just after *Niagara*, a brilliant idea. And in *Niagara*, which is a beautiful film, Hathaway wanted to cast James Mason instead of Joseph Cotten. The association of Mason and Monroe is so modern and interesting that it makes Hathaway much more than just a good craftsman—it gives him a sharpness, a flair, that has never been studied.

Henry King worked a lot more on his screenplays than is generally known. In the Scarecrow Press book about King, Gregory Peck says that the last draft of *Twelve O'Clock High* ('49) was completely written by Henry King—all alone. And Peck also says that for *The Bravados* ('58) King changed two things: He made the man whom Peck was chasing innocent of the rape. That was not the idea of the screenplay; it's a beautiful change. Peck said the change was for religious reasons—King hated the idea of someone seeking vengeance, so he made him guilty by the very idea of revenge. And then King thought of the twist at the end where the Peck character goes to confession, because King was a truly religious man. King made those two changes because of his moral values. They completely altered the film. One of the ideas was a little heavy and sentimental, but one of them was superb—making *The Bravados* one of the rare films where the hero is wrong throughout the whole film.

PM: Does a director rate higher for you if he could also write?
BT: There are two or three types of directors who write. The directors who write their own screenplays—[Joseph L.] Mankiewicz, Delmer Daves, many people—are writers. And sometimes they are writers on the screenplays where they are not [credited as writers]; Delmer Daves told me he wrote a lot of things on *Pride of the Marines* ('45), for instance.

The second type greatly influences the writer, in different ways. It's not as though these directors are actually writing, but they give a kind of direction. That's Hitchcock, Hawks, Lubitsch. . . . It's nearly like writing.

Then you have the director who does not write but whose style will change certain things, and whose style, therefore, becomes almost like writing.

PM: When you are watching American movies, what do you regret missing out on the most—in the translation? Not strictly the language, but in the cultural aspects.

BT: It's difficult sometimes. I think we miss less now because we are more used to things and have read a lot. We lose things in the dialogue, of course. Things that we once thought were good lines we now realize were very used, sometimes very tired jokes. Maybe we lose certain colloquialisms—although on some subjects we seem to know more than the people making the films . . . for example, about jazz, or certain facts in Westerns, or films taking place in the South. I have an impression that I could be more accurate in terms of southern behavior and accents than they were in *Home from the Hill* (Vincente Minnelli, '60) or *The Long Hot Summer* (Martin Ritt, '58).

PM: How about . . . just cultural subtleties?

BT: I miss them. Although in some ways I think somebody in Milwaukee is as far away from Hollywood and the people making the films there as a Frenchman. [Laughs.] The Americans created a lot of genres that had codes that could be read immediately by everybody in the world—at least, the most important things. Sometimes we broke the codes before most Americans. The Western, for example, was being written about seriously in Italy, England, and France before the US.

You always miss things. You miss things most of all in the most literate films— an adaptation of a well-known book when some screenwriter had a good sense of colloquial dialogue.

PM: Why is it that American critics took Hollywood pictures so much for granted for so long? There was a dearth of serious appraisal. I know, from the book I just finished about George Cukor, that Cukor was revered by the French in his lifetime, but was apoplectic about being ignored by film festivals in his own country. In the sixties he had to hire a publicist to promote his name. . . .

BT: I think the Americans were late. I don't know why. The serious criticism started in England and even in France. . . . Even your book of interviews with screenwriters comes so late—look how little information there is about the thirties, how much is lost! Because, in America, Hollywood was entertainment; it was not taken seriously.

But some of the filmmakers were taking films seriously. Somebody like [W. S.] Van Dyke was writing theoretical articles in '34, '35, and a book about the making of *Trader Horn* ('31). A cameraman, John Alton, was writing what might be the first book by a cameraman, *Painting with Light*. This is a subject I wondered about when I wrote my essay about Robert Florey in the book. I studied a film of Florey's called *The Preview Murder Mystery* ('36). The film is full of flaws, but sometimes brilliant and visually sometimes extremely brilliant. Why, I ask in my article, did a man like Florey, doing that little B film at Paramount, why was he shooting a scene with a cop questioning a subject, with a circular tracking shot, the people all in shadows, except for a few moments when there is a lamp in the middle of everything that gives off flashes of light—so that the people go from shadows to light according to the camera movement? It's a shot that is complicated, very expressionistic. The public that would see that film on a double bill would never notice. Practically no serious critic—*Variety*, yes—was even mentioning the B film. Why was Florey doing that! Was it to prove something to himself?

PM: Was Florey an artist?

BT: I don't know if you could use that word. Let's say he had moments where he was inventive, inspired, and moments when he thought he was an artist but he was not because the ideas were ludicrous. I don't think he was very lucid or sharp about the elements of a screenplay; the ones he wrote are incredibly uneven, with some very bright ideas, as in the case of *Hollywood Boulevard* ('36). Florey had a love of show business and movies. Sometimes he had good and bad things in the same movie. But it's an interesting question: What pushes somebody, who will not even be noticed by the critic of the *New York Times*, to do that?

PM: According to your opinion, which was the best studio in the Golden Age?

BT: Warners and RKO, I think. I cannot say they were the best, but they made the films I prefer. For comedies, Paramount was prestigious—because of Ernst Lubitsch and Billy Wilder. But Warners had so many good films . . . and you have the impression that you can still discover hidden treasures [from that studio], especially in the thirties. RKO—because there were a lot of very good screenwriters there. The studios without stars were the best sometimes, for me, because they had to compensate with other good actors and screenwriters.

PM: Do you take producers into account in your book?

BT: Of course, although we did not have enough information to do a separate dictionary of producers. But when, for example, we write about Warner Bros., we talk about the parts played by Hal Wallis, Jerry Wald, and somebody that everybody seemed to respect and find creative—Henry Blanke.

PM: Who were the great producers at RKO?

BT: I would say, of course, Pandro Berman and Dore Schary. Maybe Adrian Scott. Certainly Val Lewton, one of the most creative producers. But it was mostly a studio full of very interesting writers—the ones who worked with Robert Wise and Val Lewton, and a lot of the left-wing writers.

PM: You are so busy these days, making films yourself. Do you still find time to indulge yourself as a critic and buff?

BT: Just before calling you, I was trying to watch again a film I once enjoyed for the camera movements: *Rome Adventure* ('62) by Delmer Daves. But if I were revising my opinion I'd say I found the acting—not only Troy Donahue, but Suzanne Pleshette and Rossano Brazzi—unwatchable. Bad acting is something I have become less tolerant of, as I said. I couldn't finish watching it.

I just received a laserdisc of *The Searchers* ('56) and watched the beginning of it, this evening, too. The disc is in widescreen. I read the notes, which say they matched the widescreen from the original VistaVision negative. It looks very beautiful, but it's widescreen—like a CinemaScope shape. In our book you'll find many things like this coming from me which are really directorial questions: In the video version *The Searchers* looks like a 1.85 ratio [i.e., 1:1.85]; now, in laserdisc, it's more like CinemaScope. I remember seeing the original film in VistaVision. What would be the proper ratio? They cannot put VistaVision on laserdisc, but the VistaVision negative is really closeup CinemaScope. This proves the film we are seeing is not the true film.

In the case of Fritz Lang, I ask in what ratio exactly were his last two American films shot—*While the City Sleeps* ('56) and *Beyond a Reasonable Doubt* ('56). I myself have seen them in 1.33, 1.85, and even in SuperScope. I know that Lang was a tyrant with the framing of a film. So I would love to have that question investigated. What is the original shape, the frame, Lang used for those films? The real one. Because SuperScope was sometimes a process done in the lab.

The same is true of *The Incredible Shrinking Man* (Jack Arnold, '57) and other films done at Universal [in the fifties]—Sirk's *Sign of the Pagan* ('54), for example, which I have seen in 1.33 and CinemaScope. Sirk said that sometimes he was doing two versions at the same time, but there must have been one that had his preference, and there must be one that was better lit than the other. It's very interesting to ask that kind of question. . . .

PM: Which American films have you seen the most often, the most regularly?
BT: I think *The Searchers*—maybe twenty-five times. Most of John Ford. *The Grapes of Wrath* ('40). At one point, *The Hanging Tree* (Daves, '59) and *Moonfleet* (Lang, '55), some Billy Wilder and Ernst Lubitsch comedies. Even Blake Edwards. I used to watch *One, Two, Three* (Wilder, '61) and *The Party* (Edwards, '68) once a year. Incidentally, *One, Two, Three* was a very good political commentary, and a film incredibly in advance of its time about the destruction of Communism. Incredibly accurate. The same with *Ninotchka* ('39). The scene where they go to the station to find the comrade: they go up to a man thinking it must be him; the man turns and salutes—he is a fascist! And *Ninotchka* was finished, I think, one month before the Hitler-Stalin pact! It proves that Billy Wilder and Ernst Lubitsch were always right historically and politically. [Laughs.]

PM: Did you have any personal disappointments, reseeing favorite films?

BT: I saw a film that I had last seen when I was eleven years old, *Gung Ho!* (Ray Enright, '43), a war film with Randolph Scott. I was horrified, because it was a most jingoistic film, with racist depictions of the Japanese. I remember loving it when I was a boy. On the other hand, I resaw a film I'd seen when I was fourteen—*Wake of the Red Witch* ('48). I still love it. I adore that film. Here is a director I would like to know more about: Edward Ludwig, a quite mysterious and interesting director. I said to myself, "Oh, I was right to see it three times when I was fourteen!" I have seen it three times since.

PM: If you do another edition of your book—ten, twenty years hence—who are your subjects for further research, whose films have eluded you until now?

BT: They would be people in the thirties—screenwriters and directors. And silent films, of course. I would love to see certain silent Walsh films, because Ford told me that one of the films that impressed him the most was *The Honor System* ('17). And I heard—though I was not there—that at the Italian film festival devoted to silent movies [Pordenone], the great discovery was not only the silent films of Cecil B. DeMille, which people now know are great, but the films of his brother William. A few people told me these films are absolutely stunning, and nobody has ever written about them.

There are many, many people whom we do not know enough about and did not include much about in our book. There are now some directors practically all of whose films we have seen, but with even these directors I have one, two, or three films I have yet to see that look promising or interesting or were, at one point, well received. That goes from John Ford to Gregory La Cava to . . . Stuart Heisler. It took me a long time to catch up with Heisler's *The Biscuit Eater* ('40); and Martin Scorsese just wrote me that he's sending me a video of *Journey into Light* ('51), with Sterling Hayden, because he thinks the film's terrific. . . .

PM: The task seems almost infinite.

BT: It is infinite. I think we are just starting the story of the cinema. A lot of territory still has to be explored. . . .

A Conversation with Bertrand Tavernier on *L'Appât*

Film Pressbook / 1995

From the pressbook for *L'Appât*, 1995. Reprinted by permission. Translated by T. Jefferson Kline.

Question: The origin of *L'Appât* [*Fresh Bait*] was a news item that inspired the book by Morgan Sportès. How does the film reflect its sources?

Bertrand Tavernier: Colo Tavernier O'Hagan was fascinated by the Valérie Subra affair and closely followed the trial. The dramatic progression from an item in the news, its subsequent development as a story and its eventual implications seemed to her to have great potential for a film.

What interested Colo in this story was to see how a group of people who, individually, wouldn't have hurt a fly, when brought together could go so far astray and completely lose sight of any and all morality. Their connection seems to have stimulated their lack of responsibility and encouraged them in their excesses. Colo Tavernier saw in this story characters who were as powerful as those in *Une Affaire de femmes* [*A Story of Women*] that she'd written for Claude Chabrol.

I'd already used a news story of a crime as the point of departure for *L'Horloger de Saint-Paul* [*The Clockmaker of Saint Paul*] and *Le Juge et l'assassin* [*The Judge and the Assassin*]. I bought the rights for Morgan Sportès's book, an exact reconstitution of the affair, which contained a mass of very interesting details, and Colo wrote a first version of the scenario, using her own memories of the trial and the precise factual details that the book provided . . . then we very excitedly coauthored the second version of the story.

In principle I was supposed to start shooting in November of '93, but then I got sidetracked by work on *La Fille de d'Artagnan* [*D'Artagnan's Daughter*] and had to put things off for a few months.

Q: What sort of changes did you make in this second version?

BT: It was after making *L.627* that things really came together. I told Colo that we had to take more liberties with the story, that we should change the dates of the original to make it more contemporary. All of the contacts that I'd made as a result of *L.627*—with teachers, with police, with educators, sociologists, and young people—all those months of discussions, research, and debates ended up convincing me that I *should* make *Fresh Bait*, that this story was infused, dictated really, by our socio-political situation. What was an exception in 1984 had become—I hesitate to use the word—merely a "daily" event . . . What's more, there'd been four or five similar incidents that year. Also, one criminal investigator told me: "If you knew the numbers of murders that are committed just to stay alive for six days in prison . . ." So I didn't want to shoot a film about an exceptional situation, but one that could happen to anybody.

There's a moment when filming a film feels like a life and death question . . . I know that might sound pretentious or ridiculous . . . I experienced the same thing when Michel Alexandre showed me the Algécos [improvised barracks] where he worked. I felt the same thing with the subject of *Fresh Bait*. I had to shoot it as a reaction against the permanent aggression of the dictatorship of money, against this feeling of collective apathy, against this abandonment of values. That's why I launched into this film before I'd even finished *D'Artagnan's Daughter*. I didn't want to put it off, which would have been better for my health. I was afraid that my passion would subside and I wanted to shoot it in "a state of emergency" as I did for *L.627*.

Q: Practically speaking, what were the differences between the film and the event?
BT: First of all, the change in historical moment caused a change in the dialogue, the behavior, and the motivations of the characters. For example, the importance that America had taken in the visual imagination of the kids. The American dream still existed in France. What was then merely a fascination has become a necessary reference, a social, cultural, and ideological reference. There are also changes linked to dramatic necessity, to differences in point of view, but we kept the dramatic plot, certain specific episodes, and the social situation of the three protagonists. I decided to take out the trial, and instead, to add what ended up being the first third of the film: the deepening of, and even the invention of some aspects of the love relationships and conflicts among the three characters in their life together and their "breaks" (the slap Bruno gives Nathalie, the story of the encyclopedia . . .) and also added back certain of the details described or noted by Morgan Sportès and to develop them.

Another difference between the film and the book: I didn't want them to go to the lawyer's apartment with the intention of killing him; in the trial, the opposite was claimed, but I found that much less interesting. I wanted to show how they fell into their own trap, that they turned to violence because of an accumulation of mistakes: the first being that they chose victims who had the same profiles as they did, who've sacrificed everything for external signs and that's all they have—as a consequence, they end up facing their doubles.

I absolutely did not want to recreate the original news item, but instead use it to present characters who might be our own kids, mine, yours; to sound an alarm about our present situation.

I think it was Simenon who wrote that once a crime has gone to trial, it's no longer about the perpetrators, but about the society that produced them and whose "unconscious" is revealed in the process. But we wouldn't want the story to become a demonstration or a thesis, but instead respect its unconscious drives.

Q: You see your characters in a way that's neither clinical nor romantic.
BT: I tried to see them freely, affectionately, without any a priori or specific point of view, like the cops in *L.627*. I wanted us to feel near them, to understand their feelings. We had to show things that were touching about them, like their terrifying lack of conscience. Their fragility, their internal emptiness. This "desert of the soul" that Claudel spoke of can never excuse them, but I wanted to go beyond the criteria of sympathy and antipathy.

I wanted to avoid making the film an affidavit or pleading their case. And especially to avoid making the film a psychological explanation of their behavior. Some things belong to the domain of the unfathomable and we have to know when to stop, close the door, and just suppose. In order to achieve this, I had to make the writing open (but with a point of view) and to allow myself to be surprised by the actors and the accidents of filming. Which happened a lot. Marie Gillain, among others, so deepened her character, she produced such explosive feelings, that I had to redo certain of the shots we'd done in the first week in order to take advantage of what was being created on the set.

As for me, I see a very clear connection between this film and the part of *La Guerre sans nom* [*The Undeclared War*] that looked at torture, where apparently normal people can suddenly go haywire.

Q: We have the impression that the character of Eric is the one you feel least like saving . . .
BT: To the degree that he's the leader. But he also has his hesitation, his weaknesses, his moment of tenderness. There are times when he's incapable of taking responsibility and wants to stop. But he's a prisoner of the image of the "chief" that he's created. They're all traversed by doubt, and I wanted the film's viewers to be with them, to passionately wish they would stop.

They're the ones who set in motion the very machine that will maim them—through stupidity, ignorance, irresponsibility, or simply because they're prisoners of the illusions, the images, of the entire panoply that they're carting about—to the detriment of life itself.

Q: The film wants to portray a certain social transformation . . .

BT: Yes. Publicity, televised images, TV ratings, an entire literature focused on money and success that has provided a vision of prosperity to those who are excluded, while at the same time condemning them to unemployment and to a feeling that they don't exist, that they have no identity if they don't possess certain signs that can only be acquired through money.

Q: So it's progress that's responsible for this?

BT: Progress? Are you sure that's the right word? Let's say, rather, a huge unraveling . . . In any case, the film makes no attempt at an explanation, quite the contrary.

But on the other hand I'm not claiming that we are not responsible. We live in a society where we've suppressed all the safeguards that were once represented by education, religion, political engagement, the responsible unions, the family. Even if it was to contest them. All we have left is a taste for social satire and a vague distrust of established order that's extolled by the media; like the show that attracted a lot of kids called "How to rip people off? Steal from your parents," or the radio commentator who tells kids how wonderful it is to kill cops . . .

Q: The characters in the film are very contemporary, without appearing to be symbols . . .

BT: I avoid "general ideas" like the plague. It's true that the three protagonists of the film are not specific cases. They belong to a state of mind that is destructive and ends up pushing them into crime. But their enthusiasms, their tastes, their unconscious, their lack of moral principles are all forged by adults and their vulnerability is aggravated by their fears and worries.

Q: The style is deliberately realist . . .

BT: All of the violent scenes in the film were very difficult to shoot. You see, I wanted to preserve a certain opacity in their behavior, to stop when doors were closed, all the while trying to pay close attention to the topography, to the precise relationships, to the way they occupy their space . . . I wanted Nathalie to always appear to be in a waiting room. You should never cheat with doors you open and then close.

Q: The rhythm of the film.

BT: Every film is a voyage, and I hate organized tours where you know from the first shots where you're going. Today we must ask ourselves questions about rhythm, in relation to the attitude of spectators vis-à-vis French film and especially in relation to the morose climate in this country. You can't simply state it coldly and pessimistically, watching the cadavres float down the river. You have to react, throw paving stones in the river, express your anger physically, feel passion. But there's also the pleasure of filming. Ever since, *La Vie et rien d'autre* [*Life and Nothing But*] I've wanted my films to be fast-paced, jolting, breathless from scenes that end suddenly and abruptly. In *L.627* I wanted the mise en scène to translate physically the material and moral instability of the cops, and in this film this mechanism that is suddenly going to go haywire. My films must adopt the internal rhythm of the characters.

Q: Tell us about your young actors . . .
BT: I loved working with them. I found them dazzling. Marie Gillain radiates truth twenty-four times a second. In her own life she's the complete opposite of Nathalie, but portrayed her with exceptional honesty, depth, and integrity. As soon as I met her at a festival in Japan, I felt that I had to make a film with her. What's more, she got along magnificently with Olivier Sitruk and Bruno Putzulu and you get that, in every scene they're in. You sense their complicity . . . I could go on for hours about Marie, Olivier, and Bruno. And about the others as well. I felt as happy filming them as I did in *L.627* . . . And it's not because you need to explore certain abysses that you fall into them.

I asked them not to read anything whatsoever about the trial or to try to copy any way of speaking or dressing, or thinking. I wanted to reinvent these characters. And also the victims. I'd been wanting to work with Richard Berry for a very long time. I sense that he could be overwhelming. Which directors rarely exploit, except for Christine Pascal in her admirable *Le Petit Prince a dit* [*The Little Prince Said*].

I'd admired the work of Philippe Duclos in *La Sentinelle* [*The Sentinel*] and Clotilde Courau who does a magnificent job in *Le Petit Criminel* [*The Little Gangster*]. Marie Ravel and Olivier Sitruk were discovered by Shula Siegfried.

Filming a Forgotten War: An Interview with Bertrand Tavernier

Dennis West and Joan M. West / 1998

From *Cineaste* 23, no. 3 (Summer 1998). Reprinted by permission.

Cineaste: Why were you interested in adapting Roger Vercel's 1934 novel *Capitaine Conan* for the screen?

Bertrand Tavernier: First, because it's a beautiful novel, which, after having been very well known and influential, had become forgotten. It's a novel I'd read and been very strongly impressed by when I was young. I did not know then that it was considered the first French novel with an antihero. Second, that war in the Balkans is totally forgotten today. It was forgotten even at the time because Clemenceau and Foch hated the idea of the second front, which was an idea of Briand and the British. They did everything they could to forget this army, and so that part of the First World War has always been hidden. This is quite surprising because this army won one of the greatest victories during the war, the battle we see at the beginning of the film, the victory of the Sokol, which forced the surrender of three countries, including the Austro-Hungarian and Ottoman Empires.

Vercel wrote very well, and *Capitaine Conan* is one of the rare novels about the war in the Balkans. When I reread it, I was attracted by the characters and the theme. I felt that it was not dated at all, neither its style nor what it was saying. Conan is not an historical character. You see Conan every night on television—in Bosnia or in Zaire, in Israel or Palestine—those young kids with machine guns. After they've been at war for three or four years, people tell them, "Now forget the gun and vote," and they are unable to cope with that. You could transpose the story of Conan to Vietnam or Algeria, with one exception, which is the fact that an army was kept active more than a year after the Armistice in order to fight another enemy.

Cineaste: You have long been interested in exploring official vs. unofficial history, and the moral ambiguities of historical situations. What new historical insights does *Capitaine Conan* offer the French?

Tavernier: Especially for a younger audience, *Capitaine Conan* speaks about something they do not know. Many young people have a total ignorance of and a total disinterest in history, which I find very frightening because, as we say in French, if you willfully ignore the past, you will be forced to relive it: "Vouloir ignorer le passé, on est condamné à le revivre." For most people, including a lot of history teachers, the period shown in the film was absolutely unknown. The film speaks of themes which interest me very much, in particular the consequences of war. The real theme of the film is how do you stop a war? A war cannot be stopped like a football game; you cannot blow a whistle and say it's over, this is the armistice, we won. I wanted to show characters who cannot adapt themselves to the new situation. They have been so caught up in violence and a certain way of living that they have lost certain values, and they cannot stop themselves. Conan's people are lost geographically and morally; in fact, the film is about people who are lost.

I wanted the film to say many things, without explaining them or being didactic. The film was difficult to write and direct because it was important that the audience not know more than the characters, or be superior to them. The film is always shot from the point of view of the people who live it, not from the point of view of a general or somebody with superior knowledge.

Cineaste: As in the scene where the soldiers on the train discuss which direction they're going based on the location of the sun?
Tavernier: I added those scenes because I was dealing with something which was not true of the novel. When the novel was published in 1934, the readers knew certain things—Sofia, the Balkans, that was something they knew. Now, when people in France see the film, they do not know where Bucharest is, where Sofia is. So I decided to incorporate this into the film, because I felt the soldiers were just as ignorant—they never knew where they were being sent.

Those men were ordered to the Danube delta to fight against the Russians; they knew nothing about the political situation. What they knew grew out of propaganda from the Russians or the anarchists. So I decided to incorporate one or two segments of that into the film: the sergeant who revolts and says, "We have been at war for seven years now; we are not at war with the Russians, they are our allies." And somebody like Norbert—he did not know why he was going, he could not figure it out. He will, one or two years after; but not right then.

Cineaste: Why are the commandos all Bretons?
Tavernier: Not all of them, only two. Because being a Breton is a status statement. The Bretons were among the biggest casualties of the First World War. There were lots of reasons. It was a very poor region of France, so a lot of people enlisted. Some of the worst casualties from the First World War were peasants. There were

many more peasants killed than workers because the workers were kept in cities to make the factories produce. The French peasantry was destroyed during the First World War, so the provinces with many peasants had enormous casualties. I also wanted to show in the film that the French Army was made up of people speaking different dialects. So you hear songs in Occitan and people speaking with a lot of different accents. The French Army was totally provincial. There were even some groups who spoke in patois, a dialect which you could not understand, like people from the North, or the Alsatians.

Cineaste: We see two Senegalese soldiers in *Capitaine Conan*; and we understand that when you were in Senegal in 1980, filming *Clean Slate* [*Coup de Torchon*], you met Senegalese WWI veterans.

Tavernier: Yes, they told me about Verdun, and, in a discussion I remember quite well, they told me about the advantage of the French bayonet over the German. The French one had a kind of hook, so when you retrieved it, it cut more flesh [chuckles]. They also told me stories about the cold. In that scene with the Senegalese, I wanted to show soldiers who had lost their regiment. It's something which happens constantly; in an offensive, soldiers get disoriented. I wanted to show colonial troops who are wounded and lost on the front. The way this scene is shot is typical of the way the film was directed: the camera is following some wounded soldiers, and suddenly behind them you see two Senegalese; then you go on with the wounded soldiers and it's like, "My God, what did I just see?" I wanted to give the impression that the scenes were not staged; that they were happening by accident and that the cameraman was constantly in danger and always trying to reveal things.

Cineaste: Your battle sequences feature vast landscapes being crossed by diminutive, antlike soldiers. How did you visualize the landscape for the film?

Tavernier: It was a great part of the project because I was dealing with landscape which was totally different from all the World War stories. It was closer to a locational landscape belonging to the Western. I felt like Anthony Mann or Delmer Daves.

The traditional imagery of the First World War is very strong—it's always mud, trenches, and plains with scorched trees. But here I was in rocky, mountainous country. That traditional imagery is so strong, however, that a number of French critics said that it was quite accurate, that I had described the muddy trenches very well. But there was no mud in those trenches! You see clearly that they have been dug out of rocks in the mountains. I wanted a very dry landscape at the beginning of the film—like something you would see in Westerns with James Stewart. That gave me a totally different visual concept. And with those vast landscapes, with that incredible light that you have in Romania, I decided on a few principles of direction: that when we were shooting the battle scenes, the camera would always be in the middle, shooting from the point of view of somebody in the action, never from the point of view of a director staging the action. I made a list of different actions, which I gave to the assistant director, and then we never rehearsed. We just took a lot of precautions with the explosions, because I always wanted them in the same shot as the characters so I could avoid the insert—the shot of people walking, and then the reverse shot of the machine gun firing at them.

Also, I wanted to keep one point of view in the film. You never have the point of view of the enemy. Never. You always see the enemies when the characters see them. That's something I learned when I made *L.627*. Keeping a strong point of view helps not only the dramatization but also the moral of the film. When you adopt a certain style and point of view, it gives shape to the scenes, and shots which do not follow that approach look different. So we were always in the midst of the soldiers. You aren't supposed to understand completely if they are winning or losing, because I think that's what you feel when you're in the middle of a battle. You see very little of the enemy and never have an action with a real beginning and a real ending. Everything's fragmentary.

Cineaste: Did any previous war films influence your approach to *Capitaine Conan*?
Tavernier: Maybe unconsciously. I've always been, if not influenced, emotionally marked by several beautiful war films—*La Grande Illusion* (it's not exactly a war film, but it's set about the same time); *Les Croix de Bois* [*Wooden Crosses*], a French film; and Kubrick's *Paths of Glory*. There were many important films about the First World War, but the only war film I showed my cameraman was John Huston's *The Battle of San Pietro*, a documentary I admire tremendously.

Cineaste: You mean specifically in terms of thinking about your film?
Tavernier: Yes, in thinking about the moral of the film, about how to show the violence, how to shoot the battle scenes, and trying to show the effects. I asked to see a lot of wounded soldiers, a lot of corpses—to always see the effects. Most of the time you don't see the real action, only the consequence of the actions. I recall very well, when I was a press agent, a meeting between Alexandre Astruc, the French director, and Raoul Walsh. Astruc kept questioning Walsh on how he had done those incredibly well-shot scenes in *The Naked and the Dead* and especially *Objective Burma!* And Walsh answered something to the effect that, "I shot but never rehearsed." He sent people into the action until it was good. If there was something good, he kept it, and he was constantly cutting in his head. He said something I still remember, "Always use the diagonal. It will give a depth of focus and help the movement. There will always be a contradiction, an opposition

between the sets, the props—the trees, the rocks—and the people who are moving. Never be frontal."

Cineaste: Have your people move diagonally through the landscape.
Tavernier: Yes. Always consider the framing, the camera movement and the movement of the characters in terms of the diagonal. It changes the movement; it changes your perception. It gives a bigger intensity to things, and at the same time you create a better relationship with the landscape, because you see more of it.

Something else I always try to do is never to keep the same distance between the camera and the character. Because, especially in a film like *Capitaine Conan*, the danger is symmetry and being slick. When you do a perfect tracking shot with the guy walking, you always have a danger of composition in the shot, the danger of being academic. I wanted to shoot the film in a state of urgency, like *L.627*. I told lead actor Philippe Torreton and Alain Choquart, the cameraman, that the rhythm of the film would be provided by the character of Conan. Conan must almost always be moving, and sometimes moving faster than the camera. At least three or four times, he goes out of the frame. He walks and then, whoosh, he goes out of the frame, and we are left looking for him. I tried to set it up so that neither the construction of shots nor the relationship between one shot and the next would be predictable. There are very few shots and reverse shots.

Cineaste: For instance, you never show us the face of the soldier who is left standing, either in shell shock or dead or paralyzed. We see him from behind, and then the camera travels past him, and we never see him from another angle. He's gone.
Tavernier: He's gone because people are still running. They pass him; they don't have time to stop. The actors in *Conan* received special training from a man who had been drafted during the Algerian War. By chance he found himself in a commando unit, killing. He told us several things. One was that only in a film do you die in slow motion. In war, death is very, very quick. The most frightening thing is that you walk with somebody, you talk to him, and suddenly you turn to him and he has been killed. He's gone.

The second thing he told us is that you have very little blood on you because when you cut a throat, it's so fast, that if you have blood on you, it means that you have not been fast enough, and so you are in danger. At the moment you cut someone's throat, you are looking for the next person to kill. So, in fact, I show very little. At the moment when I have a guy putting a knife to a throat, the camera pans and it's on something else. People may feel that they've seen a lot of blood and throats being cut, but it's not true. This former commando told us that this was the impact and the aura of violence—that enormous rapidity. So I tried to avoid a typical movie kind of violence.

Cineaste: Does military service inherently lead to the corruption of a man's life?
Tavernier: I would not say military service. War and violence can destroy you. I never deal with such a general question in a film; I try to avoid that. Certainly in *Conan* there is never one word saying that war is awful or disgusting. But the war in the film destroys practically every character. The people who can escape are those who have something behind them; they have a backbone. For Norbert it can be the desire to go on teaching, his values. The film is not pessimistic. I even added lines which were not in the novel, when Norbert says, "No, I teach now. I still try to understand"—which describes exactly what I do.

You have other characters—the generals and the people around them—who can carry on without any problem, they do not seem puzzled or troubled or suffering from anything. But Norbert can leave the war because he has values, he has a goal in his life. Philippe Torreton often said in interviews that the difference between Conan and Norbert is that Norbert was able to read, and Conan never had that chance. Conan is a doomed character, a victim. He did not enlist; he was drafted. He was good, he was applauded, he was decorated, and then he's dropped. And he doesn't understand. He spent the best years of his life in Romania, in Bulgaria. He was a king and suddenly he's nobody. And that, for me, is frightening. That's how war can change the values of the system and how it can destroy. Conan pays for that. It's the story of someone who dies from the virus of war.

Cineaste: That's a point you suggest when you frame his hometown from behind the window that says, "Mercier, Conan et fils" [Conan and Son, Haberdasher—eds.]. That claustrophobic village life was all he had to return to after his experience in the war.
Tavernier: Yes, it's unfortunate that civilian society never knew how to use Conan's qualities, because he had things in him . . .

Cineaste: Leadership characteristics . . .
Tavernier: He had a leadership charisma; he could have been used for something. It's a waste that his qualities had to be used for killing. Maybe he would have been something great in the village; but nobody asked him, nobody tried to find anything in him. That's the tragedy of Conan and what moves me in his character.

Cineaste: Would you comment on the character of Madame Erlane?
Tavernier: The character exists in the novel, except she never comes to Bucharest, she only writes letters. Bringing her to Bucharest is better. First, because you observe a very important thing—class differences. The wives or fiancees of soldiers like Conan and Norbert are not rich enough to travel on the Orient Express. She can. Second, it allowed me to show an evolution in the characters. She starts as

somebody who is a bit arrogant, bourgeois, totally lost. She doesn't understand reality and keeps complaining about crazy things. But then we see her as a mother, and I feel that the whole story of Conan's attitude towards her son is very beautiful. During the battle, when Conan gives grenades to Erlane, this is a gesture to Madame Erlane, because two things can happen—either Erlane will die during the fight, or he will survive and be executed later. For Madame Erlane it's much better that he die in battle than be executed, because, in the kind of society in which she lives, having her son shot as a deserter would have made her life abominable. And the kid does not redeem himself; he dies with a bullet in the back, which means that he was still not courageous. This is something which allows me to contradict one of the great themes of the American war film—the coward who redeems himself at the end of the film. Erlane doesn't. He doesn't do anything. But Conan and Norbert both behave like gentlemen.

Cineaste: Dinner scenes are a recurring motif in the film; why do you like them so much?

Tavernier: [Laughs] It's not that I like them; I hate dinner scenes, because it's very complicated to do shots of people around a table. But they are important in the first part of the film because food is essential to the army, and I wanted to dramatize something in Vercel's novel—the fact that the whole army is starving and Conan's men are eating very well because they steal and loot. They are like people during the wars in the Middle Ages. They behave like Vikings, so they survive. It's terrifying, but in a war the people who survive are criminals.

In the second part of the film, the meals are kind of ritual scenes in which the officers—the people Conan despises and who didn't dare criticize him because he was so useful to them—are suddenly regaining their power. This often happens during a meal, because it's a moment when everybody meets and you can assess your power. I'm sure that Vercel did not invent those characters in his novel. I'm sure he met that Major Bouvier, who is one of the most frightening characters because he's so stupid, so happy with himself. This major's vision of justice is terrifying. He doesn't see the necessity of an advocate, of a defense counsel. He embodies perfectly what Clemenceau meant when he said that military justice is to justice what military music is to music.

Cineaste: Do you see *Capitaine Conan* as an effective indictment of military justice in general, or specifically of French military justice?

Tavernier: I would say that I start by dealing with things happening in my own country; but when you hit, if you are true enough, I'm sure the meaning is universal. Everything that Conan says about military justice is true. As we say, "Il a une connaissance du terrain" [he knows the territory well—eds.]. His appreciation of the army system is totally just, and in a way he is sometimes more against the system than Norbert, who is more idealist. In fact, the film is about two persons who are trying to fight the system. One, Norbert, is trying to fight it with a very humanistic approach. He thinks that he can change and reform the system by being fair, by being generous, by being indulgent. And he is. And he's useful, because if he was not there, seven, ten, fifteen people would have been shot or sent to prison for life. So he saves people. But he fails.

Conan is fighting the system with everything. He's defying it and he will fail, too, because the system is so strong. The strength of the military system is to refuse to deal with the truth. This is very clear in the case of Erlane. When Conan is fighting for this deserter, he gives the priest some very good material for the defense: that the man responsible for the deaths of thirty-seven people is, in fact, De Sceve, because he gave a mission to somebody who was unable to do it. The notion of being responsible is very important to Conan. The priest doesn't dare deal with it, because if you were to accept the idea that the people who give the orders are responsible for the deaths, then it would be the end of the system. The general who has slaughtered so many people would have to be judged. This was done during the French Revolution. That was the only moment in French history when they sent generals to the guillotine, the only moment of freedom we had [laughs]. But it's true that, in a way, in his attitude, Conan has a moment when he indicts the system. He totally shows the contradictions of the system.

An Interview with Bertrand Tavernier

Richard Phillips / 1999

From World Socialist Web Site, July 10, 1999, https://www.wsws.org/en/articles/1999/07/ sff2-j10.html. Reprinted by permission of the author.

Richard Phillips: Before discussing *It All Starts Today* [*Ça commence aujourd'hui*], your latest film, could you briefly describe how you became involved in the film industry and the directors that had the greatest impact on you in the earlier part of your career?

Bertrand Tavernier: I always wanted to be a director, ever since I was about thirteen or fourteen years old. I think perhaps it was John Ford's *Fort Apache* and *She Wore a Yellow Ribbon* that suddenly made me realize that the director wrote with images. I had read a lot of Jules Verne and Jack London when I was young and learnt that they painted with words. When I saw Ford's films I realized the director painted with moving images. All of Ford's main characters are part of a collectivity and this really appealed to me. They are not treated as great heroes but people trying to do their best for everyone under difficult circumstances. Ford's approach to history, of course, is not mine but he is a much more complex figure than commonly appreciated and not as conservative as people think. Also, I later realized that he was influenced by F. W. Murnau and the German Expressionists in the same way that many directors influenced me. I had a notebook in which I kept photos from films by directors that I liked. This included John Ford, William Wellman, and others, so it was not a bad beginning. Then I discovered the French cinema—Jean Renoir, Jean Vigo, and Jacques Becker—and later Italian movies. I grew up as a big fan of American films. I loved Samuel Fuller, Delmer Daves, and many other American directors.

Later I wrote two books about the American cinema. One of them has had several editions, first *Twenty*, then later *Thirty* and now *Fifty Years of American Cinema*. It is a 1,250-page book—a dictionary of nearly six hundred filmmakers with many essays on directors and screenwriters. It also includes a study of censorship in Hollywood. It was co-written with Jean-Pierre Coursodon and I think it is a good book. The other book is called *American Friends*. This has interviews with many American directors from John Ford to Robert Altman, to Robert Parish and Roger Corman, and many others who had not been interviewed before. It also includes people like Sidney Buchman, the writer of *Mr. Smith Goes to Washington*, and Herbert Biberman, director of *Salt of the Earth*. There is a big section on the blacklist. I got to know practically everybody who was blacklisted and interviewed many people—John Berry, Joe Losey, Abe Polonsky, and others. In two years I will do a sequel called *European Friends*, which will have interviews as well as essays on Michael Jean-Pierre Melville and many others.

The first director I worked with was Jean-Pierre Melville. I was studying at the Sorbonne and I interviewed him. After that I quit my studies and became a third or fourth assistant director. Unfortunately I was a very bad assistant director. I was awful.

RP: Why do you say that?

BT: Because I was bad, there is no question about that. Melville terrified me. He behaved like a tyrant on the set and I was miserable during those weeks. In the end he told me, you will never succeed as an assistant director. I think he was right but he presented me to the film producer and suggested I become a press agent for the company that produced Melville's films, which I did.

After that I became an independent press agent with my friend and this was very satisfying because it meant that we could work on the films that we liked. We worked more like film buffs than normal press agents, not concentrating on the stars but on the directors and writers and the meaning of the film and its place in the history of cinema. We also provided detailed information and extensive interviews with the directors. We worked with many, many directors this way—French, Italian, and American, including some old-timers like Raoul Walsh, Howard Hawks, and John Ford. We also publicized new films that we discovered; films that we reissued, like *Gentleman Jim* and *Make Way for Tomorrow*; the films of Ida Lupino and many others.

And so I learnt about film. Then I did my first film, *The Clockmaker* [*L'Horloger de Saint-Paul*], which took me fourteen months to get the financing for. It was shot very quickly and with a lot of passion. The film was released in 1973 and won the Prix Louis Delluc and the Silver Bear award at the Berlin Film Festival. It was a success. Since then I have made more than twenty films. Mostly it has been very difficult to get money for their production. Every time it was the same story as with *The Clockmaker*—the stories were rejected; no one wanted to finance the films I wanted to do. Two of my biggest successes, '*Round Midnight* [*Autour de minuit*] and *Life and Nothing But* [*La Vie et rien d'autre*], were turned down by everybody.

Although '*Round Midnight* was not turned down by the producer, he could not find a studio. They did not want to do a story about jazz, about a black guy and particularly about an old black guy. They just didn't want it and yet the film got two nominations for an Oscar and one of the nominations won. *Life and Nothing But* won the Best Foreign Language Film in England, the Special Jury Award by the European Film Academy and Cesar awards for Philippe Noiret as best actor. It also won the Best Foreign Film by the West Coast critics. But nobody had wanted to put the money up for this movie. The same thing happened with *L.627* and almost all of my films.

RP: You mentioned that you interviewed blacklisted Hollywood directors and screenwriters. Can you comment on the Academy's award to Elia Kazan?

BT: I knew Kazan very well. He was someone I did a long interview with and I worked as his press agent on *The Arrangement*. I accepted that work on the condition that he would speak to me about the blacklist, which he did. I admire him as a director, or at least I admire some of his films tremendously. I think that *Splendor in the Grass*, *Baby Doll*, *A Face in the Crowd*, and *Panic in the Streets* are marvelous films, but I think that his political behavior was shameful. When I interviewed him he only gave some partial explanations for his actions but he didn't tell me everything.

Contrary to what many people said at that time, I don't think Kazan did it for money. It was more complex than that. It was as if he wanted to become more American than the Americans and this is how he could do it. I don't buy his claim that he did it in order to be anti-Stalinist. This is nonsense, as Martin Ritt put it, how could informing to the government about a small group of theatre and film actors and writers really hurt Stalin? This is something that I cannot accept, nor what he wrote in the *New York Times* about his actions. At the same time I cannot condemn all his work. I think *America, America* is a masterpiece and I think that out of his guilt he made some of the best American films.

Secondly, I don't think it is right to blame Kazan for everything. What about the people above him—people like Louis B. Mayer and other studio moguls who introduced this blacklist, and the agents who accepted and enforced it? These people are rarely quoted or written about. They are not attacked. Kazan behaved very, very badly, there is no doubt about this, but the blacklist could not have succeeded without Jack Warner and others. I think it is important to reveal all the others responsible for the blacklist. At the time, when I was doing the interviews for my book, I tended to concentrate on the people who behaved well, who are sometimes forgotten, people like Fred Zinneman, Robert Wise, and Otto Preminger, who has not been given due credit.

When I was promoting *'Round Midnight* I met a press agent who had been a communist and he told me that for many years Preminger had worked with him.

He said that when the FBI came to Preminger's office he refused to cooperate and drove them away. Dalton Trumbo always said that Preminger was the first to break the blacklist. The Academy never acknowledged the blacklist, they never said they were sorry about it and they never paid a tribute to the people whose careers were destroyed. They should have made a kind of global honor to the people whose careers were broken in the US—John Berry, Jo Losey, Abe Polonsky, Jules Dassin, and others.

RP: Could you explain what it was like working with Dirk Bogarde on *Daddy Nostalgia* [*Daddy Nostalgie*] and Dexter Gordon in *'Round Midnight*, both films now regarded as memorials to these great artists?
BT: Dirk Bogarde's contribution to *Daddy Nostalgia* was enormous. He was very literate, biting, but warm and funny and we got along very well during the shooting. I'd admired Dirk's work for many years and he mine. In fact, he had been part of the jury in Cannes that gave me the director's award for *A Sunday in the Country* [*Un Dimanche à la campagne*] but we had never actually met even though I had worked as a press agent on several Joe Losey films. I loved Bogarde in Losey's films, *Accident*, *The Servant*, and *King and Country*—but I also liked him in earlier films like *Hunted* where he is terrific. Bogarde was a very brave actor who wanted to experiment and worked to break his matinee star image. He fought to appear in *The Servant* and immediately agreed to work with someone who had been blacklisted.

One of the many important contributions he made to *Daddy Nostalgia* was the scene where he was in the car at the gas station talking to his daughter. We had just finished shooting the film but I felt that something else was needed and I remembered a conversation with him where he talked about pain. I called and asked him to write a scene about what it means to be in pain. Colo Tavernier, my ex-wife, had written the screenplay and it was brilliant with moments of great delicacy, but the scene Bogarde wrote is wonderful. I think I only changed one line and we shot it. It was marvelous. In a way he was like Michael Powell, someone who had no frontiers and was ready to work with anybody in the world. He disagreed with the attitude that sometimes prevailed in Britain, that British cinema should be an island onto itself. He always looked for serious and challenging work.

Dexter Gordon was tremendous but in a different way. He was very literate with a sharp sense of humor, a great knowledge of film, and incredible admiration for actors like George Sanders, Richard Burton and James Mason. Dexter said Mason sounded like tenor saxophone. He contributed thirty or forty lines to the film. The discussion "Do you like basketball?" was his. It was difficult though because we had to prevent him from drinking and many times the line between the screenplay and life was not clear. When he was drunk we could not work with him, we just stopped filming. Despite these problems he had an incredible relationship with the camera. It was as if he felt the thing, and we never did more than three takes for the dramatic scenes. He was always right and had a quality that sometimes takes some actors twenty years to achieve. When the film was released in America, Marlon Brando sent a letter to Dexter in which he said that for the first time in fifteen years he learnt something about acting. Dexter read me the letter over the phone and said, "After that who needs an Oscar?"

RP: Most of your earlier films, or at least those before *L.627*, are introspective. They are about death or people coming to the end of their lives. *It All Starts Today* is about the beginning of life, about teachers and very young children, with the main characters determined to change the situation they face.

BT: This is true. My first films were concerned about death and generally involved older people; they were never about people my own age. Probably this was a John Ford influence. He is perhaps the only American director who did lots of films about old people. It is only now that I have produced films about young people. I suppose there was a moment that produced a change for me and I had to find another relationship with the audience. I was now dealing with a new audience who was watching mainly American films, an audience that was much more ignorant and not interested in history.

Today a new generation of American filmmakers has emerged who are ignorant about the history of their own country, let alone the rest of the world and so we have action movies lost in their own technology and therefore not influenced by anything important. These are movies produced by people who have never opened a book, and it shows. They're dead films, because they all look and feel the same. This of course is a very, very bad situation. I didn't like it, but the change in the social and political situation in my own country demanded that I produce films that were a bit different, less lyrical, less contemplative, more urgent, more based on the notion of freedom, energy, and drive. I had to put myself in danger, even make my own internal revolution. My films now have the same kind of energy as the main characters—Daniel in my last film—but also in *L.627* and *Captain Conan* [*Capitaine Conan*]. The films travel at the same speed as the main character. In *L.627* we get the same feeling of instability.

One of the greatest compliments on my later films came from Alain Resnais who said these were films where you did not know what the next shot would be. This is because I am dealing with characters that do not know themselves what is going to happen next. My direction has to follow and create this atmosphere. In fact, I rarely produce movies that go from shot, to reverse shot, etc. I always try to avoid that. Either I do a long take, a complex camera movement, or I will break the scene with an unexpected close-up. I try to work that way, to get away from the rules and be free from formal conventions. Often as a director gets older the films became more crafted and softer. As I get older, my films have become more violent, more biting, faster than before. I am very proud of the films I've made and there is not one that I would say that I don't agree with or would change. Ken Loach and Bob Altman would also probably say the same thing about their films. This is rare. Many directors look at their earlier films and say that were forced to do this or that, and if they produced the film again they would change part or all of it. I don't feel this at all.

RP: You said that there was a turning point in France that produced a change in your films. Could you elaborate?

BT: It was the coming of the extreme right, the betrayal of Mitterrand, and the feeling that people had lost their grip on reality and did not want to find it, that produced this change in my work. Today most French politicians try to ignore reality, they act as if they are totally autistic. This makes me very, very angry. For me there are things that you just cannot remain silent about.

My father was a writer, who published a resistance literary journal in Lyon during World War II and he provided sanctuary for anti-Nazi intellectuals. My father always insisted that words were as important and as lethal as bullets and that writers (and therefore filmmakers) had real responsibilities to their audiences in this regard. I've never forgotten that. So I believe that every artist and intellectual has a moral responsibility to be faithful both to his characters and to his art; to tell the truth. If we were making films in the way the politicians work we would be out of business very quickly.

I learn so much from making films. Perhaps it is best to use what Michael Powell said in his memoirs, that he made films in order to learn. This is my approach. I knew nothing about pre-schools before making *It All Starts Today* but what I discovered made me very respectful of teachers and all those people who are fighting for the future.

Daniel, the head teacher at the school, is a hero but he is a hero who also makes mistakes. He is not some sort of Rambo of the school. He doesn't behave well with his girlfriend's son. He slaps him; he doesn't understand him. He makes a mistake with Mrs. Henri, which has dramatic consequences after he throws her out of the school. So he is not always right, but he is one of the unsung heroes of our time, ignored by political power, ignored by the people above him in the institutions, ignored by the media.

The media refuse to speak about such people and even when they produce a TV series about teachers it is so untrue it is ridiculous. There is nothing real about it. In fact, there is a series on French television about a teacher but the classes only have about ten kids in them and he is in a different city every episode. It is totally mad and there are never any consequences, yet people are dying as a result of government decisions. This is the reality.

The misery facing many workers, and especially in the area where the film was made, is not abstract—it kills people every day. Of course it is much more fashionable to be cynical and not be involved in the social fight—one doesn't talk about teachers and the problems they confront. But these teachers, social workers, and many others are preserving little islands of civilization, of life and happiness, in our society. For years when teachers and principals were fighting against the government they were told "this is not your job, you have to teach the children how to read and write." But how can you teach children who have not eaten, or are beaten up? Does the action of a teacher simply stop at the blackboard?

I have a great admiration for these foot soldiers, those that are fighting and suffering. As Kipling said, tell me the story of the foot soldier and I will tell you the story of every war. And these are the people who play the most crucial role in society, the key economic role. I am sure that there are people like Daniel in Australia and every country. The film tries to show this.

RP: The film portrays clashes between Daniel and local government officials and a mayor who claims to be a communist. What are your feelings about the generation of 1968 who have became part of the establishment and are imposing cuts to social programs?

BT: It is true that we have a lot of people who have betrayed, compromised, or accepted power. Some of those who were Maoists in 1968 now own advertising agencies, or others that said they were Trotskyists are running unions or have positions in the government. A lot of French intellectuals, who were right wing before 1968, then became communists, then Maoist, and now they say we have to be nonpolitical without ever acknowledging that they were wrong in the past.

RP: It is almost as if your film is a reaction against this.

BT: Absolutely. The film is saying that these politicians are not taking any notice of ordinary people. It tries to listen and respect what ordinary people are doing every day of their lives.

RP: What has been the response to the film in France?

BT: The reaction was incredible, a huge and unexpected success, and very well received from the communities, teachers, social workers, and educators. We have received thousands of letters and messages saying that the film is right and totally authentic. I even got a letter from a woman working for the electricity department. She told us the department did cut the power off to many houses in the fall and did not reconnect them during winter. In fact, since this film, there is going to be a law passed making it illegal to cut off the electricity to people who cannot pay their bills. Some teachers even told me that they had wanted to quit but have decided to continue. One said the film gave them another three years of courage to fight. I even received a letter from a psychiatrist who deals with teachers suffering from depression and he is using the film a lot and with great results. There have also been reports that some teachers who have seen the film have driven away the government inspectors from their schools. This is a great victory.

RP: And what was the reaction from the government and the education minister?
BT: I showed the film to the education minister but there was no dialogue. He told me after the screening that he thought the scene between the teacher and the inspector was very accurate. He said he loved the scene with the truck and then he went away to eat some sandwiches. I wanted him to meet the teachers from the area or somebody connected with the school but there was absolutely no dialogue with him. Nothing happened. The social welfare minister said the film was totally right and that she was working to change things. This has yet to be proven.

RP: Finally, can you provide some background on *The Other Side of the Tracks*, the film you made in 1997 in response to the government's anti-immigration laws?
BT: At that time sixty-six film directors signed a statement declaring that they would disobey the Debré Act, a law proposed by the right-wing government against immigrants. The law said that if anyone knew immigrants that did not have legal papers to stay in France, they were obliged to tell the police. I did not start the protest but I immediately signed the statement of protest. We all received a letter from the Paris housing minister saying we knew nothing about the problem of integration; that we were spoilt children and should live in these areas of high immigration for one month. The minister said we would see how terrible it was in these areas and change our minds. Each of us was assigned an area and so I decided to go with my son and meet the people from this area, in Montreuil, just outside Paris. We found many people outraged by this letter and so we met. We discussed things and I asked what could I do. I said I am not a politician, the only thing I could do is make a film about it and so they agreed. This film was a tremendous experience and I spent six months living in Montreuil. I met some incredible people and go back very often to meet and have dinner with them. In fact, one of the reasons why I cannot stay longer in Australia is because I have to return for a baptism on June 26 of a little baby from this area. I am the godfather of the child, which was named after the film's editor.

There are many things that I will never forget. One man I interviewed is Senegalese and he made some fantastic comments on integration. At one point he said integration should mean the right to live where you want, the way you want. "Do

I ask Chirac," he said, "if he is integrated, and who integrated him?" It was such a wonderful way of throwing the ball back to the people who keep talking about integration. The film had an important impact and the government allocated more money to the area because of the film. They now have proper basketball courts and other facilities.

Although I know that a lot of my films have played an important part in creating a discussion on many subjects, it is difficult to know the exact effect of my films because the results are not always so easily seen and I don't always keep track. But all the people concerned say that my films are true and are real and accurate. I am very proud to have achieved this—to have the imagination to make such films. Of course as the director this is my job, to invent and to dream. As Michael Powell said, we have to dream and invent, and out of this process produce something that will change the world.

RP: And your next project?

BT: I am working on a documentary about people condemned by what is called the double penalty. This is a law that prosecutes people who have broken the law, many of them for minor offenses, but who are doubly prosecuted because they are immigrants. I have been with them for a year, interviewing and collecting material. I also want to work on a screenplay; a kind of black comedy about the people who were doing films for German companies during the Nazi occupation of France. I don't know whether I can get the screenplay; it is something that I will work on.

The Spirit of Resistance: An Interview with Bertrand Tavernier

Sandy Flitterman-Lewis and Richard Porton / 2003

From *Cineaste* 28, no. 2 (Spring 2003). Reprinted with permission.

Cineaste: Life during the German Occupation is still not fully understood in France—not to mention the United States. Is this why you thought it was important to clarify these matters in *Safe Conduct* [*Laissez-Passer*]?

Bertrand Tavernier: Partially, yes, although there have been, especially in the last twenty years, a number of films on the subject. There haven't been many films, however, on the impact of the Occupation on the French film industry. In recent years, there have been two films that touched upon these matters—Bernard Cohn's *Natalia* (1989) and *Le plus beau pays du monde* (1998) [*The Happiest Place on Earth*], written by the well-known dramatist Jean-Claude Grumberg. The latter film had a very interesting subject—it dealt with a very shocking episode involving an actor who, while he was playing the lead in a film, was sent to a camp because he was homosexual. In order to finish the film, they had to record his voice while he was in the camp.

But that dealt with only one episode and I wanted to have a wider scope in my film. What interested me was the question: "What would I have done in the same situation?" Of course, it's always a matter of ego for directors to find a subject that hasn't been touched upon by other filmmakers. And there really have only been these two—and they both dealt with very special instances of persecution and less with the daily work of people in the film business. I was interested in people who were not protected by their status as stars—that's why I didn't deal with the special plight of actors. I wanted to deal with the foot soldiers of filmmaking. And, in my recent films, I've been particularly interested in various types of foot soldiers.

Cineaste: Such as the teacher in *It All Starts Today* [*Ça commence aujourd'hui*]?

Tavernier: Yes, the teacher or the cop in *L.627*, the people in *Life and Nothing*

But [*La Vie et rien d'autre*], even the characters in *Capitaine Conan*. These people are never the generals. I've never told a story from the point of view of the generals, but always from the perspective of people in the trenches. That's an intellectual explanation, but I'd also reacted quite strongly, and instinctively, to some of the stories Jean Aurenche and Jean Devaivre told me. Sometimes you just want to make a film because you react very strongly on an emotional level to something you've read or heard. For example, I wanted to re-create this scene with the bombs dropping and the babies being saved from the nursery. That was something I've never seen in a film. The nurses and doctors have left their posts. It's somewhat symbolic of the state of France at that time—when everyone in charge had left his or her posts. Even though I didn't shoot it that way. People at first go there for selfish reasons to protect their own children. When they discover other children, they change and become altruistic. I found this evolution both fascinating and meaningful.

Cineaste: Did Aurenche tell you stories about life at Continental Films?
Tavernier: Yes. Some of these stories are told in Aurenche's memoirs, *La suite a l'ecran*, which was published by the Lumiere Institute. It's a superb book and very funny. A few of the scenes which turn up in my film, like the lunch with Greven in the restaurant where he's asked if he knows any Jewish screenwriters, are included in this book. Aurenche also told me that this was very frightening—one of the worst moments of his life.

Cineaste: Did Aurenche find temporary refuge in a brothel as is depicted in the film?
Tavernier: Yes, he told me about that as well as stories about the poor man who hunts cats and was then beaten to death. By the way, the man who plays that part is not an actor. I interviewed him for my documentary, *The Other Side of the Tracks* [*De L'Autre Côté du périph'*]. Since he was jobless, I gave him a small part. What I love about the film are the very quick shifts in tone from comedy to something truly horrible. The character of the gangster was Jean Cosmos's idea. It was based on his cousin who was with the French Gestapo and made Jean's life miserable. Every time he met Jean, he asked him, "Why aren't you in Germany?" And Jean said that this man boasted of beating up, and killing, the famous actor Harry Baur. I think this is the first film which makes allusions to the fact that Harry Baur was killed by the French Gestapo. It's a bizarre, and tragic, coincidence, that two of the actors who died during the war—Harry Baur and Robert Lynen (he was in the Resistance and tortured by the Germans)—were the stars of the sound version of Duvivier's *Poil de carotte* [*The Red Head*].

It was a crazy period. This was a time when a man named Pierre Caron, who directed a film called *Pension Jonas* in 1942, had his director's card revoked on the grounds of "imbecility." [Laughs.] The man was trafficking with the Germans. He sold them railway tracks that couldn't be fitted together. So they complained after he sold them a lot of useless railway tracks. [Laughs.] In fact, he was a crook! He finally found refuge in Spain. *Pension Jonas* developed a cult reputation because of this.

Cineaste: You mentioned in another interview that no one took the effort to interview Greven before his death.

Tavernier: That's true. This is something that both puzzles and exasperates me because the man was the head of UFA before the war in 1936 or 1937 and then was appointed head of Continental by Goebbels. He went on working within the German cinema until 1972 and no one ever bothered to research his role in these events or interview him. There are a lot of questions left unanswered—like how he could employ someone like Jean-Paul Le Chanois, who was known as a Jew and a Communist—and who was wanted under his real name, Jean-Paul Dreyfus? Everyone knew that Dreyfus was Le Chanois. A man who was wanted by the Germans worked for a year and a half in a German production company!

Cineaste: Didn't he brag that he had a Jew working for him?

Tavernier: Yes, all the time! It's in my film. And many people said that he called Le Chanois Dreyfus openly in front of other people. How could a German production company make films that didn't have a hint of Nazi or pro-German propaganda? And how could they produce a film based on a book by Emile Zola, a writer hated by the Nazis? There are many mysteries. The purpose of the film was not to solve them. That would have been untrue. But I try to show that you can never accept anything said by a character as gospel. When Greven says to Aurenche that he wants to work with Jewish screenwriters, you've previously witnessed a scene with a composer forced to resign from the studio because he's Jewish. This is the opposite of what he says during his conversation with Aurenche.

Cineaste: It's linked to the paradoxical nature of the French film industry during this period.

Tavernier: It's part of the paradox of the times, which I wanted to capture. I wanted the camera to observe the events—the feelings and the emotions—of those times, as if it wasn't burdened with the knowledge we have today. Most of the characters have only a fragmentary knowledge of what's going on. One of the best compliments I received came from a young woman, who in a Q and A after a screening remarked, "Mr. Tavernier, I feel that I've been parachuted into that period." Usually, when I do a period film, it's as if I was looking at the inside of a house from the outside. In this film, I was inside the house.

Cineaste: How did you achieve this degree of realism?

Tavernier: That was my obsession—to make sure that the camera was always in the middle of events, never observing from an exterior or detached point of view. I never wanted the camera to be a witness who knew more than the characters. When I directed a scene, I had to forget my knowledge of events in order to preserve the characters' own uncertainty.

Cineaste: The ability to capture fleeting moments is especially striking in the sequence when Aurenche's future girlfriend witnesses a bus packed with Jews speeding down the street.

Tavernier: Yes, this is something my co-screenwriter, Jean Cosmos, witnessed. He was walking in the street one day and suddenly he saw a bus. I wanted this to come as a surprise. You've just seen people queuing for food and no one reacts or is angry. Just one young woman sees this, and she's totally puzzled by what she's seen. I wanted to include horrifying details that almost seemed to happen accidentally. Life was proceeding with all of its little problems and suddenly you were confronted with something terrifying. Since people are used to seeing horrifying images on screen, I had to be very economical and avoid being preachy. My problem was that Devaivre never saw this, so I couldn't link this incident with his character. I invented certain things, but this would be too serious an invention. So I used a trick, transmitting this information through a young woman played by Maria Pitarresi, who's connected to his character.

Cineaste: How did you cast the two leads—an important decision given the fact that they are playing actual historical figures—one of whom is still alive?

Tavernier: I never use a casting director and do all the casting myself. I find it a pleasure. I go to the theater frequently and spend a great deal of time meeting actors. In this film, I'm using many actors I've never worked with. For a long time, I wanted to work with Jacques Gamblin, who plays Devaivre. I've seen Denis Podalydès on the stage of the Comédie Française about twenty times and always admired him. I'm very proud of the casting, since there are about 119 roles in the film and I don't think there is one mistake. Some of the actors, such as the man who plays Charles Spaak, I've worked with before. He played a totally opposite sort of character in *Capitaine Conan*.

I wanted to show that some of these actors, who don't get many chances to work in films, are very good and have a very wide range. Among the actresses, Marie Desgranges was brilliant as Portia in a production of *The Merchant of Venice* and I discovered that she could sing very well. So I added the moment where she sings a Kurt Weill song. Marie Gillain had played in *Fresh Bait* [*L'Appât*] and I think she's wonderful. It's very much an ensemble film; it's not uncommon to have ten or fifteen actors in the same shot. I often thought of Robert Altman's *Nashville* when shooting the film. When I had a problem, I always thought, "What would Altman do?" You always have the feeling that Altman is in the middle of the action; he avoids looking at life from a distant, exteriorized point of view and captures the incredible energy of living in specific moments.

Cineaste: And you also use overlapping conversations that are reminiscent of Altman.

Tavernier: Yes, I love that. I wanted actors who were able to speak quickly and move quickly.

Cineaste: You've moved from the very intimate, contemporary narrative of *It All Starts Today* to the epic, historical scope of *Safe Conduct*. Do you like to alternate the scale of your projects?

Tavernier: Yes, but there is one link. I had a desire to bring the audience as close to the people of the forties as they were to the children of the previous film. I wanted the audience to view the characters of *Safe Conduct* as contemporaries. But I love to alternate. Even when I was shooting *Capitaine Conan*, I was working on a documentary about immigration with my son Nils that's never been shown in the United States. I went from working with a very elaborate set and an enormous crew, special effects that I'd never had before, to Lyon where it was only me and my son operating the camera. I love this sort of contrast.

Cineaste: Although you had been familiar with Aurenche's stories for years, I understand that the structure of the film came together once you heard Devaivre's anecdotes.

Tavernier: Yes, all of the stories Aurenche told me—since he was a screenwriter—pertained to events that occurred before films were shot. Screenwriters never came to the set, or at least very rarely. Something was missing, and Aurenche couldn't tell me about relationships between the people making the film. He had a working relationship with Autant-Lara, and perhaps I could have explored that. But I don't think I could have gained much from pursuing that angle. When I met Devaivre, he immediately filled in the blanks and provided all that was missing in that story—how the films were made and the frenetic atmosphere of the studio. I wanted to convey both the bleakness and colorlessness of the oppression, as well as the incredible energy and craziness that prevailed during that period. People weren't alone and frightened in a room; it was completely the opposite.

Cineaste: Alain Resnais's *Night and Fog* [*Nuit et brouillard*] deals with the contrast between the bleakness of the period and daily life.

Tavernier: Yes, but Resnais's film is difficult to compare with my film because it deals with the Holocaust. No one in my film is really connected with the Holocaust, because the cinema world was more protected. But I agree that Resnais deals with these oppositions. That film is a total masterpiece.

Cineaste: You're a great cinephile and I'd imagine that you were attracted to this project because of your fondness for certain directors who play a role in the script. Are you, to take one example, a fan of Maurice Tourneur's films?

Tavernier: Yes, I like some of his films, especially his silents, and some historians like William Everson think he's as important as Griffith—citing, for example, *The Last of the Mohicans*, which he codirected with Clarence Brown. His best film from the wartime period is *La Main du Diable*—it's quite a remarkable film. Devaivre liked him a lot and worked with him several times.

Cineaste: Although Clouzot is not a character in your film, the subversive nature of *Le Corbeau* [*The Raven*] is alluded to. Recent scholarship has made much of the fact that, despite being produced by Continental, it's very critical, albeit allegorically, of Vichy.

Tavernier: It's very critical of the status quo, especially of informers. It's incredibly adult, strong, and ambitious for its time. At the time of Vichy, it features an atheist character. It refers to abortion, and the emphasis on the sex lives of the characters is incredible. After the liberation, the film was unfairly attacked by some critics, especially Georges Sadoul who said that it reminded him of *Mein Kampf*.

Cineaste: That seems like a serious misreading.

Tavernier: The puritanical attitude of some elements of the left, especially the Communist Party, was absurd. They were trapped by the myth of the positive hero. They assumed it was conveying a degrading image of France. I don't think that was true; although the film is critical, it's also quite compassionate. So they invented this notion that it was a German conception of a typical French town. This was a total lie; the film was never released in Germany because it was considered too pessimistic. In many respects, it could be considered a film of the Resistance.

Cineaste: It's noteworthy that the characters who triumph in *Le Corbeau*, such as the abortionist, are all outsiders.

Tavernier: Yes, it's quite remarkable. Many of the films released by Continental had strong satirical elements; they're anti-Church and antibourgeois.

Cineaste: Of course, after the war Clouzot was attacked as a collaborationist.

Tavernier: Some of the directors at Continental were forced to sign contracts because Greven had taken control of French productions. If directors didn't sign, thousands of people would have been out of work. For Clouzot, the situation was different. He agreed to be the executive in charge of screenplays—he was not signing a contract for one or two films but for a job. That being said, everyone agrees that, once Clouzot had signed on, he behaved extraordinarily well. He protected Jews, and you can't reproach him for anything. You can only criticize him for having accepted the job.

Cineaste: This goes back to the question you posed earlier. How do you think you would have behaved under such circumstances?
Tavernier: Maybe I would have behaved like Aurenche, who refused to work for Continental. Like Aurenche, like Prévert, like Pierre Bost and some other screenwriters. On the other hand, some of the screenwriters who accepted, like Charles Spaak, behaved very bravely and decently. You can't find any political mistakes in their screenplays.

Cineaste: Your film makes clear that, in the midst of the war, people accepted work at Continental for all kinds of reasons.
Tavernier: Yes, for all kinds of reasons. Sometimes you have to question historians who have a scholarly approach to history that is merely based on documents instead of life. There has been a tendency to attach the label "collaborator" to everyone who worked at Continental and this is not true. Something very interesting happened after the film was released in France. I received a phone call from a woman named Rosine Delamare, who is one of the greatest costume designers in France. She said that she had seen the film and loved it. She told me that she worked at Continental on six films including *Le Corbeau* and *Au Bonheur des Dames* and remarked, "You totally captured the atmosphere of those sets." We started talking and I asked her, "Did you feel that you were a collaborator?" She replied, "No, we had to work. After 1942, if you found any work it was German. I was working with directors I had known before the war on films with very decent, interesting screenplays. And I was active in the Resistance. Like Devaivre, I rode one hundred miles on a bicycle to report to my superior. When I started my first film, it was only at the end of the shoot that I discovered that I was in a German production company."

That means the reality was much more complex than people realize. The Germans and Greven were smart. Another reaction from a viewer I liked was from someone who said she never realized how difficult and complex every daily choice became during this period. At least half of the people involved just wanted to survive. Most of them acted very decently, a few were genuine collaborators, and a few were trying to resist.

Cineaste: While most of the reviews of *Safe Conduct* in France were quite favorable, it seems that some critics, particularly those at *Cahiers du cinema* viewed the film, not from a historical perspective, hut through the lens of old debates between the New Wave and the "tradition of quality." From all appearances, they wanted to reduce the film to a debate between *Cahiers* and *Positif.*

Tavernier: They saw it only through that lens and that, for me, was totally disappointing. They said it was an attack on the New Wave. The last line of the editorial commenting on *Laissez-Passer* was, "The New Wave is the great 'absence' in the film." This is like saying, "The New Iranian Cinema is not a strong presence in *Paths of Glory.*" Or "*Salt of the Earth* should have made reference to the Coen Brothers!" These people are a million miles away from the realities of the creative act. No one is going to spend three years of their life making a film about two styles of criticism.

Truffaut said that no one makes a film merely to attack another artist. It would be easier to write a pamphlet. And I admire the New Wave. I worked as a press agent for Godard, Chabrol, Varda, Demy, and Rozier, and I fought for them. *Cahiers* can't conceive that you can be interested in both Truffaut and Autant-Lara.

Cineaste: I wonder if Truffaut pulled a number on us. Many of us became interested in film through his essays and took his denunciations of Bost and Aurenche for granted.

Tavernier: Yes, but even with Truffaut you have to go deeper. It's much more complex. First of all, Truffaut never attacked the films made during the forties. He attacked the films of the fifties. And in the fifties he wrote a very good review of Autant-Lara's *La Traversee de Paris* [*Four Bags Full*]. In 1976, he wrote an incredible foreword to one of Andre Bazin's books in which he said that you can speak of a New Wave—even though the phrase hadn't been coined yet—when discussing the French cinema of 1940 to 1944. He claimed that more than eighty important films, or masterpieces, were made during that time. At a time when the Italian cinema was almost totally fascist, he maintained that the French cinema almost totally avoided being Petainist. The people editing *Cahiers* now don't seem to be aware of this. I found this horrendous. There's something degrading about it. It's as if there was a fatwa issued against some filmmakers that you weren't allowed to defend.

Truffaut was right about some things and wrong about others. I think he was wrong in choosing Aurenche as a target. As the director Paul Vecchiali said, Aurenche was the figure during that period who comes closest to the spirit of the New Wave. He was right in that many films made during the fifties were quite stiff and academic. For example, the films Marcel Carné made during the fifties were incredibly bad and dull. But Truffaut was unfair to some people, and even he changed his mind later on. So his disciples, *Cahiers* among them, are being totally fundamentalist.

Cineaste: But, *Cahiers* notwithstanding, the cinema of the Occupation is being rediscovered in France.

Tavernier: Yes, *Cahiers* never devoted any articles to the French cinema of this period and it reveals a great ignorance. They never studied the directors and all of the contradictions. Jacques Siclier, on the other hand, wrote a tremendous book on the cinema of Vichy. Noel Burch and Genevieve Sellier have written an excellent book in which they totally rehabilitate Autant-Lara and observe that some of the films written by Aurenche were strongly feminist, and some, such as *Douce* [*Love Story*], are about class struggle. And they are! It's a shame that people don't know them here. They should be shown in this country and available on DVD, along with the films of Jacques Becker and Robert Bresson.

Cineaste: Although it's not as ambitious as your film, a recent movie such as *La Guerre à Paris* also attempts to deal with this period.

Tavernier: Yes, and of course there's Costa-Gavras's film, *Amen*. But already, even in the forties there were films such as the overlooked *Retour a la vie* [*Return to Life*] (1949). That's an episodic film, and there's one section by Clouzot, which deals with the return of a prisoner that's extraordinary. And a film like *La Traversee de Paris* makes a strong statement while being very funny. As you can see in my film, it was a revenge of Aurenche against suitcases. He made that film about two people who were forced to carry enormous suitcases around Paris, just as he did during the Occupation.

Cineaste: How did you come to work with Aurenche on your first film, *The Clock-maker* [*L'Horloger de Saint-Paul*]?

Tavernier: Since *The Clockmaker* dealt with conflicts between the generations, I wanted to work with a screenwriter who was older than myself. I needed someone who could invest a lot of time in the project and who wasn't so fashionable that he'd take off after eight weeks and wouldn't be around for rewriting. I looked at a lot of films made by older screenwriters. I found Maurice Auberge, who had worked on several films with Jacques Becker, and whose work was incredibly modern and sharp—not at all old-fashioned. And I also discovered the team of Aurenche and Bost through *Douce*. I was impressed that they included a line encouraging "impatience and revolt" in a film made in 1942.

Cineaste: Wasn't that line cut by the censors?

Tavernier: It was cut after a month. The complete version played for about three or four weeks and that line inspired a lot of applause. Then the scene was cut. The censors were very smart; they were smarter than many of the critics. The scene was restored after the liberation. It's a very strong scene. My diary in the journal

Projections—published in English—includes my meeting with Devaivre, an article on *Douce*, and reflections on the death of Aurenche.

Cineaste: In certain respects, you're functioning as a film historian, as well as a filmmaker, in *Safe Conduct*.

Tavernier: I never wanted to make a film that was just about the cinema. It's possible to appreciate this film and get caught up in the emotions of the characters without knowing anything about Le Chanois or Aurenche. You can understand the spirit of resistance, even if you don't know who is who. Some young kids in France just saw it as an adventure film, although it gave them a desire to learn more about the period and the films. Part of my job is to pass on to an audience the discoveries I made while making the film—as well as the passion and curiosity I experienced while making those discoveries. When I was making *The Other Side of the Tracks*, I filmed a very old worker who talked about his experiences in factories and his life as a Communist. The man was incredibly moving. When I filmed him for the last time, he said to me, "Continue and transmit." It was one of the most incredibly moving moments in my life. The pleasure of making a film involves communicating a little bit of that spirit to the audience.

Cineaste: Historical memory?

Tavernier: Yes, if you succeed in making an historical film it won't be merely historical. The spirit of the Resistance did not die in 1945. You can adapt it very easily to today's concerns.

Cineaste: Of course, along with your passion for French cinema, you also have a long-standing interest in Hollywood cinema. This is even apparent in your recent statement on the refusal of the State Department to grant a visa to Kiarostami, in which you invoke Billy Wilder, among others.

Tavernier: I was horrified by what happened to Kiarostami. And I adore Billy Wilder and always view his films with pleasure. It was wonderful how he was able to retain his integrity over all those projects. I'm particularly fond of one of his less-known films, *Ace in the Hole*. That's a masterpiece—and so contemporary! We met several times; he was a great admirer of *The Clockmaker* and *The Judge and the Assassin* [*Le Juge et l'assassin*].

There are several films that look even better now than when they were made. Not only *Ace in the Hole*. There's also *The Grapes of Wrath* and *Salt of the Earth*. And there are several extremely strong Frankenheimer films—*Seven Days in May* and *The Manchurian Candidate*. These films seem brand new. Frankenheimer's last film on LBJ, *The Path to War*, is a masterpiece. Outside of the documentaries of Michael Moore, this is the best American political film of the last ten years. This last film is incredibly moving, because you have the feeling that, despite certain mistakes in his career, he retained the political commitment of the sixties—the commitment you find in *The Manchurian Candidate* and *Seven Days in May* is in every frame of *The Path to War*. So many other directors capitulated; it's not that they made bad films, but you feel that they're washed up. But you get the same comfort watching Frankenheimer's work as you do watching the films of Ken Loach—the comfort that some directors have not sold out.

An Interview with Bertrand Tavernier on Documentary Filmmaking

Isabelle Meerstein / 2006

From *Point of View*, no. 22 (March 2006). Reprinted with permission.

Isabelle Meerstein: Mr. Tavernier, thank you for accepting this interview on the morning of your return to Paris. I would like to ask about your documentary work. What is your approach to editing for the documentary; how much footage do you discard, how much do you keep in the finished film?

Bertrand Tavernier: Well, that depends on the film. Generally, we are faced with a lot of footage, and I am no exception to this rule. And so we need sometimes to take our time to find out how to organize the material.

For *La Guerre sans nom* [*The Undeclared War*, 1992], I had forty or fifty hours of material that I reduced to four hours. I cut and cut. Some things are easy to discard, such as uninteresting moments or people. So, there are those things that at first glance you have to get rid of. They amount to 20 percent or 30 percent of all the footage.

And then, you have to discover organically the structure of your film, it's in there, somewhere. That architecture cannot be imposed from the outside. We hadn't decided on a structure before the shoot. We were not merely illustrating a point when we were shooting *The Undeclared War* or *De l'autre côté du périph* [*The Other Side of the Tracks*, 1997]. You have to find your structure at the editing stage. We applied to both films more or less the same principle: switching between two ways of narration. Going from an all-encompassing one that tells a collective story to an individual story, so you tell the story of the group and then you interrupt it suddenly to focus on one single experience. Then you go back to something more general, before switching back again onto one single person, and so on. And so, at some point in our editing process, for both *La Guerre sans nom* and *De l'autre côté du périph*, we had discovered recurring topics, which in turn introduced us to so many parts under so many themes. For instance, in *La Guerre sans nom*, the following themes emerged: grub, fear, exactions, torture, and seeing one's fellow soldiers dead. So you find your structure little by little.

But there are certain things that escape a clear discrimination, I mean when something forms the core of a subject, it shows up both in a theme and in a character, so you leave it in both. You leave those things both in the collective drama and in the individual drama. In short, that's it. It requires you to grope your way, it takes time to reach it, to find it. Time to manage to keep that impression of paths that cross. Ultimately it's that individual emotion.

IM: Do you always work with the same editor?

BT: Well, I try . . . but sometimes, there are things in the way of that. For example, both *La Guerre sans nom* and *De l'autre côté du périph* were edited by Luce Grunenwald, but she died just after finishing that second film. She died because of a mistake during a liver transplant, so I could no longer work with her. Then I took Sophie Brunet. Very often I take people who can go from documentary to fiction, people who are able to alternate between both, and who take pleasure in doing so. That's Sophie Brunet to a T. Luce had been the assistant of my editor Armand Psenny for years, and then she became my editor. As for Sophie, I met her when we were producing *Veillée d'armes* [*The Troubles We've Seen: A History of Journalism in Wartime*, 1994] by Marcel Ophüls. She was the editor of Marcel Ophüls. So I told myself that if she could survive Ophüls, then she would be able to survive me! And that was it.

IM: Can you tell me, please, about the use of sounds in your documentary practice, live sound and those background sounds that are so present in your films?

BT: Very often, I go back to a place to try and get more. In *La Guerre sans nom* I was working with the sound engineer who works on all my features. We had gathered a lot of live sound; great ambient sounds, individual sounds very useful for the editing. While shooting in Algeria, the Algerian sound engineer had little experience of live sound because at the time, in Algeria, most was done in post-sync. If they needed a live sound, they would ask a French guy to come over. And yet, he managed two or three lovely ambient sounds.

There are times I want to keep the ambient sound even if it is aggressive. That sometimes compels us to be acrobats! And sometimes, in my documentaries, this led us to make mistakes; sometimes the mics were badly placed; we were less experienced but in the end, it all came out all right.

IM: There is always quite a strong texture, with music too . . .

BT: Yes, I work a lot with musical moments. The purpose is to give some breathing space, to offer openness, calm, distance, and lyricism inside the narrative. I also include a lot of songs. In *La Guerre sans nom*, there was no original music. Instead, we had songs the participants were referring to, like songs the soldier told me they used to listen to during meal-time. They were listening to Gloria Lasso singing *L'étranger au paradis*. Or Yves Montand; I included several of his songs. The soldiers also listened to Sydney Bechet's *Petite Fleur* a lot.

But there was one thing I did not do. I ran into a conflict over a song with an executive of the production company that was doing *La Guerre sans nom*—not Mr Guérin who was great, but someone else. There was a man, a male character in the film, a worker, who said that prior to taking part to all those battles,[1] he used to sing all the time. He worked in a factory. And there was a song he used to sing often, *C'était mon copain* [*He was my buddy*], the famous song by the late Gilbert Bécaud. And then, there came a day when, having seen so many of his buddies dying in the dirty war, he said: "I will never sing again." And *that* exec was telling me that I *had* to include that very song in the film! So I told this person: "That's the very thing I will never do." When a bloke says he will never sing that song again, I won't put it in, no way. He refuses to sing it. I would use another song; I used *Un jour, tu verras* [*One day, you'll see*] sung by Mouloudji. I believe I was getting the same result, the same melancholy. There is a guy who says: "I cannot bear to hear that song ever again" and then you include it!? I find that despicable! All of a sudden, you just would violate the private life of one of your characters. I am very reluctant to do such a thing. Oh, it would certainly have "paid off" emotionally, the viewers would have had tears in their eyes, but the price to pay was very questionable to me!

IM: And this leads me to another question about the way you approach reality. You are obviously not a TV person who seeks to induce a very strong emotion, a shock in the viewer to get attention. How do you bring about an emotion? What is an emotion made of, according to you? How do you seek it, also, regarding your characters?

BT: I try to understand, yes, I do. I try to let someone speak, to give my characters the time they need to speak at length. And, yes, that gives a style that is not even remotely fashionable nowadays on TV. What is hot on TV is this: people you let utter only two or three sentences, you try and get them to say two or three very striking things. That's all fine for TV shows such as *Envoyé special* [on the French public channel France 2], for reportages. But for a documentary, I think that's not it at all! A documentary involves coming to an understanding of your characters. I very often deal with people who have never been given a voice, I mean an opportunity to say things in their own words. With them, I cannot just take a sentence, just like that, just for the sake of the point I want to make. I must respect their way of thinking, of reacting, and sometimes, their hesitations. Because a hesitation in their speech is the very thing that will give the scene its emotion, that thing they find hard to say. If I shoot and keep only the emotional sentence such as someone crying and if I don't show the way he/she holds his/her tears, struggles with their emotions, I lose very important things: what I lose is that very groping for one's thoughts. I lose a palette of sentences, of words, which belong to his/her profession, to his/her origins or culture and so, no, I don't feel like cutting it out! In *Histoires de vies brisées* [*Stories of Broken Lives*, 2001], I even went very far in that direction. I was a bit compelled to do so because some material we had shot went missing: cutaways. We had characters, men and women who had been hunger-striking for forty days. There was a great urgency in them. They wanted to speak. They had to speak. Everyone could see it was very difficult. I didn't have to encourage them to speak. I *had to* let them speak. I had to respect them. It had to go far, they had to get to the bottom of what they wanted to say, to release it all. For example, at the beginning of the film, one of the participants is speaking. And little by little it builds into an extraordinary emotion. But it becomes such an intense emotion thanks to the fact that we have taken our time, that we have given them all the time they needed.

There are people who work for public channels in France who tell me: "We will buy your film when it has been turned into an audio-visual product." That is to say when those moments of listening have been cut out. That makes me really mad! I am also enraged by the fact that in our world, we are so scared to just listen to someone who is speaking, so scared that we want to turn that into "cinema," into a *show*! And so, we cut instead to documents such as photographs, archive excerpts, objects. Ah, I can't believe it! When someone speaks, don't you know? You just do *not* interrupt them. Ah, but in some TV talk-shows, what do they do? They make it a priority to interrupt people non-stop! In some broadcasts, it's even become a trademark. There are presenters who have built their notoriety on interrupting their guests systematically! I am for letting the viewers listen to those who are speaking. In daily life too. I like to be listened to sometimes and other times I feel like giving someone else the space to speak and be listened to. It really is worth taking five more minutes without interrupting, without cutting it out, in order to try and understand what is happening. And that is always *complex*, it *cannot* be summarized into five or six striking sentences.

IM: From a practical point of view, where do you position yourself physically in relation to the camera and sound recording, when you are in that process of listening?
BT: I *never* hold the camera. First of all, I am not a good camera person. A few times I happened to hold the boom, yes, and to deal with the sound recording, but it's not my thing, really. What I want is to be close to people, and to look all around me in order to see the context, and to catch a good cutaway opportunity.

What matters to me is to be the one who is listening. Often, I have by my side my son, Nils, who, unlike me, handles the camera very well. He's great. He's very quick. Sometimes, he would cut too soon. And yet, once he did not listen when I said: "Cut!" and he was so right. There was someone who burst into tears in front of the camera and he let the camera roll and that was good because that moment when the person was weeping was excellent. I trust Nils very much. I'm relaxed with him. I let him shoot the way he feels like it. Now and then, I would ask him for a specific shot but generally I focus essentially on what's happening in the scene. To answer your question more precisely: I am beside Nils. Sometimes also, I am opposite the person I am speaking with so as to let her/him see me and not speak and gaze into the camera lens! I need to be in contact with the person I am listening to. Or at other times, the camera is behind me with a long lens. Or a wide angle if I need to appear in the shot. And also, Nils moves around. He moves in. Or if the camera is on a dolly, he zooms in with a similar effect, and he frames the shot in several different ways, maybe over-the-shoulder, or close-ups if that's what he feels the shot needs. But very often, he will position himself so as to be comfortable. He will handle the camera, carry it or put it on a tripod, then he feels something is going on or I signal to him to go closer and so he does. We get on really well. It's special. The shots he did for *De l'autre côté du périph* or for *Histoires de vies brisées* and the shots other people did, nobody can tell the difference. So it means on the one hand that there is a great, obvious unity, and on the other there is a way of seeing, a common vision in all those films.

Another thing that is very important: as far possible, I try not to meet the participants prior to the shooting. I try to avoid meeting them in order to prepare them, to talk with them beforehand. I really think this is bad for a film. That is the lesson I learned from Marcel Ophüls who used to say: "You must never meet your protagonists and talk with them before the shooting."

In the case of *La Guerre sans nom*, how did we select the participants? We still had to see if their story was a bit interesting, so there was someone whose job was to determine this. Georges Mattei was the researcher on that film. You see, if you have someone telling too much of what they have lived through, when we reach the shoot, this person will feel he or she has already said it all. That has happened to me. I remember that man who had practiced torture in Algeria. He had in later years been so disturbed by his experience that he had seriously envisaged becoming a monk. And he said that to us before the shoot. Of course, when the camera was on, he would not say it again. We tried hard to get him to repeat his experience, but to no avail. It was just too late. The moment had passed. So you've got to be extremely careful with that kind of stuff, you must never dry up your witnesses, your participants. You must take great care. And if when you are shooting, you don't get anything because it's too early, your participants and you don't know each other yet, it's too close to the first meeting, what do you do? Well, of course you see them again, but you won't speak of *the* matter. One, two, or three months later, you get back to them. [You have had time to build trust in the meantime.]

With my documentaries, there are a few very clear rules: the participants know, I tell each person each time we are filming that they can come back whenever they feel like it if they realise they have not said something they wanted to, or if they are unhappy with something, we would always welcome them. The people can also watch the rushes, they can drop in the editing room to see how they have done. They let me know what they think, and I take them onboard—or not! But I do not hide anything. I tell my participants: "This film is also *your* film, so you have to feel we haven't come here to film you against your will, or that we are going to distort what you say. You can check." The greatest compliment I got came with *La Guerre sans nom*. After the screening, all thirty participants said they felt we had *perfectly* respected what they wanted to say, even though we had cut so much out. They could recognize themselves in the film. They had not been misrepresented. There was nothing they had regrets about.

IM: That is a compliment indeed. And finally, I wanted to ask your definition of a critical mind?
BT: A critical mind is something you must keep ticking on at all times when you make a documentary. It is to tell yourself: "What this person is telling me, it's great, but is it accurate?" It is so only when you can back it up with one, two, three, or four other people. So exercising your critical mind is not to sacrifice everything straight away and accept immediately a detail that can be striking, or funny, or tragic. Or suddenly very shocking so as to make a show. It's about constantly questioning everything, doubting everything. Not "Is he telling me the truth?" because that's too simple, because there are always several kinds of truth. It's to tell oneself: "Isn't he painting too black a picture of the situation?" or the opposite: "Isn't he embellishing the facts?" Or: "Isn't this too picturesque a detail?" For example, the fact that quite a few French conscripts were given World War I rifles in the Algerian War of Independence. But then you hear the same story from a guy who did not and could not have known the first guy. And a third, and a fourth who was somewhere else. So you tell yourself: "Ok, that's not *too* good to be true. I can keep that." And anything that has been told only once, I mean by one single person, I discard. So to have a critical mind is this: to tell yourself that the person you are filming, who is certainly innocent, is he or she to be believed just like that? No, you have got to get to the other side, to hear the story from the opposition. When the young lads were complaining about the police in *De l'autre côté du périph*, we got to hear what the other party had to say. You must get the other version, the other point of view!

Notes

Isabelle Meerstein wishes to acknowledge Niamh Sweeney, administrator of Alliance Française de Cork, Ireland (AFC); Nora Callanan, president of the AFC; and Professor Richard Raskin, former editor of *Point of View*, Aarhus University, Denmark. She dedicates this interview to the memory of Ms. Laure Ecker-Tripier, the late cultural attaché of the French Embassy in Dublin.

1. The French government called the Algerian War of Independence (1954–62) *les événements*, "The Events; The Troubles"; hence the title of the film, whose literal translation would be "the war without a name."

Interview with Bertrand Tavernier:
I Believed in Robicheaux's Visions

Elise Domenach and Philippe Rouyer / 2009

From *Positif*, no. 578 (April 2009). Reprinted by permission. Translated by T. Jefferson Kline.

Elise Domenach & Philippe Rouyer: Why did you wait so long before making a feature fiction film in the United States?

Bertrand Tavernier: It wasn't for a lack of proposals. I received lots of subjects. In particular a scenario for *LA Confidential* that was different from Curtis Hanson's version. But despite my love for James Ellroy, I didn't see what I could have brought to the project that would have been better than a lot of American filmmakers would have done. And as I had no desire to have a career in the US, if I was going to do a film here it would have to be on my terms and with a subject that I'd thought of myself. I'd had a very good experience on *Autour de Minuit* [*'Round Midnight*], thanks to Irwin Winkler, who supported and protected me. With him, I'd started a project on the subject of blacklisting. I'd asked Abraham Polonsky to write the screenplay. But I never succeeded in getting what I wanted. All the scenes ended the same way by making the protagonist right. I never stopped asking whether he was sometimes wrong, but it was impossible. I ended up by abandoning the project. And Irwin Winkler ended up shooting *The Blacklist* as we know. I have to say that the creation of the scenario was done in the American way: the screenwriter goes off by himself and incorporates into his script more or less the desiderata of the filmmaker with whom he's met. But I've always done things differently. My screenwriters do two or three scenes and submit them. I critique them, they make corrections and we go on like that.

D&R: So that's how you proceeded with *Dans La Brume électrique* [*In the Electric Mist*]?

BT: Yes, I'm the one who initiated the project. I chose James Lee Burke's novel and looked for an American producer since I'd seen too many people lose fortunes trying to do without one. I tried contacting Irwin Winkler, who didn't answer, before proposing it to Michael Fitzgerald, who, with *Wise Blood*, *The Pledge*, and *Three Burials*, had put together a very impressive film list. The financing was done by TFI International, a little bit of money scraped together in Louisiana and the rest, money that Fitzgerald got from Kazakhs. He was the one who suggested the screenwriters from *The Pledge*, Jerzy and Mary Olson-Kromolowski, assuring me that they knew the South really well, though he's Polish and she's of Danish origins. I met them and read a beautiful adaptation of *While I Lay Dying* by Jerzy. I was supposed to do the film with Sean Penn as producer. But they quarreled and it never got made.

D&R: When you wrote the scenario, did you know the terrain?
BT: Before writing a word, I insisted on going to New Iberia to see what it looked like. I also wanted to meet Burke with whom I'd exchanged some emails over a two-year period. That allowed me to discover the Holiday Inn with its seedy little pool where I immediately decided to film the first scene with Balboni. You always associate the Mafiosi with palaces. There, between the fake plants, the plastic pool chairs and the kid on the swing, I right away had a site that was both common and extraordinary. I immediately hit it off with Burke. During that first visit, he invited me to stay with him. We drove around a lot, which allowed me to discover lots of different places, such as Robicheaux's house and the bait shop where Dave and Batist sell lures. Burke introduced us to a bunch of people, like the sheriff Sid Hebert, who was very useful in our site research, and even did some screen tests on him. We didn't end up using him in the film, but the actor Gary Grubbs used him as a model. With different people we met I was able to test my idea of making the novel into a present day film. Everyone approved of the idea, considering that it was more credible that Balboni would be diverting the federal disaster relief from Katrina than that he be trafficking porno films.

D&R: Did Burke approve this change?
BT: Absolutely. Burke was open to everything. He refused to write the adaptation of his novel himself despite my repeated entreaties to do so. But he told a whole raft of anecdotes about the region, and allowed me to keep in my film this interweaving of past and present that I so loved in his novel. We ended up with a screenplay that I wasn't quite satisfied with. After trying three different versions, I went back to Burke and asked him to write a different beginning. I had a body that the police had found near the road, with all these police cars, cops talking on their two-way radios, an opening sequence you've seen thousands of times. I wanted to move the body and put it in the bayou, in the middle of the mist with a voice off talking about something else. Four hours later, Burke sent me the text. I followed him to Montana to work on the scenario. He changed some things, cut

others and gave me what I hadn't succeeded in getting from my own writers: an ending in a voice off. And Burke also gave me two or three lines which are among my favorites.

D&R: Did Tommy Lee Jones participate in the writing?

BT: Yes. After all these edits, he thought some of the scenes look too much like TV shows, so we reworked the whole thing together. Tommy was freaked by having to explain things and absolutely didn't want speeches. Which didn't prevent him from appreciating that his character occasionally used arcane words like when he says to Balboni that he's "metastacizing." All this work of rereading with Tommy Lee Jones was very exciting. He had an obsession for the musicality of words and he could cut and reduce things constantly, sometimes spending days hunting for the right word. One day during the shoot, I told him I needed an additional scene between Bootsie and Robicheaux and the next day he brought me the scene of the salamander. I didn't have to change a comma. To play this scene, I knew that Tommy had worked very hard by himself. As soon as we'd finished a shot, I'd see him go off behind the house to work on his lines, coordinating his words and his gestures. He was so thorough that in two takes, we were done. Tommy told me that he'd hated working with Paul Haggis, who'd work up to thirty takes. I gave myself a limit of three, like Don Siegel. And I succeeded, wrapping up the shoot in forty-one days. I almost always agreed with his suggestions. There was only this one day when I got really angry because he wanted to invent new complications between the characters. For example, Amber Martinez became one of the girls he'd given money to at the bus station. I threatened to drop the whole film. The important thing for me was that the plot should never overshadow the characters, and that we didn't want any silhouettes having a role in the action.

D&R: Wasn't it more complicated making this movie not being from the South, or even American?

BT: In my first encounter with Burke, I understood that I'd need to immerse myself in Louisiana. In all my films, I try to get inside a place, a period or a profession that are foreign to me before starting the project. People who know the country will tell you that the Cambodia of Holy Lola was beyond authentic, that you could really feel it. In this case it was more complicated. Burke's characters are welded to the world they inhabit. So we had to film these places through Dave Robicheaux's eyes without ever giving the impression that we admired or were surprised by the countryside. So the fact that I was French meant I had some serious work to do. But maybe I ended up with less arrogance than some Hollywood directors. A bunch of people told me that, even in terms of the local accents, the film was the truest to the region of anything that had been done. And Tommy Lee Jones, who's from Texas, was very helpful in this. For example, I'd imagined that at the end of the film that, when Dave's truck arrives, Mary Steenburgen would run out to meet him. But Tommy explained that in the South a woman would never leave the porch where she's waiting for her husband. On issues like this I always took his advice.

D&R: In France you're known for always choosing your actors. Did you have to go through a director of casting for this film?

BT: I used three! If I knew from the outset that I wanted John Goodman, and quickly decided on Peter Sarsgaard, I had to see a lot of girls before hiring Kelly MacDonald. With her, we immediately went outside the usual agreements. For the secondary roles, we had a long and thorough search. I chose local actors who'd not done much film work. Sometimes a bit of theater. Tommy Lee had two terrific ideas which I immediately adopted: Buddy Guy, one of the great bluesmen, for Hogman Patin and Levon Helm, the former drummer for the Band, as General John Bell Hood. Burke, who's a great specialist on the Civil War, thought he looked a bit like Robert E. Lee. He told me all about Bell Hood, explaining that, like Lee, he was opposed to slavery. And in that he's the double of Robicheaux, who had been in Viet Nam, an honorable man fighting for a horrible cause.

D&R: Isn't it a paradox to want to film from Robicheaux's point of view with a French cameraman?

BT: Not at all. I had an excellent cinematographer in Chris Squires. For the lighting I totally trusted Bruno de Keyzer. I saw him extricate himself from some very tricky situations in *Un Dimanche à la campagne* [*A Sunday in the Country*] and *La Vie et rien d'autre* [*Life and Nothing But*]. He'd been recommended by the people in the labs whom I'd asked for names of cinematographers who, in short subjects, are in charge of the negatives. We saw rushes that were completely uncalibrated, with ridiculous colors and violet faces, but he told me: "Not to worry! I know what I've got on film. It's exactly what you described in Paris."

D&R: And what were your instructions?

BT: To play with a mix of light and shadow in the tradition of film noir; with the added difficulty of not being in an urban setting but instead maintaining the luxuriance of the foliage which had to appear suffocating. That forced us to modify certain settings, like the one in which they discover the cadaver in the barrel. Originally that was also supposed to be in the bayou, but Bruno told me that he was at the limit of his visual resources. So we imagined this little port, which would allow us play with the lighting. It's an unexpected setting, but, visually one of the best sequences in the film. During our preparations, we'd gone over the lighting in every scene with Bruno: the sense of sanctuary in Dave's house, the atmosphere in the bars with few sources of light . . .

D&R: How did you shoot the fantastic scenes?

BT: I had a very precise idea of everything: The discovery of the general's camp, for example, that I wanted to do in a single shot. We had to search a long time to find the setting that would allow that and that that could be lit by Bruno. I didn't consider it as fantastic. I believed in Robicheaux's visions, the way Buñuel believed in ghosts. I was very interested in making this general plausible. One evening, after a dinner and a few drinks, Tommy Lee suggested adding some white and yellow flashes to a Steadicam shot. I was afraid the members of the team had heard him and that I'd have to fight with him about this as well, because what I wanted was a more naturalistic effect. I'd never done anything about the Civil War, so I enjoyed filming a Confederate camp. I'm really interested in the Civil War and Ken Burns's immense documentary. It's the cinephile in me: to want to succeed in making a film that's inspired by Mathew Brady's photographs.

D&R: Did you see a connection between your cinephile side and the idea of places connected through their histories?

BT: It was more the cinephile side: the choice of a mise en scène that was dictated by the settings and universe of Burke, all of whose books I'd read. In a general way, when I'm filming, I no longer feel like a cinephile. I want to be carried away by the places where the action happens and by the characters, without being influenced by memories of other images. There are always moments in the film that contradict this position. Those are the violent scenes that are inspired by the dryness with which Mann, Walsh, Fleisher, or Hathaway treat them. I wanted to have the opposite of this riot of special effects, the slo-mo's, the explosions that in so many contemporary films transform the film into a video game and empty it of any sense of consequence. I wanted to rediscover, in the shootout at the Club Léon or in the fight in the restaurant, the sense of duration which gave such weight to the drama of *Raw Deal* or *Narrow Margin*; that's why I insisted on shooting the first outbreak of violence in a long take whereas the editor wanted to add some montage-cuts. I have to confess that I had some pretty violent disagreements with him. He didn't want me to film wide-angle shots. He thought I didn't cover myself enough. Like the fishing scene, which he wanted me to re-film with a close-up of an important line of the dialogue. I disagreed completely. I wanted to capture Dave's gesture and Bootsie's reaction behind him. The most stimulating discussions were

with Burke, who is a true film lover and with my production director, who knew
Ozu's work really well.

D&R: How did you choose the production director? Usually he's the head cameraman . . .
BT: Bruno is very demanding, but also very flexible. When he works outside of
France, he knows he can't bring his team. So I asked Steven Soderbergh to help us
choose our technicians. He's the one who recommended Paul Ledford, the sound
engineer who did all of the direct sound for the film, which we kept in the final
mixing because it was sublime. We had our first meeting at the Holiday Inn. I
wanted him to tell me if we could shoot at the pool outside, since the hotel was
surrounded by three highways. But before coming to meet me, he'd gone on the
Internet to study an aerial view of the surroundings in order to anticipate sources
of noise. For example, there was an auto body shop a hundred yards away that we'd
have to close. From that observation alone I decided that he'd do the film. And I
loved working with him.

D&R: And why Marco Beltrami for the music?
BT: Because of Tommy Lee Jones's *The Three Burials of Melquiades Estrada*. When
I went to see him he was amazed: it was the first time a film director had come
to see him before beginning a film. He spent a month in Louisiana researching
instruments and drums. He's one of the only people who knows the music of Alex
North and Jerry Goldsmith, who were his teachers. Like them, he has a very wide
register and an amazing knowledge of orchestration.

D&R: So what did you ask him to do?
BT: A very rhythmic and energized music for the present tense of the film. And
very piercing sounds for the past when it mixes in with the present. I also spoke
with him about the composition of the orchestra. I didn't want a symphonic orchestra but more one with a rhythmic base that would incorporate elements from
Cajun music. He used the accordion for the melody and a rhythmic instrument
for the beat. He borrowed some zydeco blues and used a washboard that you play
with a kind of thimble.

D&R: Did he play some of his themes for you?
BT: No, he came to see the film when we were shooting in New Orleans and we
talked a lot. Then I returned to France to do the editing. Until all the legal details were worked out, I was barred by the producer from talking to him. He told
me later that this was very hard for him. But he recorded each instrument on

a separate track so that I could make what I wanted out of it. And he was nice enough to record two other pieces in case I'd need them. I used one of them for the credits.

D&R: After the Handel aria.
BT: Precisely. I chose that aria after a long search. I listened to some Marin Marais, to some Bach. One day, Philippe Meyer suggested I listen to *Dixit Dominus* by Handel in the Gardiner version. It's a prayer for the salvation of the dead. Unbelievably beautiful. Moreover, the lyrics corresponded to the end of the film. Right from the start I knew I'd need a different kind of music for this ending. I also wanted some Cajun songs, like Michael Doucet's "I walked by your door" which I love. In fact I carefully chose all the music of the film.

D&R: Roberto Silvi, the editor with whom you had such heated arguments, was not your choice?
BT: I trusted Michael Fitzgerald, who otherwise suggested really remarkable people such as the scene designer Meredith Boswell. I wanted her because I'd seen her work on *The Three Burials*. She was perfect. When we were looking for someone to play Bootsie, she's the one who suggested Mary Steenburgen, whom I adored. But to come back to the editor, he was a super technician but I didn't find him very creative. I was bored in the editing room. And then, I missed France and my children, despite the wonderful people I'd met in Louisiana. So I started over from scratch with Thierry Derocles. And in five minutes we'd resolved all the problems. I had to go into debt to do this, since TFI didn't want to pay for this. But I don't regret it. I made the film I wanted to make.

Tavernier: A Biological Film: On *La Princesse de Montpensier*

Philippe Rouyer and Yann Tobin / 2010

From *Positif*, no. 597 (November 2010). Reprinted by permission. Translated by T. Jefferson Kline.

Philippe Rouyer & Yann Tobin: Let's begin with Mélanie Thierry, who is a revelation in the title role . . .

Bertrand Tavernier: There wasn't any name that jumped out at us. Gerard Moulévrier, the casting director, introduced me to several young actresses, among them Mélanie. From our first meeting, I liked her as a human being. She was among the first to do a screen test and did so with a handicap: she was late because of a baroque story of a traffic ticket and a taxi and so she was very wrought up. But when she settled down, she was terrific. I'd wanted to do these auditions with the chief cameraman and with Grégoire Leprince-Ringuet and Gaspard Ulliel, whom I'd chosen from the start. That allowed me to run through some dialogues, to begin to think about mise en scène, and to get an idea of what I wanted in the princess from a list of things that were missing in the various actresses. Vahina Giocante did some very interesting work for us and I knew that she was physically right for the part. But she lacked a certain childishness. Others didn't have the haughtiness we needed. And others failed to get the changes of tone needed within scenes where Marie has to transition quickly from a seductive and even teasing manner to that of an offended aristocrat. Mélanie succeeded in all of these emotional changes without any sign of effort. When we tried out various costumes, we were entirely convinced. After the auditions, we saw her in Tennessee Williams's *Baby Doll*, and she was excellent. Monique Chaumette, her partner, told me: "She's a Stradivarius, you'll get all you ever dreamed of from her."

R&T: Did you work a lot on her character with her before the shoot?

BT: We saw each other for read-throughs and discussions. I saw her alone, once, to answer her questions. She was eager to learn everything, discover everything, she did very intelligent and diligent work, beginning with mastery of the language. But all of our actors were very good at this: at first they were afraid of the dialogue, but once they got into it, they enjoyed it enormously. At each go, we discovered new meanings and new feelings to explore. That's Jean Cosmos's great strength. His immense and unknown talent comes from his wide literary culture but also from his open-mindedness. I hired him for *La Vie et rien d'autre* [*Life and Nothing But*] because I found that in the TV films he'd written, the language of people who exercised certain professions had an authentic ring to it that is without its equivalent in French cinema—except perhaps in Aurenche's work, or Prévert's. After the war, he worked for a long time at the Ministry of Reconstruction, where he'd rubbed elbows with masons and surveyors . . . Our goal was to find a language that was mid-way between the parlance of the times and our own. We knew we had to avoid the pseudo-historic veneer of some scripts. And also the conventional way of having these dialogues played. It was as if, since it was "historical" the actors were supposed to talk louder! As though in the past there were many more introverts than today. And that's why I chose Grégoire Leprince-Ringuet. I knew he would bring some modernity into the way the lines were spoken. In Guédiguian's *L'Armée du crime* [*The Army of Crime*], he's always spot-on.

R&T: So when you were casting you were trying for a sort of bouquet?
BT: Exactly. After having chose Grégoire and Gaspard, we had to find the girl and the third boy. That's when we discovered Raphaël Personnaz, whom we'd already assigned to another role. When we saw him in costume, my assistant Valérie Othnin-Girard pointed out that he had too much class to be a supernumerary and that we should try him as the Duc d'Anjou.

R&T: What about Lambert Wilson?
BT: He was added fairly late on. The producer wanted a well-known actor so we had to go looking for one. We considered Fabrice Luchini. I like him but in *The Hunchback* he had refused to do a lot of physical things. Our stable master, Mario Lurraschi said that we'd never get him on horseback.

R&T: So the challenge was to avoid using stunt men instead of the principal actors?
BT: That's right. So they had a strenuous regime of physical fitness: gymnastics, horseback riding, fencing. I wanted to do a lot of long takes to show that we hadn't resorted to using stunt men before shooting any of our actors in close-up. In general, I avoid stunt men like the plague because inserting them in the shot breaks up the action exactly when you're at the most spectacular moment. In the battle

scene, these moments are blended in with the others: a horse collapses under the blow of a pike, but just before, in the same scene, two horsemen are thrown from their saddles and one is killed with a sword blow. And when the horse falls, we do a pan to catch Gaspard who's galloping up and gets unsaddled.

R&T: Was all that in the storyboard?

BT: No, we rehearsed it all on the spot after having more or less worked it out in the stables with Mario Luraschi and Alain Figlaz, who coordinated the fights. Then we had a day of rehearsal, on Sunday, with the extras. So when we shot it, all we had to do was rework what we'd rehearsed, given the disastrous weather conditions we faced: an icy rain which was coming straight at us and froze us immediately. If you stayed too long in any one spot, you got stuck in the frozen mud. I was terrified that the next day none of our extras would come back; their clothes hadn't had time to dry. But they were all there: the stunt men, the people we'd hired locally who provided us the savagery and violence we needed.

R&T: The battles really look authentic.

BT: That's one of the things I like best as a director: to shoot outside and give the impression that it's an expensive film when we're working with severe budgetary constraints. As we set out, we did a lot of research before finding the battlefield site. I wanted to film in a valley with a river running through it, muddy ground, groves of trees and rocks: a bunch of obstacles that prevented the viewer from having a clear perspective. Afterwards, we burned some wagons and some tents. This gave us thick black smoke and the explosions. It was the period when the first cannons were used. By introducing all these elements and with the help of Chris Squires, my cameraman, we were able to give the impression there were thousands when there were only a hundred of them. It was a bit like *Captain Conan* where we gave the impression of having seven to eight times the numbers we actually had.

R&T: So you didn't want large numbers of actors?

BT: No. Neither for the extras nor for the explosions. I wanted them to have an impact on the characters and on the shots. Bruno de Keyzer and I wanted "a biological film" not a big numbers film. I think that's a lazy man's solution: as soon as you don't have the means to do something right, you fall back on large numbers of extras. But that way you lose texture and reality. I was thinking of Kurosawa's battles and Orson Welles's *Falstaff*. The complete opposite of Ridley Scott's *Robin Hood*, where you never know where the people are, and you have the feeling everything was arranged in post-production. The battle scenes that impress me seem to have been torn out of their surroundings, with visual perspectives that limit one's horizons but increase the energy of the combatants. I'm thinking, for example, of the battle scene in André de Toth's *Monkey on My Back*: with very few extras, it gives the impression of endless carnage. For me, the battle scenes were a way of revealing things about the characters. When you see Montpensier, this very young man, fight with such courage and then see him totally disarmed before his child bride, you're even more moved. We talked with Grégoire about this. We wanted to undo the stereotype that threatened his character: Montpensier is neither a weakling nor a jealous cuckold. His suffering is greater.

R&T: One of the strengths of the film derives from the heroine's relations with men, especially Chabannes and her husband . . .

BT: Even with Guise: she gets carried away but then stops cold. I told Gaspard and Mélanie that when they're together they should give the impression that they could make love right away before our eyes. And that each time, Marie's character stops. Not out of fear, but because there's something blocking her: her love for Philippe, her religious education . . . I don't want to know, but I told Mélanie that she must know. Guise is driven purely by desire. But with the three others, it's more complicated. I wanted there to be moments when you'd have the impression that things could very well work out between her and her husband. Whence the idea that she'd go find him in his chamber—something a woman of the sixteenth century never would have done. It's a very audacious act. They make love and in the morning they're totally at ease with each other. She makes all of this effort out of love and respect for him. He's not the brute that one might have made of him. He doesn't try to rape her, and that touches her even though she doesn't know how to respond to it. In this respect, I was, from the start, opposed to the idea of film noir with a *femme fatale*. The more I worked with Cosmos, the more we discovered the opposite: Marie is anything but a seductress. She's a character who is torn, confused, and who's looking for a way out.

R&T: So you totally rewrote the scenario you'd started with?

BT: The first version was written by François-Olivier Rousseau, but Jean Cosmos and I gradually rewrote it from A to Z. We didn't say: everything must go, but in rewriting one scene we ended up having to change the next . . . At one point we asked ourselves: how come there's not a wedding night of love? I can't simply declare that there's no way to show it: a man and a woman who do not know each other marry. How does this work? Didier Le Fur told me: "The first night of love was always public." Great! After that I was curious to follow them, to know how they looked at each other. I told myself that they wouldn't have been able to speak to each other. Philippe tries to be gentle. What's he going to say to her? That he's going to try to forge a path that is going to be difficult. That's a way of saying that he loves her, that he'll pay attention to her.

R&T: And this approach dictates that you use very young actors . . .

BT: That's what excited me the most about this project: the vulnerability, the innocence, a childlike side to them, but also times when they're wounded and constrained to be adults. That provided an exceptionally dramatic development of Marie's character.

R&T: That's the pre-feminist aspect of the film . . .

BT: Yes. We tried to understand how a young woman would be able to react and to find her own way. None of this was in Madame de La Fayette's novel, which is anything but feminist! For me, her entire moral doctrine is expressed in what Marie's mother (Florence Thomassin) tells her daughter: "Love is one of the most inconvenient things in the world." This is a sentence taken from a letter written by Madame de La Fayette. So it's what the author thinks; it's not taken from one of her novels but from her correspondence. She makes her heroine die because the mere fact that she can entertain this kind of thought constitutes a "lack of good sense" (the last sentence of the novel). So I took this more feminist approach, and there will probably be two or three scholars who will reproach me for it. That said, I thought about the author herself when, during her "education," Marie asks to learn to write. That was a very subversive thing to do at the time, almost revolutionary! The great majority of noblemen didn't know how to write and could scarcely read. "The Duc de Guise," Didier Le Fur told me, "is the equivalent of a gang leader in the Paris suburbs of today!" Fights, absolute scorn for people who are educated! I thought about Marie's desire to learn to write in terms of the shock Madame de La Fayette's friends must have felt when she began publishing her novels. Not only did she not sign them, but in certain of her letters, she denies having written them and attributes them to men! I also wanted Marie to try to learn things about herself: does she risk damnation because of her feelings for Guise? So I told Cosmos: it would be great if she wanted to learn the reasons for this war . . . The entire film takes place from her point of view. We encounter this entire historical period through her eyes and she knows no more about it than today's audiences. She is forcibly kept out of all the important decisions; she sees only the consequences: her husband leaves or comes home; they've won or lost. I wanted her to try to learn what her husband is fighting for and why she has to be alone sometimes for two years at a time. So Jean wrote those dialogues about faith. The evocation of these metaphysical questions moves me a lot. That's perhaps a consequence of my catholic education!

R&T: Let's talk about Chabannes.

BT: He represents our point of view—Jean Cosmos and myself—and allows us to tie the various destinies of these characters together. He's at the heart of all the relationships. He sees everything. We had in mind certain personalities of the sixteenth century who had this ability to understand the world around them: Montaigne, Erasmus, the warrior-teachers you find in Rabelais. He provided us a character who anchors the story. He is disenchanted yet maintains his hope: if he were loved, he could begin his life anew.

R&T: Marie understands too late that she didn't appreciate him enough.
BT: Like all young people who lack lucidity. She gradually discovers that Chabannes represents lasting happiness . . . the opposite of Guise.

R&T: But at the same time, despite his withdrawn nature, he gets caught up in the story.
BT: Yes, that's in Madame de La Fayette's novel. He wants to remain outside of things, but each of the other characters involves him in turn: Marie, in making her confessions to him and in asking for his help (which is simultaneously cruel yet touching); Montpensier, of course, and even Guise! At one point I said to Lambert Wilson that he must have been angry: you asked for it! You're going to ruin your life, so too bad for you!

R&T: Was the sequence of scenes all worked out in advance?
BT: No, never. I may have one idea while we're writing, but it's often countered by the choice of setting, which will dictate certain principles of mise en scène. For example at the Chateau de Plessis-Bourré, with its little bridge, and then the vaulted passageway that leads into the courtyard, I thought: Marie will have to enter this vaulted passageway and stand between the Montpensier family on the bridge and the Guise family in the courtyard. She should be far enough away so that she can't hear what is said, but close enough to guess that it's about her! The topography of the setting, the way the space will be filmed, the position of the characters in the shot ultimately provides me with a vision of where the film is going without having to discuss it at all. That was decided when we saw the setting. Afterwards I worked things out by watching how the actors moved. We often rehearse very early in the morning, before they've set up the lighting. The actors aren't quite fully awake yet so lots of things happen in an instinctive almost animal way. We're no longer thinking about what we'll do. I really believe in this way of doing things. Once we've completed the preliminary work, done our reading and defined the important points, it's important, when you start a scene, to begin with something purely physical, not at all intellectual. Both the actors and me with the camera. In this way we can discover what's going to be the heart of the scene, the movement of the sequence.

R&T: You brought a touch of irony to the film with your choice of Raphaël Personnaz to play the role of Anjou, the future Henry the Third . . .

BT: Yes, he's miles away from the image of the twisted madman that extremist catholic propaganda gave us, and that was challenged by Dumas and more recent biographies. Yes, he's serious ("I'll cut your head off . . ."), with brusque changes of tone which are a challenge but also a joy for the actor. "If I were king I'd disobey myself. . . ." Raphaël managed all of these with complete aplomb. And he's a terrific horseman, which was crucial. He had a long scene on horseback with Guise that I wanted to film in a single shot: I'd shown them Bud Boetticher's westerns where there are three-minute scenes on horseback, at different distances but where you can always see the horses.

R&T: A tour de force for the actors.

BT: The entire cast had a great time together. They'd responded to each other, cut each other off . . . Mélanie told me she'd never worked with a more generous actor than Lambert Wilson. Raphaël was irresistible, even in the horrible conditions we had to work with, under a tent during a storm! And when he says disgustedly, while eating his kippered herring during his Polish lesson, "I think we pay too dearly for the privilege of our birth!" It's all true: he was king of Poland for two days and fled! It's worthy of Dumas! It's also from Dumas that I learned that at this time there were no rules for dueling. They did anything they could to wound each other. So that allowed me to add anything I wanted: they punched and bit each other. . . . We're not yet under Louis the Thirteenth with d'Artagnan!

R&T: The reading of the final letter, which is constantly deferred, allowed you to keep the suspense right up until the end.

BT: What I really liked, thanks to Cosmos, was that this letter was taken up by several different characters: Chabannes, Philippe, Marie. The letter ends up by linking all the protagonists of the story.

R&T: You end as you often do with a voice-over.

BT: I love that! Very late on I decided it should be Marie's voice: so I called Cosmos and had a hard time convincing him. In the end it was the first time she speaks using the first person pronoun. We'd never heard from her the least letter or declaration. She explains her choice: it wasn't for me to do but for her. In the same way, I wanted the snow at the end, which creates a shock. Likewise, I'd wanted the autumn scenes to reinforce the emotions in certain other scenes. We were fortunate: we always shot at the right moment! The whole thing was meticulously prepared and luck or heaven was on our side. So I took advantage of all this good fortune to add some shots and some mute sequences. I was afraid that Marie, all alone as she was in this chateau, should be seen as someone being punished by her husband: it's a magnificent but very austere setting. And so I decided she needed a companion, someone her age, a cousin or servant who would accompany her everywhere. The character of Jeanne, who's barely mentioned in the scenario, appears in several mute scenes, using looks and smiles. So I'd ask her to react to things: she's a character whose only function is to react, but each one of her reactions enriched both Marie's character and the atmosphere of the film. They laugh together, dance, eat chestnuts (which allowed me to use Mélanie's laugh, which I love). The simple presence of this character ensures that we can accept that Marie be alone in this castle without it being seen as a sad or punitive situation.

R&T: What specific problems do historical films present?

BT: The most essential thing is to succeed in making the camera a contemporary of the characters and their emotions. I try never to privilege the idea of "reconstitution" of the interior feelings of my characters. In certain films, otherwise very estimable films, that can make me raise an eyebrow. I have the impression that we try to hard to be exact about a historical period: we can pay too much attention to a chandelier or a writing desk or some accessory, whereas I want to discover this furniture with the character. I believe it's this way of seizing the whole ensemble at once that gives you the feeling of the times. It's not because we focus on one "authentic" detail that a shot will be right. The behavior of the characters should be exempt of any respect of anything than can give the accessories priority over the essential thing, which is the character! I was delighted when Didier Le Fur told me, "There was no such thing as good manners at the time." When Philippe and Chabannes enter Anjou's tent, there is a parquet floor laid out and covered by superb rugs. I asked Le Fur whether, when they entered the tent, with their muddy boots on, they should be careful of the rugs, or if there are valets to take their boots off. "No, they don't give a damn!" The code of good manners comes much later. If they get dirty the servants will clean them! They don't wipe their feet before entering, drip on everything, and if they take off their coats they just throw them on the floor: someone will pick them up. Such things immediately set the tone: as soon as Philippe appears, he throws down his cloak and someone enters the frame and picks it up. There's a total lack of respect vis-à-vis clothes that today could be exhibited in the Museum of Costumes! The characters should behave with the furniture and costumes (which are, of course, not period pieces, but contemporary pieces) just as we do with our things. Or maybe we're more careful than they were . . .

R&T: Yes, because we have fewer servants!

Interview with Bertrand Tavernier on *Death Watch*

Antoine Royer / 2013

From DVDClassik website, January 27, 2013, http://www.dvdclassik.com/article/
entretien-avec-bertrand-tavernier-autour-de-la-mort-en-direct. Reprinted by
permission of the author. Translated by T. Jefferson Kline.

Antoine Royer: I might sum up *La Mort en direct* [*Death Watch*] as the meeting—I would even say the amorous meeting—between a dying woman thirsty for life and an evil eye (with all the multiple meanings of this term), in a film that anticipates yet refuses futurism to inscribe itself in a kind of ancestrality, that is, in the very duration of things. Would that summary satisfy you?

Bertrand Tavernier: Yes, that's it. In any case, it's the story of a paradoxical love, between this woman who was made for happiness and who is looking to protect her freedom from the intrusion of the media, and the man who, in fact, exploits her and who, by dint of filming her, falls in love with her, and his guilt ends up by trumping his mission. And in the end, the story of love gains the upper hand and becomes a true love story between Gerald Mortenhoe and Katherine.

AR: So in fact, if we come back to the different (and apparently paradoxical) aspects that at first seem to define the film, this character of Katherine, this "dying woman thirsty for life" could not have been brought to life by any actress other than Romy Schneider.

BT: I never imagined that anyone else could play the part. There were about two pressured days when I was asked to meet Jane Fonda, and I immediately abandoned the idea of using her. I tried to see her at Cannes, and I immediately saw that there was a total contradiction—as there so often is with American stars—between what she said to the press ("I'd like to do some French films, to support young directors") and the fact that she was unreachable. I had to leave my name ten times along with proof of who I was, and I finally decided the whole thing was absurd. Why give in to people who were already trying to get me to take Richard Gere instead of Harvey Keitel? And so it was Romy. It was really Romy right from the start. In fact there are three or four things that constituted the film from the beginning: Glasgow, Romy, Harvey, and perhaps also Antoine Duhamel, partly because of *Pierrot le fou*.

AR: Did you already know Romy Schneider?

BT: I'd met her when Pierre Rissient and I were press agents for Claude Sautet. We'd gone to bat for *Les Choses de la vie* [*The Things of Life*] and *Max et les ferrailleurs* [*Max and the Junkmen*] not against the press—the films had been very well received—but against a fraction of people—who are now beginning to change their minds—who take thirty or forty years to recognize a great filmmaker: *Cahiers du Cinéma* where there's a group of intelligentsia who sovereignly despise Claude Sautet. Pierre Rissient thought François Truffaut was partly responsible for that: he said that Truffaut was spreading rumors about Sautet in the US to prevent his getting distributed there, but I don't know how true that is. I know that Truffaut asked Sautet to look at the editing of his films and get his advice. But anyway, as a press agent, I'd met Romy. You could see right away that she wasn't going to help promote the film: she was withdrawn and was afraid of expressing herself because she thought she didn't speak French very well, that she wasn't cultivated or intelligent, but Pierre Rissient and I tended to focus on the director when promoting a film. So we focused more on Romy and on Sautet, whom we had defended. Claude Sautet was one of the first personalities I'd interviewed, and the first article I wrote in *Cinéma 59* or *60* was on *Classe tous risques* [*The Big Risk*]. The film was disgracefully received although now we understand what a great crime film it was in those years, an extremely bold movie, the equal if not better than the best Melville films. So I knew Romy through Sautet; we'd met and spoken and I'd found her amazing in *Max and the Junkmen*. I was also the press agent for Deray's *La Piscine* [*The Swimming Pool*] so we saw a lot of each other, though I can't say I knew her well. But when I went to see her to propose doing *Death Watch*, she immediately agreed to do it.

AR: Before, in your summary of the film, you said that Roddy fell in love with Katherine while filming her. And that's the impression I get from Romy: it was enough to film her to succumb to her charms.

BT: Oh, yes, completely, me too! We couldn't help falling in love with Romy when we filmed her. All of us. It was impossible not to be bewitched, captivated. But she had something else: an incredible strength, something of Verdi's heroines, and I thought that in France she'd been given roles that were too ordinary, that she performed magnificently, of course, but I was convinced she could go way beyond the figure of the young woman who'd been wounded and was struggling to protect her freedom, as she'd so beautifully done in *Max and the Junkmen*, or in Visconti's *Il lavoro* in *Boccaccio '70*. On the other hand, I had some reservations, given her reputation and rumors that had spread about things that had gone wrong with certain of her films, in particular, Alexander Petrovic's *Group Portrait with a Lady* with Pierre-William Glenn as cameraman. But I think it had something to do with the director's psychological approach. So I had a certain amount of apprehension: she was intimidating all the same.

AR: And yet she got entirely wrapped up in the film, to the point of signing notes to you with the name of her character.

BT: Yes, she signed Katherine. She'd told me, "I will be your Katherine without self-pity." She sent me letters that she signed Katherine and enclosed dried flowers in them. I had an enormous collection of letters, and I haven't been able to find them for the last two years. Maybe they were lost when I moved, or maybe I left them in things I loaned out—books that were written about me, for example—or when people came by to consult my archives. I don't know. In any case I really regret losing them. It was an extremely touching collection . . . She thanked me for the way I'd directed her in a scene when the entire team was focused on David [Romy Schneider's son, who had recently died in an accident—Eds.]; she sent me poems in German by Brecht, by Heine, that I had to have translated immediately because she expected a response!

AR: You mentioned David. So you think the subject of the film, this woman hunted by pressure from the media, was particularly touching for her. For example, it seems to me that Alain Delon had been considered for the film but that he'd refused partly because of their history together.

BT: The role of Gerald Mortenhoe was originally intended for Philippe Noiret. But he had to undergo surgery, so I thought of Delon, who behaved marvelously: he didn't keep us waiting, he gave us his answer the same day, explaining that he thought it would be better if he didn't take the part, that he would have led the film viewers in the wrong direction. Which was very much to the point. And yet perhaps it hid the fact that he found the role too thin, though I don't think so. I thought he was entirely sincere. Given his relationship to Romy, people risked having fantasies about them and the whole point of the film would have been obscured. And I don't know by whom or how the idea was introduced of having Max von Sydow play a role, which we decided very late on: I think I met him on the set. I was beginning to prepare the film when Philippe Noiret had to withdraw.

AR: You mentioned earlier three requisites for the film: Romy Schneider, Glasgow, and Harvey Keitel, who had the reputation of being box-office poison.

BT: People didn't like him. There were rumors that he was very difficult to work with. It's true that he asked a lot of questions, and insisted on certain things, and he's a Method Actor. He never wanted anyone in his field of vision. He never wanted to participate in the "Making of," because he doesn't like giving away his favorite recipes. I was accustomed to working with actors like Noiret, Rochefort, Galabru, Marielle, Marina Vlady, who, given their culture and way of doing things, have already figured out the answers to questions they might have before we start shooting. Harvey, like many American actors, is someone who comes from a more narrow acting culture: for example in his theater work, he would do only American plays; the European repertoire was entirely unknown to him. If I compare him to someone like Noiret, who'd acted with the Théâtre National Populaire, and who knew the meaning of "troupe" and had had roles in plays by Calderon, Lope de Vega, Shakespeare, Corneille, Victor Hugo, Brecht, Pirandello, which provided him with a much more open mind about the possibilities of the theater. Romy had that too. Whereas Harvey asked questions all the time, some of which were useful but could also be exasperating. For example, he'd arrive in the morning saying he wanted a suit of clothes that would allow him to go film in the sewers, and then afterwards go off to the Claridge. He was supposed to be ready to work, but that was an argument he simply wouldn't listen to. So I was pretty stuck. I couldn't satisfy his request and it was our marvelous costumiere, Judy Moorcroft, who'd worked with James Ivory, who went to see him and came back saying, "It's OK, I've worked it all out. I gave him a necktie that he put in his pocket. He's got the same costume as yesterday but now he knows he can go to the Claridge." You can laugh at that, I can just see Noiret smiling, but when we had to do a long take, to have him struggle with his vision, to embody that feverish quality . . . one take was all we needed and that was really great. And that's why I believe that his requests were never dictated by ego: he always put the quality of the film first.

AR: Yes, because Roddy's character could have been very dark, but Harvey Keitel takes it in another direction. I was talking a minute ago about malevolence, and here Harvey Keitel has a more mischievous look . . .

BT: That immaturity, the childish side that causes him to get manipulated, is what makes his character so touching. He doesn't appear to be conscious of what he's doing: he's playful and then explodes. Otherwise, he'd just be your run of the mill bastard. I hired Harvey for his smile. The first time I saw him, he was coming into the restaurant with a big smile and I said to myself, that's him, that's Roddy. There was something about him, and when I told him he looked like John Garfield, he looked surprised because, like many American actors, he doesn't know much about film history. Garfield had that malevolence combined with innocence, some weight of guilt about him.

AR: The same physical density . . .
BT: Physical density, yes, and that feeling that he's not from a middle-class background but comes from a working-class milieu. That was Garfield's great contribution: he introduced into American film the image of the working-class hero, but in an entirely different way than James Cagney. Keitel has that, and it's very evident in Scorsese's *Mean Streets*, that "right out of the gutter" side, and I found it really beautiful—quite the opposite of Harry Dean Stanton. That glint in his eyes was exactly what I wanted and what other directors disliked about him. Like in Nicholas Roeg's *Bad Timing*, for example, with that haunted, guilty, terribly serious air. But I wanted to make him smile. I wanted him to look and to smile. He was afraid at times that the shots wouldn't be meaningful enough, so he'd try to add some prop, chew on something, grab a cracker, but I'd tell him, "No, just use your eyes. You don't see me eating anything when I'm filming, do you?"

AR: That's funny. That's the second time you've made a parallel between Harvey Keitel's character's look as he films within the film and your own as the film director. Can one say that *Death Watch* is first and foremost a film about the morality of the look, or of "looks": the character's, the spectator's, and the film director's?
BT: Yes, of course. That's definitely something I was thinking about as I was filming. I was denouncing the manipulation of the look, the over-dramatization of a society that sells itself to the cult of the image, without consequences. I had to weigh those consequences for my own role in the process. That's why that I thought a lot about framing and about camera movements: all those tracking shots that move us from subjectivity to objectivity in a single shot.

AR: That's exactly what I was getting at—the question of subjectivity. We're living at a time when TV has shown us Mr. Everyman; with films using found footage, we are constantly assaulted at the level of subjectivity. Whereas in *Death Watch*, you don't use it consistently so that when you do, the effects are more precise and meaningful. I'm thinking in particular of two shots: the one where Katherine takes off her wig while Roddy is watching, in a subjective shot, and then this shot is multiplied subsequently in a non-subjective shot on the control screens at the TV studio. Or the gripping shot when Katherine flees from the market. You have a tracking shot in which Katherine arrives from the left, then turns and takes the axis of the tracking shot, so that the shot becomes a subjective shot for the spectator who is following her. She's trying to escape the Death Watch and we, as audience, are not letting her go.

BT: Indeed, I asked myself a lot of questions about the meaning or the reception of these shots. I didn't want to be too didactic: this shot, for example, changes. Within one shot you have an objective POV of someone running away so that you have two POV changes within one shot. The shot you've mentioned is one I'm fiercely proud of. It's one of the first times we used what was still called at that time a "Panaglide"—the grandfather of the Steadicam. In any case it's the first time it was used in French film. It's a magisterial shot that took advantage of the magnificent scenery of Tony Pratt, and we did it in only two or three takes. Everything was constructed, but we gave it a curious sense of life through an injection of Indians, hippies, and all kinds of ethnic minorities. And the person chasing her is Robbie Coltrane, who was unknown at the time and afterwards became a superstar in England. When *Death Watch* was released in England, the English press noticed Robbie Coltrane and went crazy when they saw his name in the credits. But concerning the changes in POV, I was very impressed by Michael Powell's *Peeping Tom*, in which there were innumerable passages from objectivity to subjectivity, but also, in a certain sense, in *Rear Window*. These two films had a big impact on me and influenced me.

AR: Right. Through the use of these shots we were just mentioning, the film succeeds in putting the spectator in a most uncomfortable state, pretty close to what you find in Powell or Hitchcock: a paradoxical state—or at least a dual position—between our first empathy as spectators which moves us to want her to escape, while at the same time a voyeuristic urge that causes us not to want to lose sight of her.

BT: I tried to include myself and my feelings in this process, and not to remain cloistered from it. At a certain point, it's evident that Roddy doesn't understand things unless he's filming them, and that was also true of me at a certain point and in a certain way: I discovered what I wanted to express by making an unfiltered image of it.

AR: The first time I saw *Death Watch*, precisely because of this feeling, I thought that since Katherine couldn't escape from the spectator's look, that inevitably we'd watch her die. And then in the final sequence, with simple camera movements, you demonstrated a delirious elegance.

BT: Well I don't know about that, but I didn't want the viewer to see her death. She was Antigone: we didn't see her death but learned about it afterwards from Max von Sydow's character. That's something that is repeated fairly often in my films, like the murders in *L'Appât* [*Fresh Bait*], for example: a very important element of the plot that we don't get to see. In that, I certainly didn't want to be like the people I was denouncing. At one point the character said, "Leave me alone!" and I didn't want to disobey the character. You find the same thing in *Ça commence aujourd'hui* [*It all Starts Today*], when Philippe Torreton goes back to the apartment of the mother of the little girl and she asks him to stop. So the camera stops. *Death Watch* was probably the founding moment for me in respect to the characters' desires: if a character doesn't want to be seen, I don't show him. I'm not going to betray him just to accentuate the spectacle.

AR: I understand the moral force you assign to your own look in what you're saying. And that made me think of Jean Renoir, who said that the only reproach he would make of *Grand Illusion* was that it didn't prevent the Second World War. Would you reproach *Death Watch* for not having been able to prevent the delirious sensationalism of reality TV?

BT: I'd be very upset if I succeeded in preventing anything whatever. I feel very lucid about the power of a film. Renoir himself claimed that a film director should have the arrogance to believe that he can change the world but the modesty to believe that if he succeeds in deeply moving four people, it's a victory. Just as for novels and plays, the important thing is to ask questions. The question of reception can't really be included in the work. It depends on the way the work will be exploited, understood and, as Prévert said, in the reception of any work there's probably 90 percent misunderstanding. What's important is to take a stand, to be a voice that's heard, which speaks out against the status quo. But the film has had an effect over the years. It provoked reactions from people like Paul Virilio [cultural theorist who studies the speed of technological change], and from sociologists, philosophers who add a lot to the debate. But a film shouldn't be judged simply by the effects it produces. Can you understand the power it would give me if I made a film that upset the order of things? In particular, I made a film that was hailed as one of the most accurate things that had ever been done about the police [*L.627*]. Do you think that the minister of the interior at the time had the intelligence to take account of the things that were denounced in the film as preventing and paralyzing the operations of the police? For example the culture of the prison guards and the use of statistics? It's only gotten worse since the film was released! I went to see Sarkozy, who was then minister of the interior, to talk to him about specific abuses, for example the equipment of the police officers that didn't allow them to follow a criminal into the Metro because the computer programs that had been developed by the police didn't include the possibility of going into the Metro. Which meant that if you were working on antiterrorism, you would lose your contact if you wanted to take the Metro! I explained all this to him and I could see that it didn't interest him one bit. So of course when you make a film like that, you'd hope it would have some effect. But the politicians ignore the cinema, and each time I've made a film about a precise subject, I discovered that I ended up knowing a lot more about the subject than the government agencies created to manage it. How can you hope that a film will have any effect when you've got people like that in government? Another example: I showed *Captain Conan* to two ministers of national education, and neither one knew that the war had continued after November 11 and that 500,000 Frenchmen had continued ti fight and many died after the Armistice . . .

AR: Yes, but in a way, what you're pointing out is a problem of education, and the work of a filmmaker is also to participate in spreading consciousness and information about such things . . .

BT: Yes, it's to illustrate things that have astonished him, surprised him, made him laugh. In general, I'm unaware of all of those things when I begin a film; they're things I discover when I'm preparing the scenario, and my work really comes down to discovering worlds that I didn't know and then communicating them to my audience. But I'm always devastated to see the way films are sometime reduced to binary oppositions—militarist or antimilitarist, for or against cops—which has never been the point of any of my films. *L.627* was even attacked for being a racist film! Okay, I was defended by Fode Sylla of SOS Racism, but when you see Raymond Depardon's documentary in which there is the same proportion of Blacks and Maghrebians, no one says it's racist. So, when I start out, it's the excitement which motivates me, because that provides an interesting dramaturgy, because that creates scenes that you don't see in the movies and shows behaviors that are original . . . To base a character, like Chabannes in *La Princesse de Montpensier* [*The Princess of Montpensier*], on the feelings of guilt for having killed a pregnant woman—how often do you see that in the movies? But that was considered in the sixteenth century as a war crime, and there weren't too many of those. So this provides for a very interesting plot and gives unusual power to Lambert Wilson's character. And the fact that a marriage is consummated in public, what weight does that bring to the relationship between two young lovers? That's what I'm looking for, the unprecedented shadings that such things can give to characters, feelings, and interactions.

AR: That scene in *The Princess of Montpensier* reminds me of what we were just saying about the morality of the spectator—what he should see and what he shouldn't see.

BT: Of course, and what I have to do is discover ways to portray these things in a way that isn't voyeuristic but instead makes the spectator uncomfortable.

AR: When you set out to make *Death Watch* or others of your films that we've been talking about, what is the driving motivation for you? The desire to create an unknown world—that you just mentioned—indignation, fear?

BT: Above all else, it's the desire to understand. You know, indignation can motivate a scene, but it can't motivate an entire film. You wouldn't want to spend ten weeks in a constant state of indignation! There are moments when it's appropriate, but indignation can give rise to anger, to sarcasm . . . In *It All Begins Today*, I filmed an inspector for the National Ministry of Education who speaks a phrase I didn't make up and which was even the marching orders of his bureau: "Work things out by yourself so that your kids can become autonomous." Okay, there, inevitably you get angry and you think who are these Doctor Strangeloves, these cretins shut up in their offices giving such orders, while the teachers are facing children whose parents are out of work, are destroyed by drink . . . Okay, yes, you get angry making a scene like that . . . and there are always going to be people who say you've dabbled in caricature, whereas I know how completely authentic these sequences are. The problem is that a good number of critics and journalists know absolutely nothing about the country they live in and they have the arrogance to decide something is exaggerated. But indignation has to give way to something else, principally the feeling of respect for the characters played by Torreton, Nadia Kaci, and Maria Pitarresi. I feel great tenderness and admiration for those people. And for Noiret's character in *La Vie et rien d'autre* [*Life and Nothing But*]. And for Romy in *Death Watch*.

AR: Indeed, there's a surprising and touching aspect of *Death Watch* and that's the writing of David Rayfiel, who'd written several films for Sidney Pollack . . .

BT: Many of which are uncredited.

AR: This was the first film you did that wasn't in French, so you teamed up with an American author.

BT: Who's marginal. I've often worked with coauthors who are unknown, not part of the system. Aurenche was an outsider, completely and unjustly vilified at the time we were working together. Jean Cosmos was unknown in film. Not to mention my ex-wife, Colo, who'd never written a scenario, or Michel Alexandre, who was a cop and whose literary experience was limited to police reports! Or Dominique Sampiero, who wrote *It All Begins Today*. And then there's David Rayfiel who was also an outsider, who occasionally signed films and who sometimes joined a film because Pollack called him in to clean up a scenario that was going nowhere. That's how he ended up writing two-thirds of *Jeremiah Johnson*. It was Pollack, by the way, who encouraged me to sign him on. I liked David a lot and I wrote about our friendship in a text that appeared in *Positif* (Number 621, November 2012). He was someone who always came at scenes from an unusual angle and who wrote one of the most beautiful love scenes I've ever filmed, between Gerald and Katherine, in which the characters never tell each other "I love you" except in French. But his way of doing it was to tell the amazing story of Robert de Bauléac.

AR: This composer who never existed . . .

BT: Ever. Though I got lots of requests from people who'd searched for references to him in magazines or dictionaries of musicology. [Laughter]

AR: I find that David Rayfiel's personal style and yours as well are evident in the lines of a secondary character, Tracey, Roddy's companion, played by Thérèse Liotard (and dubbed in the English version by Julie Christie) who reminded me of one of your favorite actresses, Christine Pascal.

BT: Yes, I can see that, though she's less cutting than Christine. I chose her so as not always to choose Christine Pascal, and then, to tell the truth, Pierre-William Glenn and Christine Pascal don't get along. It's crazy, but something like that could create tensions on the set . . . but on the other hand Glenn didn't like Thérèse Liotard either! So we had some difficult moments, especially given that, when Glenn doesn't like someone, it shows. But when he has a positive reaction, you get sublime results, with Romy, with Harvey, with Harry Dean, with Max von Sydow, though with Thérèse it wasn't easy. I took Thérèse because I'd liked her a lot in Varda's *One Sings and the Other Doesn't*, but our relationship got complicated by the fact that I was forever negotiating things between her and the head cameraman. For me she was in a sense the spokesperson of the film, who tells the story and expresses its moral.

AR: Yes, that's how I saw her: as your own commentary.

BT: She has a view of things that's deep, compassionate, and at the same time ironic. Yes, she spoke for David [Rayfiel] and me: the character allowed us to keep our distance. He wrote her a magnificent commentary, very lyrical. Okay, you always redo films retroactively in your mind, so as for Tracey, I thought I really should have chosen Jane Birken. When I look at the film now, I really like what Thérèse brings to it. She adds a lot of feeling, but I should have chosen Jane whom I wouldn't have had to dub. But it's not because you think you should have done things differently that you're necessarily right. Christine, Jane, or Thérèse all had in common that they're slender young women who display intelligence, wit, strength, and vulnerability all at once.

AR: When you were talking about David Rayfiel's style, you mentioned him as "someone who always came at scenes from an unusual angle." In *Death Watch* there's a kind of unhinged lyricism, something almost operatic and that at the same time refuses decorum, ostentation, and the spectacular.

BT: Yes. It's a love story. Lyrical and vast in its landscapes and its feelings. There was something of this in *Le Juge et l'assassin* [*The Judge and the Assassin*], but I'm one of the French directors of that period who gave the most attention to nature and landscapes, trying to integrate them into the drama. *Death Watch,* or more recently, *Dans La Brume électrique* [*In the Electric Mist*] or *The Princess of Montpensier* or previously *Life and Nothing But* or *La Passion Béatrice* [*Beatrice*] are films whose landscapes condition a part of the action. That probably comes from an unconscious influence the directors of Westerns had on me. The way Daves, Mann, Hawks, and Ford filmed nature left its mark on me.

AR: What about Boetticher?

BT: Yes, even if Boetticher's style is more refined. And I was also touched by the beauty of nature in the films of Michael Powell, whom we often forget to credit for his love of nature that shines through in *Gone to Earth, Black Narcissus,* even if it's a "studio" nature.

AR: What about the central scenes of *A Canterbury Tale*?

BT: Yes, totally. These directors have left their mark on me, which is funny, because I'm not a very outdoorsy person, but I know how to film the outdoors: horseback rides, landscapes . . . finding exterior decors that are varied and interesting.

AR: Indeed, you've recently discovered the restored version of *Death Watch.* The old DVD was pretty faded and obviously didn't do justice to the Scottish countryside.

BT: I was delighted. It was as though I were discovering a new film. I had gotten some distance on this film that I hadn't seen in fifteen years . . . The last time I'd seen it, it seemed as though it had deteriorated, dulled, and when I happened to see it on TV it was never the right format, was always missing the edges of the image.

AR: Which is particularly troubling since Scope is essential here!

BT: And suddenly when I saw the restored version I felt the same enthusiasm I'd felt when I saw the rushes of the film. We always saw the rushes mute since we didn't have a soundtrack, and we watched them at the Glasgow Film Theater. And I remember that when the audience saw the shots with the Steadicam, they all applauded. There was a certain pride in what we were filming that I rediscovered recently. It's a film where the lighting and the colors play an important role: no one is wearing colors in the film, including Romy's dress, until the sunlit scenes at the end. But before that there were some shots in which there were three or four nuances of green and the lab technicians had told me that they used certain shots in the film to show what one can achieve in terms of color shadings, as difficult to film as the color green is.

AR: In your filmography, in France, except for the last two films, there are no HD editions of your films.
BT: Yes, that's Studio Canal for you . . . [sighs] I really don't understand, because films like *The Judge and the Assassin*, *Coup de Torchon* [*Clean Slate*], *Que La Fête commence* [*Let Joy Reign Supreme*], or *Life and Nothing But* are films that . . . well, I just don't understand. From time to time I send them emails asking where they are on this, but . . . But you know that, after René Bonnell and Pierre Lescure, we've ceased having real connections between directors and the people who curate their films. Sometimes it happens in the right way: for example the people who worked on the edition of *The Princess of Montpensier* were terrific. But I have the impression that, in general, we've lost what we used to have, that is, a general policy about video and the various things that go along with it. When you want to compare things you've done in former films with more recent ones, it's almost impossible: when I was shooting *Laissez-Passer* [*Safe Conduct*], I called and asked, "Are you sure you have the rights to the films we're showing in *Safe Conduct*?" but no one in the service of current films had made contact with the people who hold the rights. There's a wall. In the multinational films there are walls. It's practically impossible, for example—and Stéphane Lerouge can attest to this—to include music that belongs to Universal in a DVD edited in the same group! People just don't talk to each other.

AR: But why? Because they don't know anything about rights or out of ill will?
BT: They're just in different worlds. We succeeded in slipping some of Philippe Sarde's music into a DVD but it was very difficult . . . But Stéphane can talk about this better than I can. I just don't understand. The idea that the video and music worlds might mutually benefit each other never seems to occur to anyone: for example, if you wanted to sell the CD of the music in *The Princess of Montpensier* in the movie theater, they'd tell you, "No, FNAC or Virgin Stores have exclusive rights to the CD." So I tell them that I don't have the impression that right now the sale of CDs is all that good, and I try to suggest ideas. But no. So sometimes in bookstores you can pair the sale of DVDs with the books they're adapted from, but CDs are impossible. It's the Berlin Wall.

AR: Let's talk about your projects: you're currently shooting *Quai d'Orsay* [*The French Minister*], an adaptation of the graphic novel done by Christophe Blain and Abel Lanzac.

BT: We've finished shooting and already have a first version of the edit. We had an idyllic shoot, absolutely marvelous, and the way the film has been edited was a real pleasure. I didn't run into any of the problems I encountered with *In the Electric Mist* or *The Princess of Montpensier*. Our connection with the people at Pathé was terrific; we felt very supported but at the same time they gave us lots of freedom to work.

AR: To conclude, Bertrand Tavernier, I'd like to have you do a little exercise which may make you uncomfortable, but for the cinephile that I am, you're both the director of some very important films and a historian of the cinema, through your contributions to some foundations, through editions of DVDs, and through works you've written about the cinema. And in particular, you and Jean-Pierre Coursodon wrote a reference book on American cinema in which, in a very few lines, you succeed in summarizing the essence of each director. So let's imagine that you were asked to write about Tavernier's style for a hypothetical *Forty Years of French Cinema*. How would you go about it?

BT: Well, you know, writing about other people is also a kind of relief from having to assess my own films. Perhaps I'm afraid, or timid . . . I'm also afraid that self-analysis might lead to some sort of block. I've seen too many people who ended up believing what the critics said about them and who began making films that are nothing more than exegeses of these others' summaries. But what I could say, despite all the variety of inspirations that produced them, that there are very precise connections between *Clean Slate* and *The Judge and the Assassin* and a few others of my films, and notably that they are films that try to escape from the notion of "plot," that are sometimes very anachronistic, which has the effect of distancing me from all the films with which I've been compared, the academic French cinema which was often too theatrical, with precise beginnings and predictable endings. I've often made very open-ended films and often have narrative lines that zigzag, a tendency that has been increasing in my work. I think that my films also refuse to subscribe to any genre, but instead take genres and try to explode them. *The Judge and the Assassin* is a film noir about a serial killer, but it's also so many other things . . .

AR: Or *Death Watch*, a sci-fi but at the same time not a sci-fi at all.

BT: Yes, exactly. I think that the majority of my subjects have not been done before, or in any case are original in their way of treating the subjects. The vision of Colonial France in *Clean Slate* is at the antipodes of the French colonial films with their tight framing and dark sensibility. I would like to say that certain films are built on others or are made *against* others: *Des Enfants gâtés* [*Spoiled Children*] seems to be the opposite of *The Judge and the Assassin*, but the contrary is really the case, perhaps in a way that's too theoretical which explains why it isn't totally successful.

AR: Well *Spoiled Children* contains the announcement of *Death Watch*!

BT: Yes, which shows why I took three years to edit it. I had the idea of it in my mind, but the production was really difficult until I found the Lebanese producer Gabriel Boustani, a curious personality with lots of bizarre habits. But I could also talk about nature and the importance of decors, landscapes, and places in my work. Neither the Ardeche nor Africa, for example, seems to be badly filmed, at least not in a conventional way. And then there's the pleasure of being with actors. The freedom to work with them. Brialy, Huppert, Noiret in *The Judge and the Assassin* . . . but all the actors in *Clean Slate* are exceptional. Stéphane Audran, for example, who recently revealed that she still knows by heart several dialogues from the film! So that's what I could tell you about my films . . .

Interview with Bertrand Tavernier

Max Nelson / 2014

From *Film Comment*, March 2014, filmcomment.com. Copyright © 2014 by the Film Society of Lincoln Center. Used by permission of the Film Society of Lincoln Center/Film Comment Magazine.

Max Nelson: The theme of this conversation—in keeping with the pace of your new film—was initially going to be "the world's fastest screwball comedies," so I wanted to start with a general question: what considerations, in your experience, go into determining the speed of a movie?

Bertrand Tavernier: Difficult question. First, I must say one thing. When I start working on a film, I stop being a film buff. I very rarely see films to influence either my work, or the work of my collaborators. I want to stick to the film I'm doing and the characters, without thinking about other films. Of course, when I'm doing a comedy like *Quai d'Orsay* [*The French Minister*], I have in mind the rhythm of great comedies like *His Girl Friday*, *To Be or Not to Be*, or Billy Wilder's films. I didn't need to see any of them again. I also had in mind something that Hawks said: a good comedy is a comedy which could, with a few changes, be directed in a more straightforward, even dramatic manner. You could take the screenplay of *Quai d'Orsay*, and with a few adjustments—not so many—you could have a good dramatic film. After all, it's a film which deals with a potential war, with—at one point—a cargo which is going to explode and maybe kill a few million people, and the danger of civil war in Africa. It's all very serious.

I also had in mind, as I said earlier, the rhythm, the pace. The pace of a film—especially of a comedy—must come from one or two main characters. I have seen films, especially recent films, where the directors try to stick with a single kind of pace because everybody told them that the audience is impatient, so you have to move fast. The film is trying to move faster than the characters. Or the film is always moving at the same speed, which is, for me, the opposite of real rhythm. Rhythm must include—even if they're only twenty or thirty seconds—moments when you break the rhythm. The speed had to come from the character of the minister, who was always in movement, always running, unable to sit down for two minutes, unable not to do anything. The rhythm also had to come organically from the character of Arthur, who always has to do something but is always rebuffed. What he does is ignored and thrown away, so he has to start again and start again. I had to get that feeling in the rhythm, and I think I got it. The rhythm of the film is really imposed, dictated, and determined organically by the character—like in *The Princess of Montpensier* [*La Princesse de Montpensier*], or *L.627*, or *Capitaine Conan* [96].

MN: Part of what's interesting about that dynamic in *Quai d'Orsay* is that you have one character within the film imposing a rhythm on another character. So, to some degree, for the rhythm to feel natural, it has to feel forced.
BT: Yes. And the rhythm is always stopping when you come to the character played by Niels Arestrup, who is always slowing the scenes down, speaking slowly . . .

MN: Falling asleep . . .
BT: And falling asleep. It's like he's saying, "You move too fast. Stop, think, wait, we'll find a solution." And that's good. He's always doing things—reading, signing, talking on the phone, or absorbing huge stacks of files—but just a shot with him, or three lines from him, allows me from time to time to break the rhythm and the speed of the film.

MN: That's one of the respects in which the film reminds me of certain classic Hollywood comedies. They always include all this buffer space, passages that absorb the shock of the manic stretches surrounding them.
BT: Especially films like *His Girl Friday* or *One, Two, Three*.

MN: These very quiet, hushed, slow scenes—like the exchange in *His Girl Friday* between Rosalind Russell and the imprisoned man.
BT: Yes. It's surprising how dramatic the background of that film is—it's the death penalty—and you laugh all the time.

MN: In some sense, it's those quiet buffer scenes that really end up being the dramatic core of the movie.
BT: Yeah. There was another director I was thinking of, without seeing the films—because, again, making a film is so exciting, so demanding, and so involving that I don't want to see other images. But I was remembering some of the comedies of Jacques Becker. I know he's not known in this country, and it's a pity, because for me he is, if not the greatest, then one of the greatest French directors of the forties and fifties. One of the greatest. One of the most underrated in this country.

I know they re-released *Antoine et Antoinette* recently, which is a masterpiece, but *Edouard et Caroline* is a wonderful comedy: very, very funny, with tremendous space, and some moments when it suddenly becomes serious. Just at the end, there's a moment when it could become a drama. It's done with such grace and elegance in the direction.

I find Becker the equal of—if not better than—even people like Hawks. He had such a wide range: going from *Casque d'or* to *Edouard et Caroline*, or from *Antoine et Antoinette* to *Touchez pas au grisbi* to *Le Trou*. An enormous range, and always with the same deeply organic quality. He was doing things which were extremely bold and extremely new, but they were done so fluidly that nobody noticed how new it was. The character of Gabin in *Touchez pas au grisbi*, for instance, pre-dates all the antiheroes of the sixties and seventies: in the way he's macho with women, or the way he wants to go to bed early. It's a destruction of Gabin's image, and of the whole romantic image of the hero. This gangster is just a bourgeois who wants to have a bourgeois wife and doesn't want to go to sleep late or have any problems. That was incredibly daring with somebody like Gabin. There are very few actors who were willing to challenge their own image like that: he had the reputation of being the great seducer, the romantic guy, the hero of all the prewar films. And then he was playing the opposite. I love that.

MN: One thing that might unite Becker and Hawks is that they didn't primarily make comedies.

BT: Becker started with dramas. His first film is a kind of tongue-in-cheek gangster film, but his second is a murder drama set in the country. He was, by the way, a great admirer of Hawks and Hathaway. During the first *Cahiers* interview with Hawks, Becker was present in the room.

MN: Do you think that the way these directors made comedies was somehow affected by the fact that they spent so much of their careers making dramatic films?

BT: Maybe. Coming out of directing dramas, they had a kind of elegant style which was very well suited for comedy. And maybe by doing those dramas, they knew how to transform a dramatic scene into a comedy.

MN: The comedies are always threatening to become dramas.

BT: Yeah. I don't know if that's true of all Hawks, though: I'm not sure *I Was a Male War Bride* could have been a dramatic film.

MN: Another striking aspect of *Quai d'Orsay* for me is structural: for increasingly long stretches of the movie—during the crisis with the ship, for instance—the film leaves Arthur altogether.

BT: He would have been useless. He is there with the other advisors, and there's a moment between him and Valerie, but there's no possibility for him to help solve the thing. I do not care about losing a character. You get him back, and you get him back with a very good scene. And at that moment, the audience has absorbed the fact that, more or less, even if he's not present, he is getting everything that's happening. He is slowly becoming a member of the cabinet, so he doesn't have to be present to know what's happening.

I find your question strange, because there are so many novels and plays in which you lose a character for twenty minutes. I love freedom. I love to be able to do what I want, not to follow a pattern where, when you have a main character, he has to be there in every moment. I've never made films where the screenplay is dictated by the plot. Especially in many of the latest films I've made, I want to give the impression that the screenplay is written by the characters. My films are often very collective; even if you have one, two, or three main parts, every character counts. I can jump from one to the other; I want to be able to build a whole film—*Safe Conduct* [*Laissez-Passer*, 2002]—on two heroes who practically never meet. I want to have the possibility of making that. It gives me a very free dramatic construction, where I can jump from one character to the other.

I'm suffering from everything that's predictable: films that look like they're coming from a three-act screenplay, or that have twists which seem to be dictated by the screenwriters and imposed on the characters. I want to get rid of all that. I want to enjoy the freedom of narration.

MN: Part of the effect in this case is that you get the sense that the characters are always reacting to events out in the world.

BT: Absolutely. Sometimes it's a challenge. In *L.627*, if I wanted to be true to the essence of the work of the police squad, I had to accept the fact that they will fail at one thing, start another investigation, and change gears suddenly to follow something unexpected. The story was starting over all the time. Normally, that's something that screenwriters hate. I had to accept it and ask myself: "What can I do to overcome something that can be problematic for the audience?" I had to be able to understand the state of mind of people for whom nothing is ever finished. The moment they think they can have some rest, they have to start again; they have to work. If you deal with that frontally, if you accept it, you can overcome the problem, even make what could have been a problem into a virtue. You find a kind of narrative which will be exciting, providing you put a lot of gusto and energy into it, and providing you never waste time indulging yourself. I did it in *L.627*, *Capitaine Conan*, and *Safe Conduct*, and I knew it could work here too. They're doing twenty things at the same time, but in the end, we must feel the progression even if what they've tried to do has stopped or failed. It's something I liked in the graphic novel: you finish one thing, and you have another problem immediately, or two problems at the same time. You have to start all over again.

MN: I think that contributes here to the film's sense of humor as well.
BT: Yeah, the repetition can be a source of fun.

MN: Another element that contributes to the tone is the very inventive use of language: everyone's talking past each other and over each other's heads.
BT: It's something that Robert Altman did brilliantly. He's one of my heroes in many ways. In *Tanner '88* or *Nashville*, he's doing that constantly. Gregory La Cava, too, in *Stage Door*.

MN: How did you make sure the comic impact of the language would carry over from the graphic novel?
BT: I think the characters were very well written in the graphic novel. It was very funny; at the same time, it felt true. That was the story of the writer's life. He told, very simply, what happened to him. And you can feel that. I wanted to preserve the energy of the novel, not to copy the way it was ordered. This is the trap. A graphic novel is not a storyboard. You must understand what is great in it, and sometimes that will mean finding solutions which are the opposite of what is actually in the graphic novel. I can just give you a detail: in the novel, I looked at Christophe Blain's wonderful drawings, and in some of them, the foreign minister is moving so fast that he has five or six arms, like an Indian god. Papers are flying. I had to keep this idea, but I didn't want to do any kind of special effect. Instead, I had him walk as if he was preceded by a kind of mini-storm. He's like the character in *Peanuts* who is always followed by dust. When he comes into a room, everything flies, and he never has any kind of look towards what's happening around him.

One of the great foreign affairs ministers, when he saw the film, said: "That is a wonderful idea. It gives the right color to the character. He doesn't leave anything concrete; he's so far away in his own vision that he never sees that he's bothering everybody. He's living in another dimension."

MN: He sets the rhythm of the space, but he's also constantly disrupting it.
BT: Totally. He creates an enormous chaos around him. Sometimes, when I was doing the film, I thought: "My God, it's a fable about filmmaking." Some directors seem to create a huge chaos on the set, but in the end, when you see the finished film, it has tremendous logic. It was very late, during the editing, that I discovered that in his brilliant speech in front of the council of security—which is a real speech—the minister is using all the formulas which he has been repeating throughout the film. It sounds absurd when he gives these lists—"*ténacité*,"

et cetera—but in the end, they are all in the speech, and they make sense. It's as if he tries out a lot of formulas verbally, and then, having created a lot of chaos around him, succeeds in doing something which is structured, organized, and incredibly well written—the most brilliant speech in French diplomacy for two or three decades. It was vilified in this country at the time, but he was totally right. Everything which was in the speech is now timeless. It's precise, intelligent, true, and wise. During the whole film, you would have a problem attributing those adjectives to the character of the minister.

That was what attracted me to the story: that the politics of individuals are more important than their behavior or their crazy way of talking. Politicians can only be judged by their effects—not by the way they dress, talk, or scream, or the fact that they contradict themselves, say stupid things, or sound emphatic and arrogant. They can be all of that if, at the end, the result is terrific. In exactly the same way, some directors can seem nasty or mean; others want to change their screenplay whenever they meet somebody. But in the end, something will happen, and it will be great.

Additional Resources

Interviews

Andrew, Geoff. "Police State: An Interview with Bertrand Tavernier." *Time Out*, January 6, 1993, 13.

Benoit, Basirico. "An Interview with Bertrand Tavernier on *L'Horloger de Saint-Paul*." *Cinezik*, April 14, 2009, http://www.cinezik.org/cinema/realisateur/realisateurs. php?compo=tavernier-ent20090414.

Carlson, Michael. "Crime and the Surreal: An Interview with Bertrand Tavernier." *Diary of a Screenwriter* (blog), July 11, 2013, http://diaryofascreenwriter.blogspot.com/2013/07/bertrand-tavernier-crime-and-surreal.html.

Challon-Kemoun, Adeline. "Filming the Skies." *Air France Magazine*, December 2013, 82–94.

Chester, Ronny, and Xavier Jamet. "La Passion Créatrice: Interview with Bertrand Tavernier." DVDClassik website, September 1, 2005, http:// http://www.dvdclassik.com/article/entretien-avec-bertrand-tavernier.

Coursodon, Jean-Pierre. "An Interview with Bertrand Tavernier on '*Round Midnight*." *Cineaste* 15, no. 2 (1986): 18–23.

Esther, John. "Cinema can open windows: an interview with Bertrand Tavernier." *Cineaste*, Summer 2011, 46.

Jaehne, K. "La guerre n'est pas finie, an interview with Bertrand Tavernier." *Cineaste* 18, no. 1 (1990): 23–26.

Kemp, Philip. "Tavernier on Mackendrick." *Sight and Sound* 4, no. 8 (August 1994): 16–20.

Lowenstein, Stephen. "Bertrand Tavernier: *The Watchmaker of Saint-Paul*." In *My First Movie: 20 Celebrated Directors Talk about Their First Film*. Penguin Books, 2000, 156–77.

McAsh, I. F. "Cleaning the Slate, an Interview with Bertrand Tavernier." *Films*, August 1982, 11–12.

Nelson, Max. "Interview: Bertrand Tavernier." *Film Comment*, March 14, 2014, http://www.filmcomment.com/entry/interview-bertrand-tavernier-the-french-minister.

Piazzo, Philippe. "Interview with Bertrand Tavernier." *Jeune Cinéma*, January–February 1997, 7–9.

Solis, Jose. "*Quai d'Orsay* Is Now 'The French Minister': An Interview with Director Bertrand Tavernier." *PopMatters*, March 27, 2014, http://www.popmatters.com/post/180274-director-bernard-tavernier-talks-to-statuesque.

Stratton, David, "Bertrand Tavernier Interview." *At the Movies with Margaret and David* website, December 24, 2008, http://www.abc.net.au/atthemovies/txt/s2454713.htm.

Wooton, Adrien. "An Interview with Bertrand Tavernier." *Guardian*, November 12, 2002, http://www.theguardian.com/film/2002/nov/12/features.

Young, Alison. "Interview: Bertrand Tavernier on *Death Watch*." Glasgow Film website, http:www.glasgowfilm.org/cinema_city/features/2810.

Books by Tavernier

La Guerre sans nom: Les Appelés d'Algérie 1954–1962. Paris: Seuil, 1992.

I Wake Up, Dreaming: A Journal for 1992. A monograph volume of John Boorman and Walter Donohue, eds., *Projections: A Forum for Filmmakers*. London & New York: Faber & Faber, 1993.

Qu'est-ce qu'on attend? Paris: Seuil, 1993.

50 Ans de cinéma américain (with Jean-Pierre Coursodon). Paris: Omnibus, 1995.

Ça commence aujourd'hui (with Dominique Sampiero and Tiffany Tavernier). Paris: Mango, 1999.

Amis Américains: Entretiens avec les grands auteurs d'Hollywood. Lyon: Institut Lumière/Actes Sud, 2008.

Pas à pas dans la brume électrique: Récit de tournage. Paris: Flammarion, 2009.

Books on Tavernier

Bion, Danièle. *Bertrand Tavernier: Cinéaste de l'émotion*. Hatier, 1984.

Douin, Jean-Luc. *Bertrand Tavernier: Biographie*. Edilig, 1988 (updated edition by Ramsay Poche Cinéma in 1997, without illustrations).

Hay, Stephen. *Bertrand Tavernier: The Filmmaker of Lyon*. Taurus, 2000.

Higgins, Lynn A. *Bertrand Tavernier*. Manchester University Press, 2011.

Nuttens, Jean-Dominique. *Bertrand Tavernier*. Gremese, 2009.

Raspiengeas, Jean-Claude. *Bertrand Tavernier*. Flammarion, 2001.

Zants, Emily. *Bertrand Tavernier: Fractured Narrative and Bourgeois Values*. Scarecrow Press, 1999.

Index

Printed in the United States
by Baker & Taylor Publisher Services